THE MAN FROM MAYBE

AN ONI PRESS PUBLICATION

ONI PRESS

THE MAN FROM MAYBE

WORDS

JORDAN THOMAS

PICTURES

SHAKY KANE

LETTERS

JIM CAMPBELL

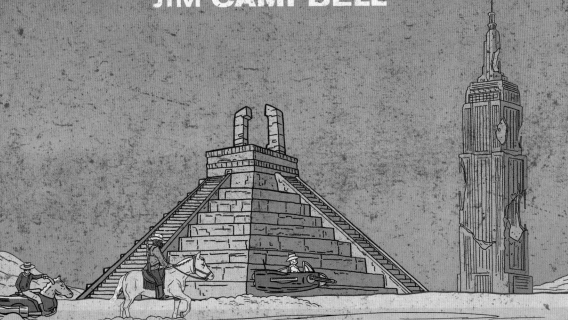

PUBLISHED BY
ONI-LION FORGE PUBLISHING GROUP, LLC.

EDITORS
ZACK SOTO AND KARL BOLLERS
DESIGNER
WINSTON GAMBRO

ONIPRESS.COM

facebook.com/onipress

twitter.com/onipress

instagram.com/onipress

First Edition: **May 2024**
ISBN: **978-1-63715-409-0**
EISBN: **978-1-63715-410-6**

Library of Congress Control Number: **2023947254**

Hunter Gorinson, president & publisher • Sierra Hahn, editor in chief • Troy Look, vp of publishing services • Spencer Simpson, vp of sales • Angie Knowles, director of design & production • Katie Sainz, director of marketing • Jeremy Colfer, director of development • Chris Cerasi, managing editor • Bess Pallares, senior editor • Grace Scheipeter, senior editor • Karl Bollers, editor • Megan Brown, editor • Gabriel Granillo, editor • Jung Hu Lee, assistant editor Michael Torma, senior sales manager • Andy McElliott, operations manager • Sarah Rockwell, senior graphic designer • Carey Soucy, senior graphic designer • Winston Gambro, graphic designer • Matt Harding, digital prepress technician • Sara Harding, executive coordinator • Kaia Rokke, marketing & communications coordinator

Joe Nozemack, publisher emeritus

Printed in China
1 2 3 4 5 6 7 8 9 10

CHAPTER ONE

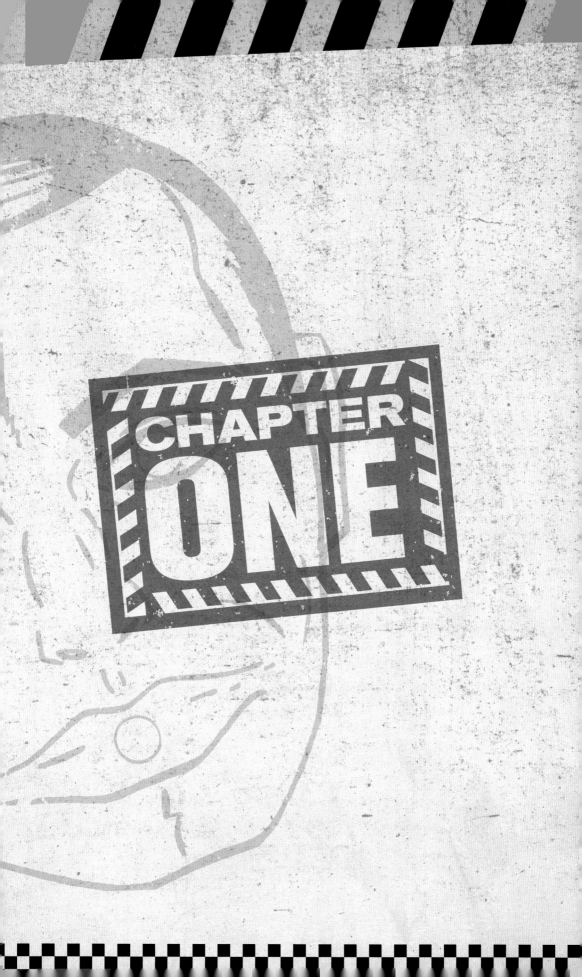

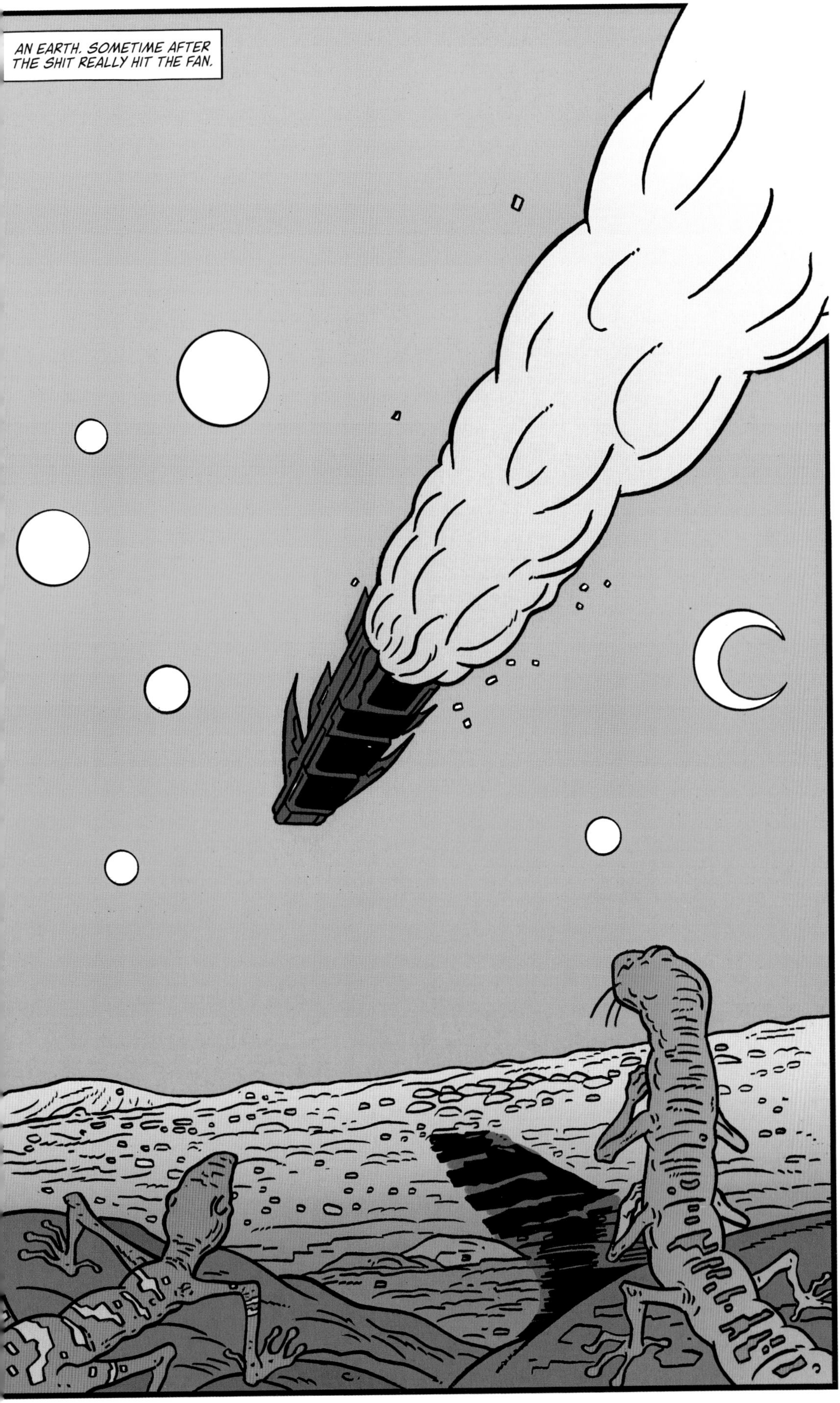
AN EARTH. SOMETIME AFTER THE SHIT REALLY HIT THE FAN.

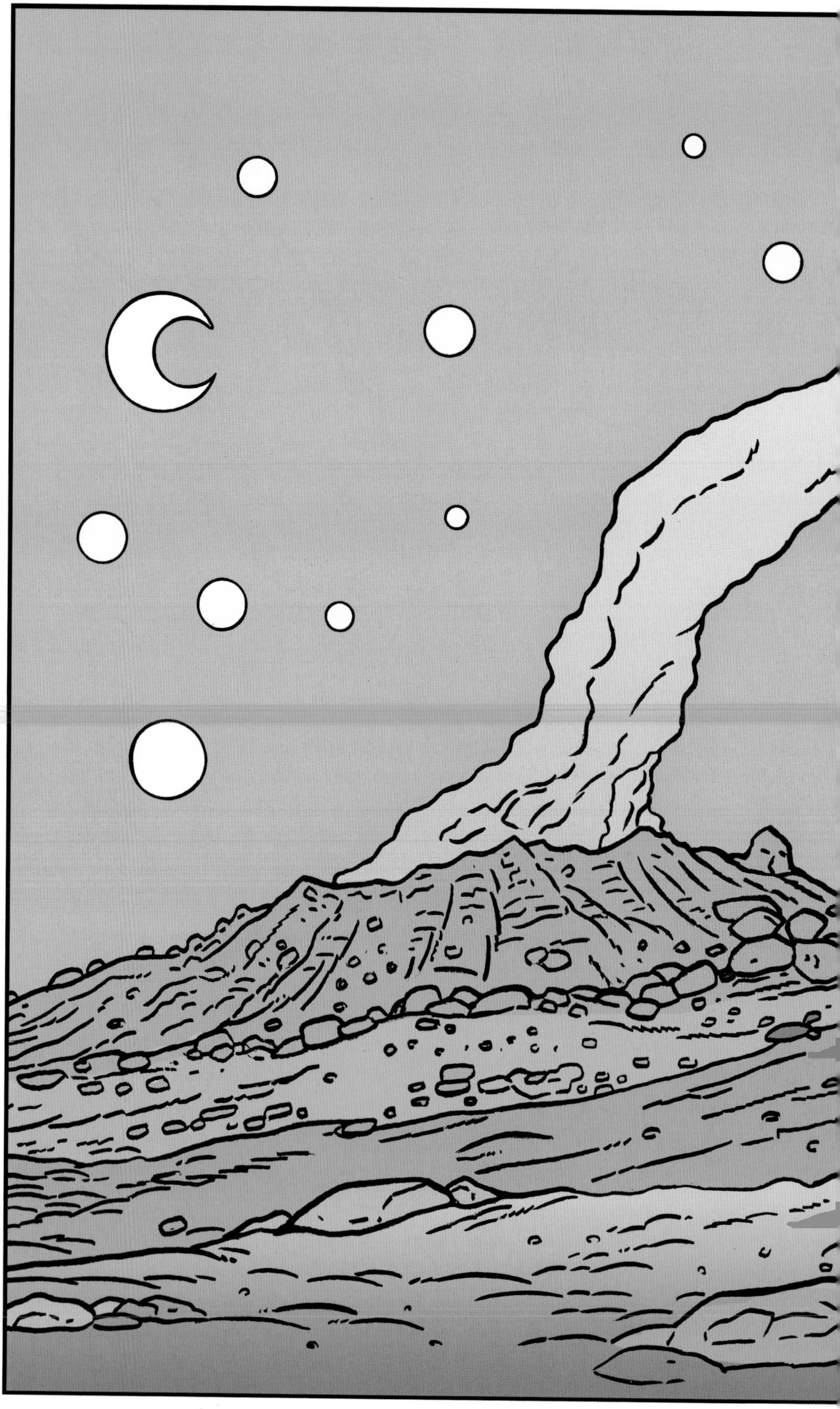

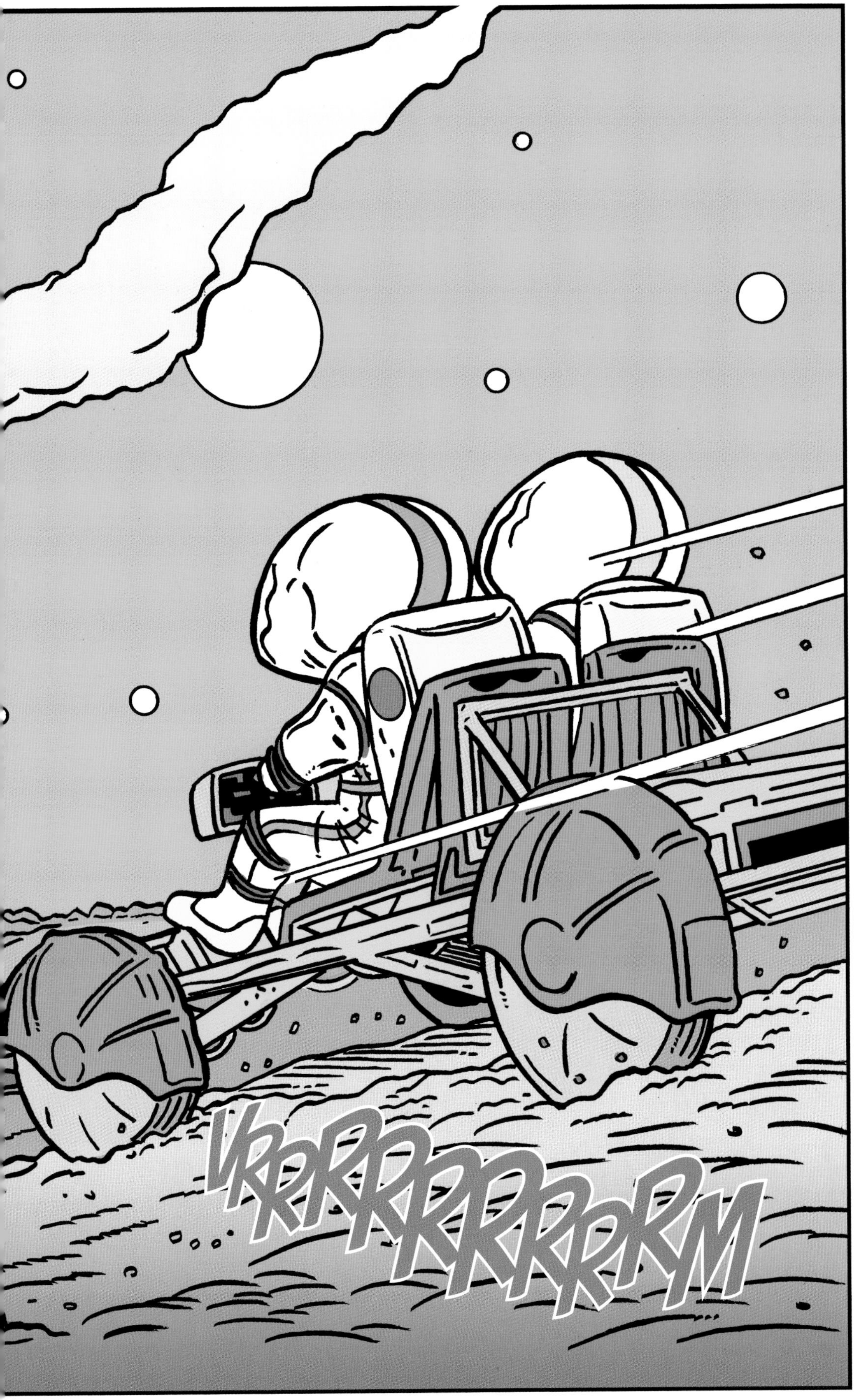
VRRRRRRRRRRRM

hsSSSs

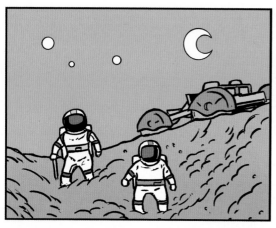

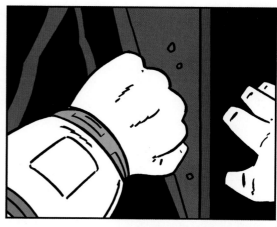

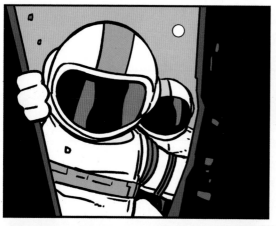

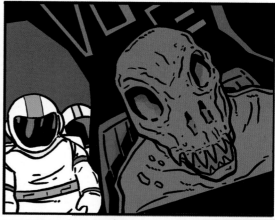

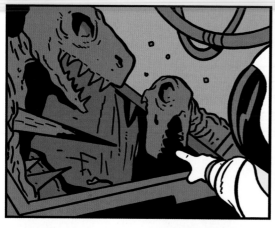

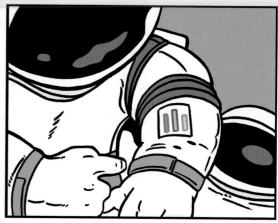

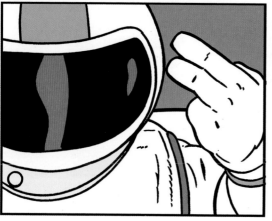

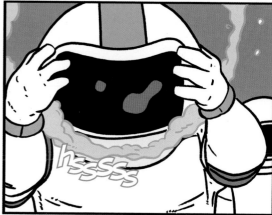

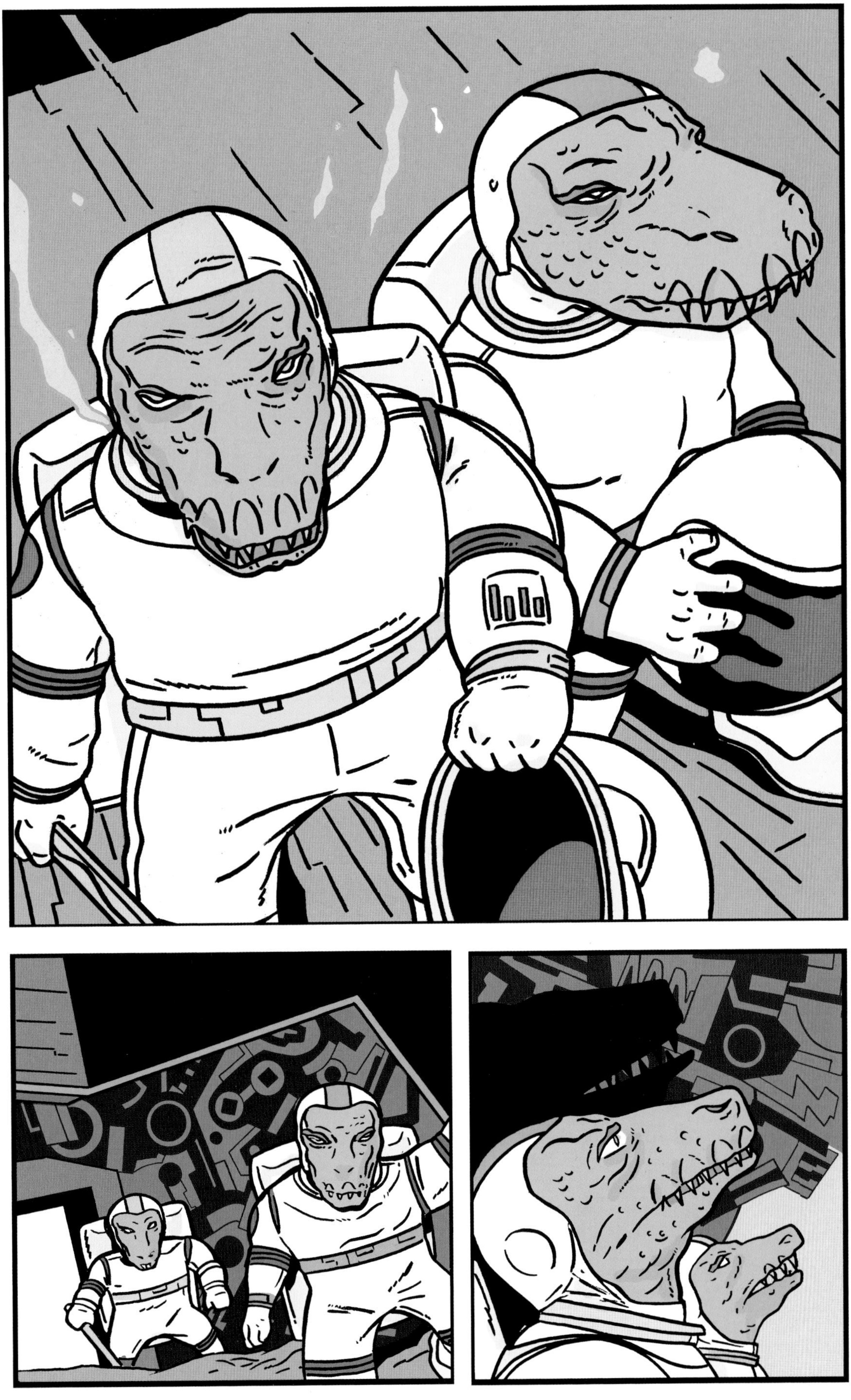

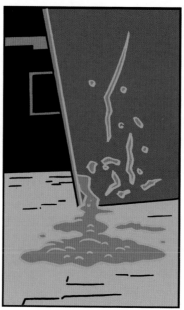

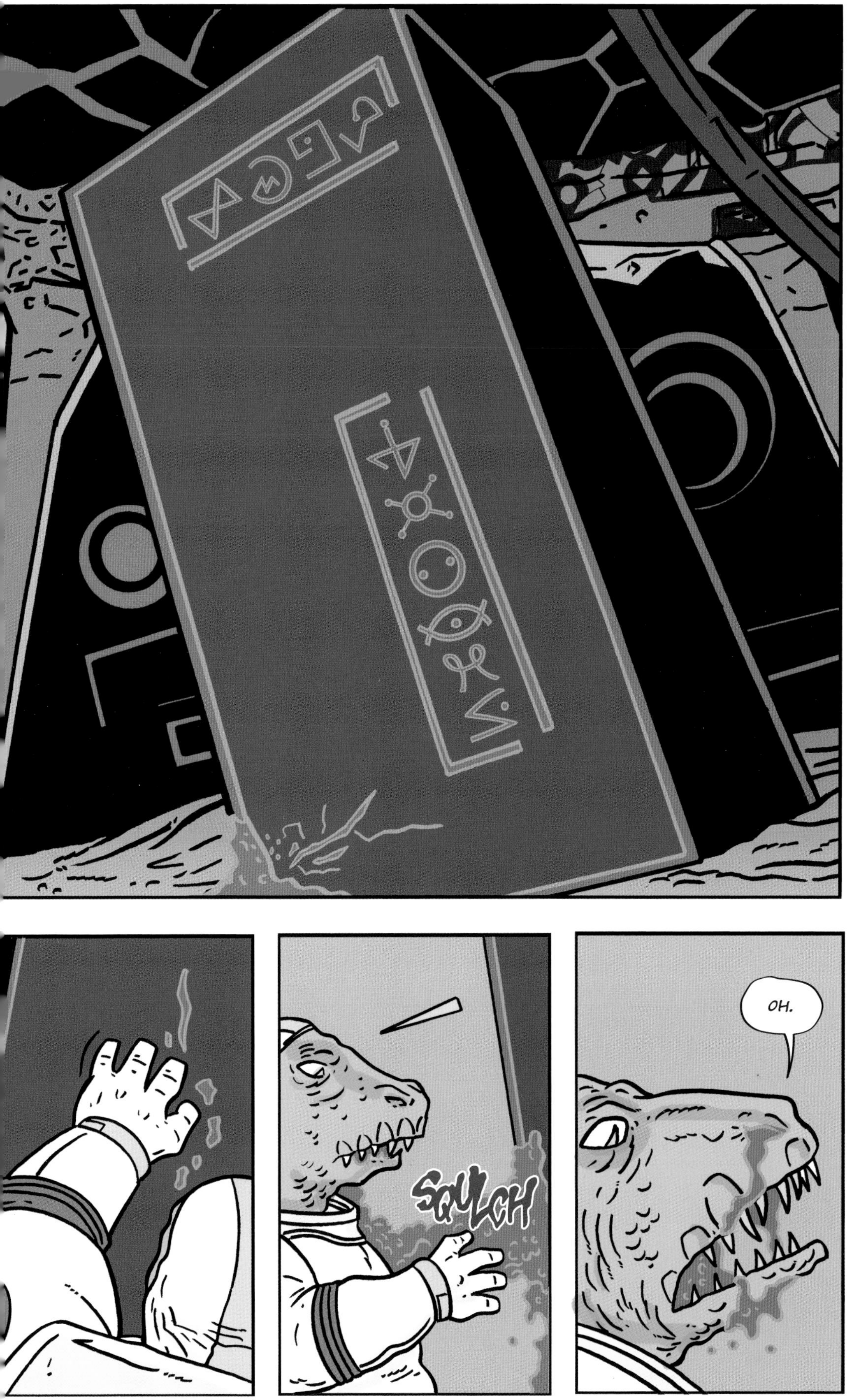
SQULCH
OH.

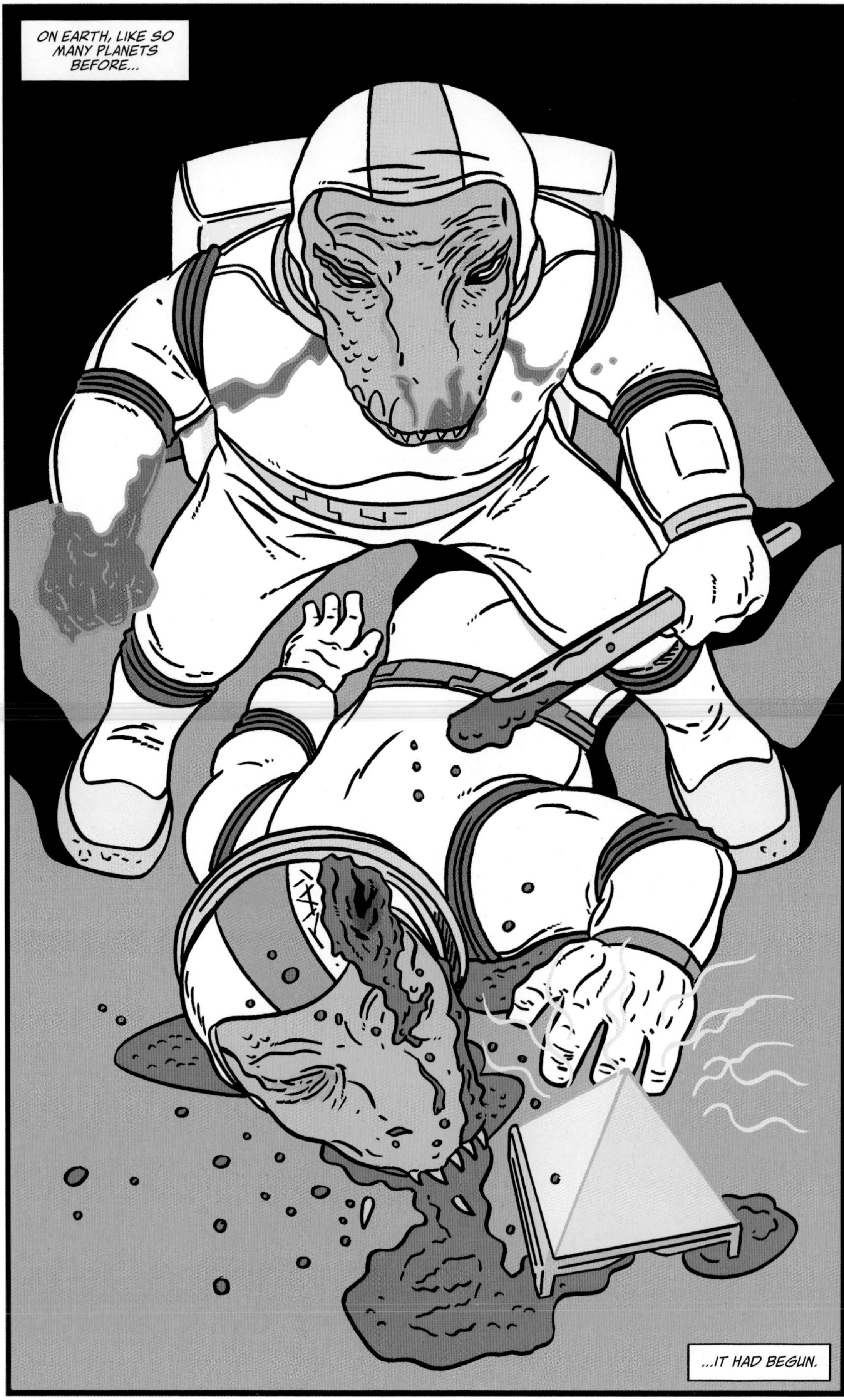
ON EARTH, LIKE SO MANY PLANETS BEFORE...
...IT HAD BEGUN.

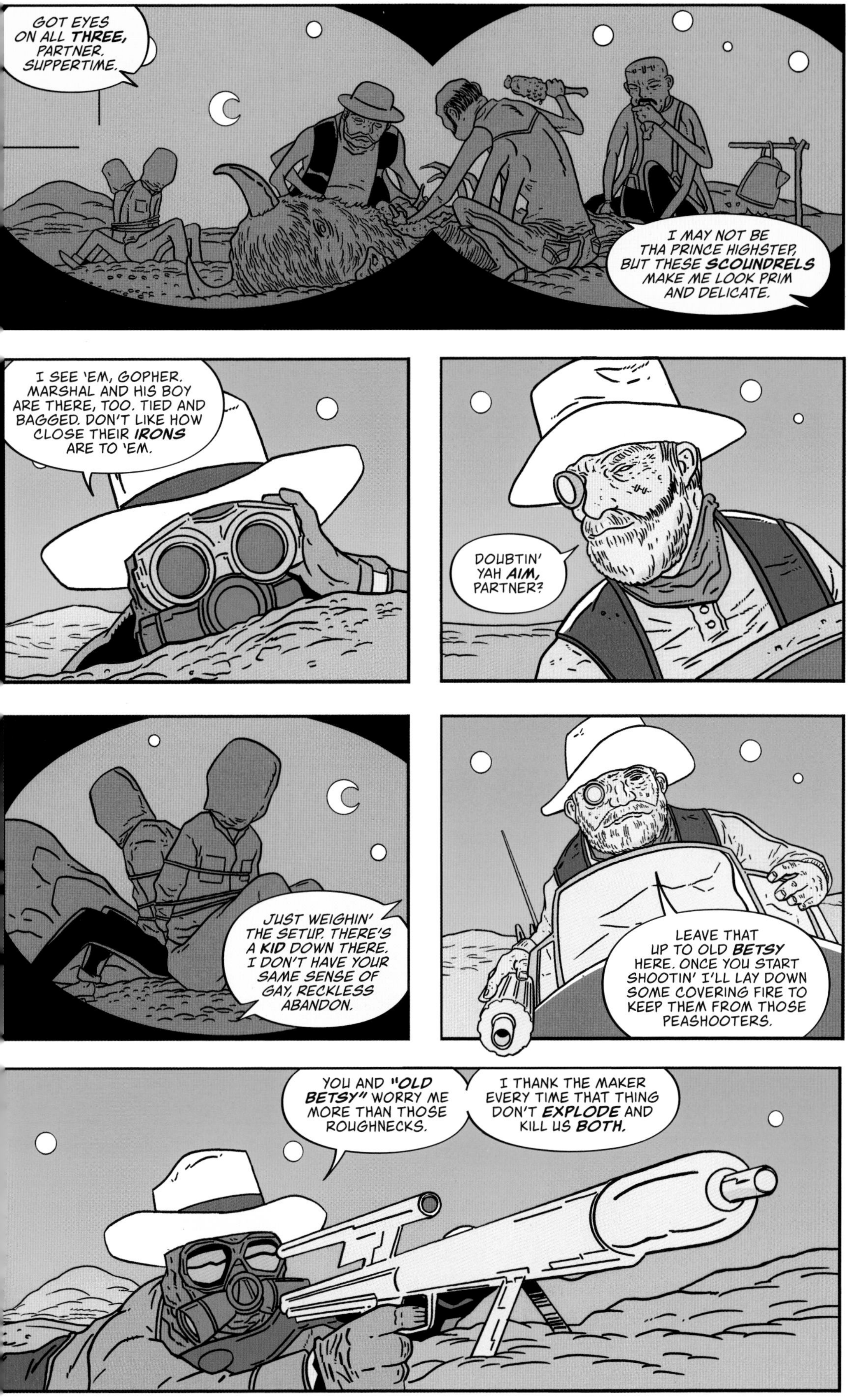
GOT EYES ON ALL THREE, PARTNER. SUPPERTIME.
I MAY NOT BE THA PRINCE HIGHSTEP, BUT THESE SCOUNDRELS MAKE ME LOOK PRIM AND DELICATE.
I SEE 'EM, GOPHER. MARSHAL AND HIS BOY ARE THERE, TOO. TIED AND BAGGED. DON'T LIKE HOW CLOSE THEIR IRONS ARE TO 'EM.
DOUBTIN' YAH AIM, PARTNER?
JUST WEIGHIN' THE SETUP. THERE'S A KID DOWN THERE. I DON'T HAVE YOUR SAME SENSE OF GAY, RECKLESS ABANDON.
LEAVE THAT UP TO OLD BETSY HERE. ONCE YOU START SHOOTIN' I'LL LAY DOWN SOME COVERING FIRE TO KEEP THEM FROM THOSE PEASHOOTERS.
YOU AND "OLD BETSY" WORRY ME MORE THAN THOSE ROUGHNECKS.
I THANK THE MAKER EVERY TIME THAT THING DON'T EXPLODE AND KILL US BOTH.

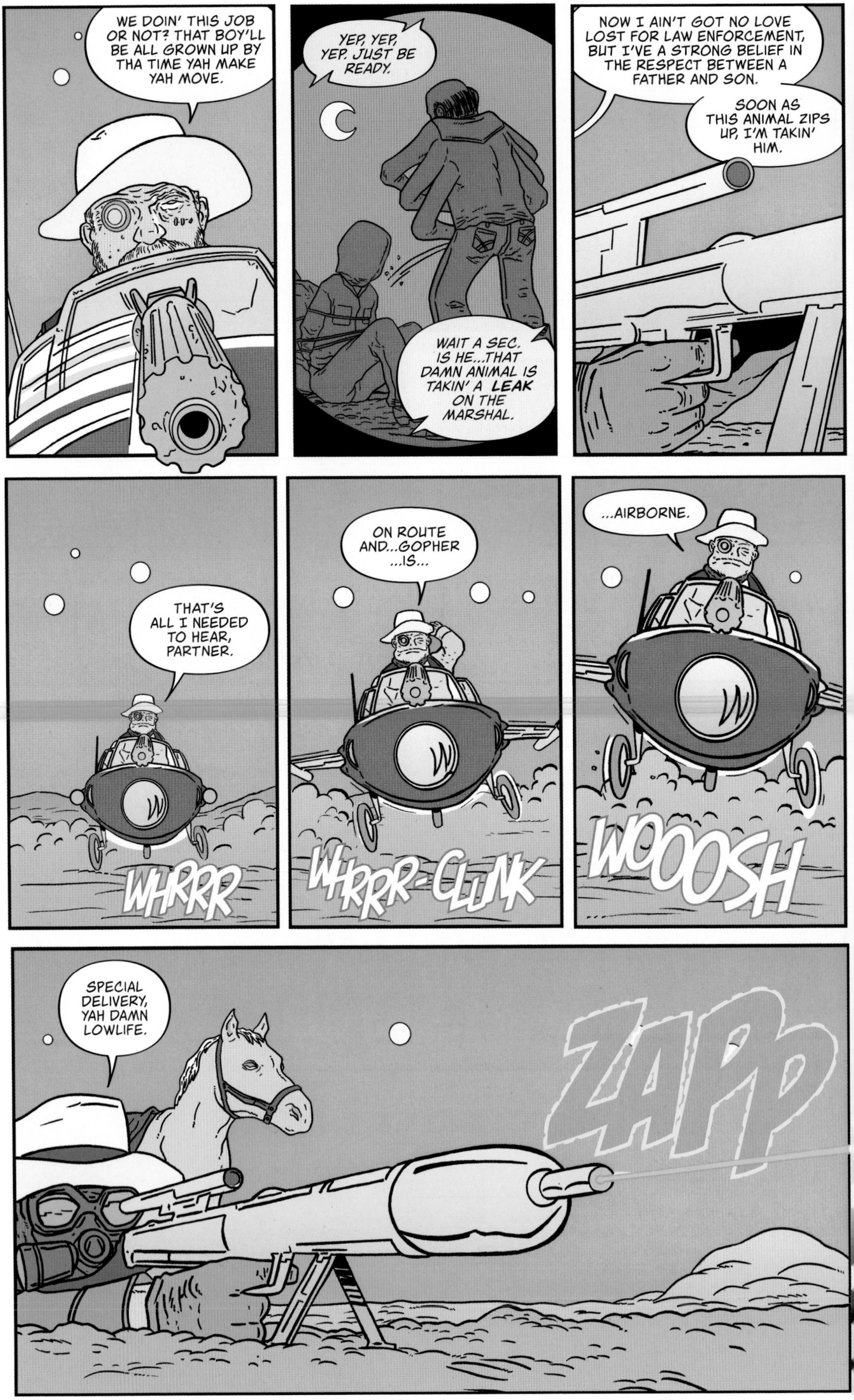
WE DOIN' THIS JOB OR NOT? THAT BOY'LL BE ALL GROWN UP BY THA TIME YAH MAKE YAH MOVE.
YEP, YEP, YEP. JUST BE READY.
WAIT A SEC. IS HE...THAT DAMN ANIMAL IS TAKIN' A **LEAK** ON THE MARSHAL.
NOW I AIN'T GOT NO LOVE LOST FOR LAW ENFORCEMENT, BUT I'VE A STRONG BELIEF IN THE RESPECT BETWEEN A FATHER AND SON.
SOON AS THIS ANIMAL ZIPS UP, I'M TAKIN' HIM.
THAT'S ALL I NEEDED TO HEAR, PARTNER.
WHRRR
ON ROUTE AND...GOPHER ...IS...
WHRRR-CLUNK
...AIRBORNE.
WOOOSH
SPECIAL DELIVERY, YAH DAMN LOWLIFE.
ZAPP

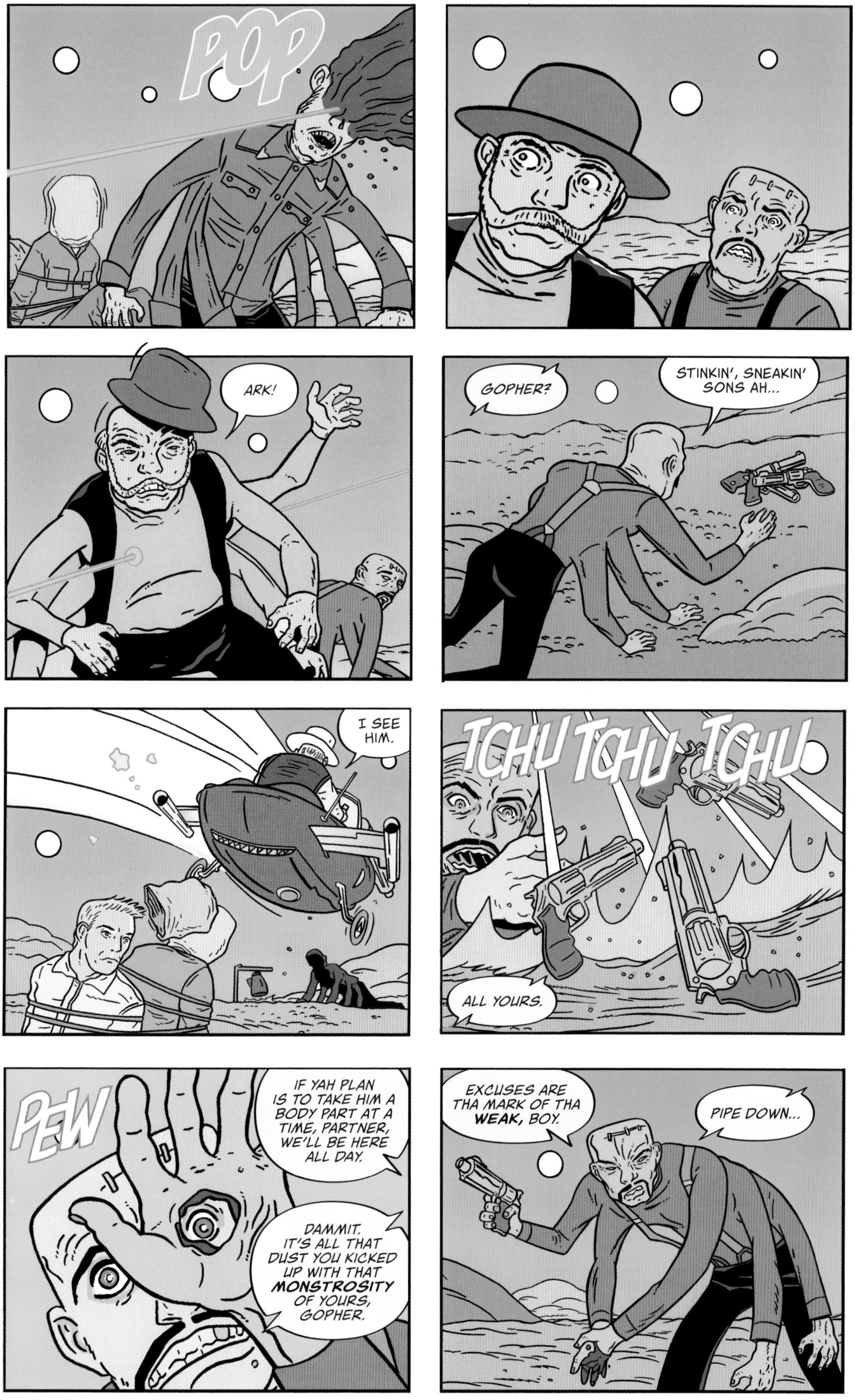
POP
ARK!
GOPHER?
STINKIN', SNEAKIN' SONS AH...
I SEE HIM.
TCHU TCHU TCHU
ALL YOURS.
PEW
IF YAH PLAN IS TO TAKE HIM A BODY PART AT A TIME, PARTNER, WE'LL BE HERE ALL DAY.
DAMMIT. IT'S ALL THAT DUST YOU KICKED UP WITH THAT MONSTROSITY OF YOURS, GOPHER.
EXCUSES ARE THA MARK OF THA WEAK, BOY.
PIPE DOWN...

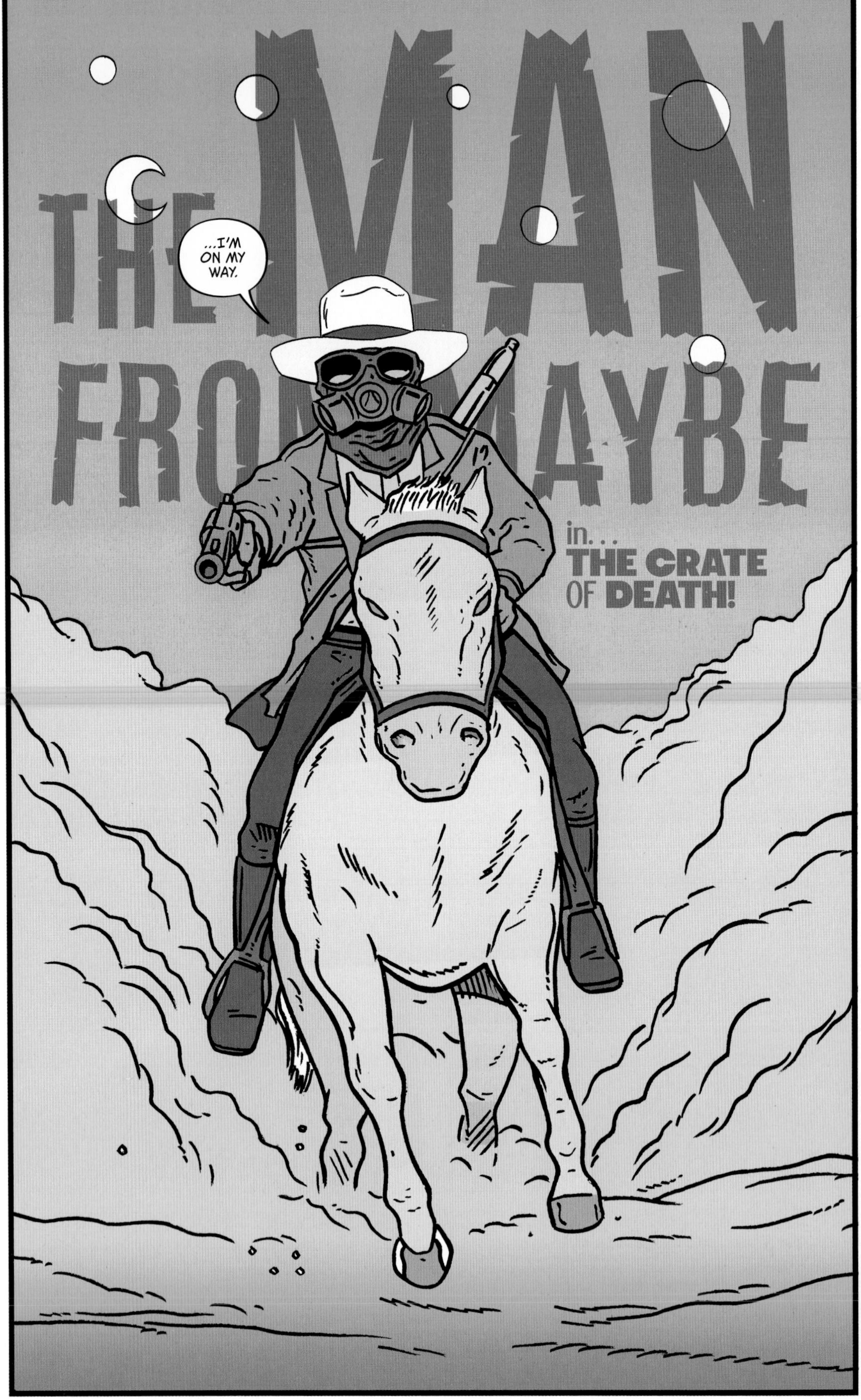
THE MAN FROM MAYBE
...I'M ON MY WAY.
in. . . THE CRATE OF DEATH!

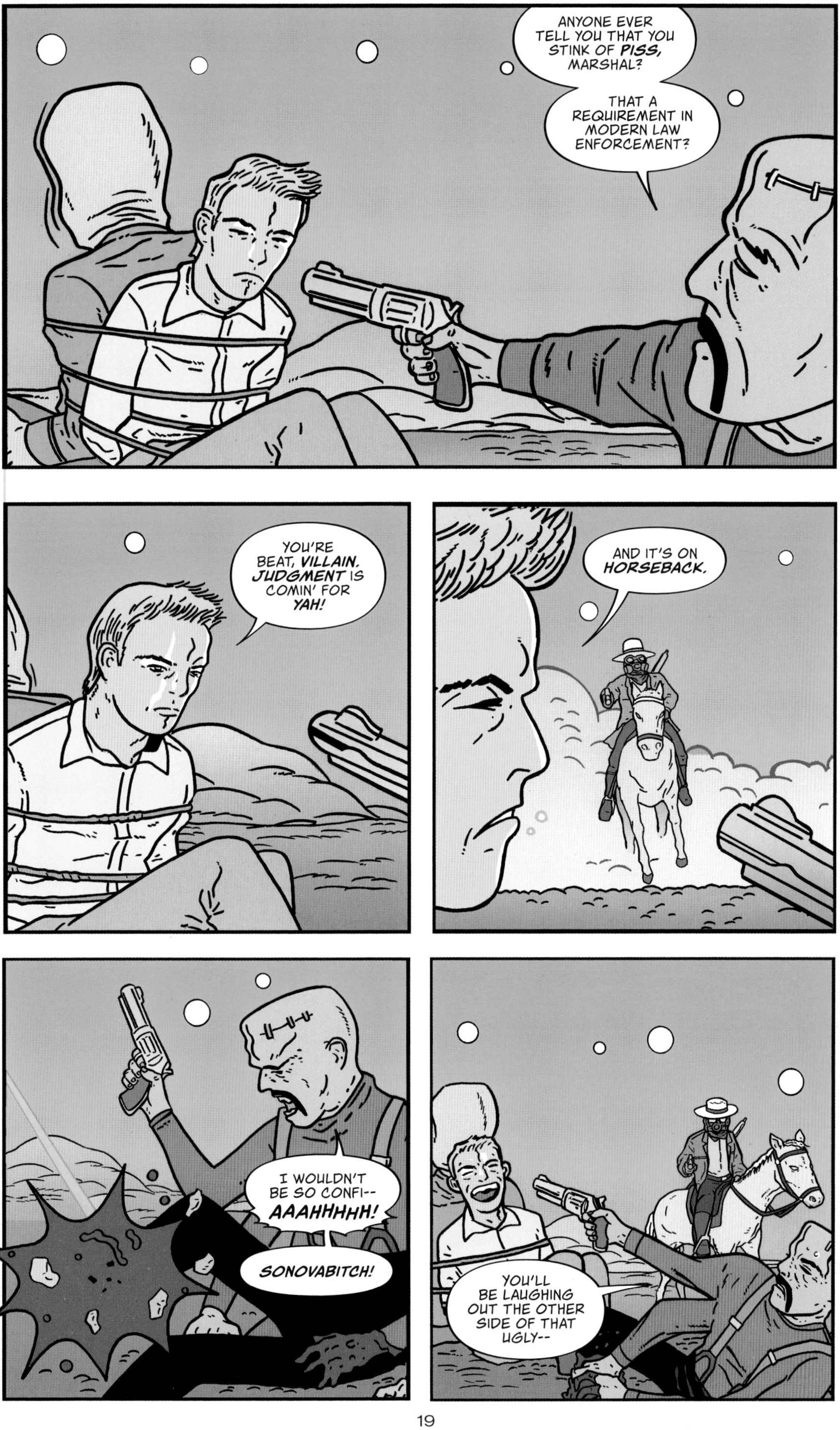
ANYONE EVER TELL YOU THAT YOU STINK OF **PISS**, MARSHAL?
THAT A REQUIREMENT IN MODERN LAW ENFORCEMENT?
YOU'RE BEAT, **VILLAIN. JUDGMENT** IS COMIN' FOR **YAH!**
AND IT'S ON **HORSEBACK.**
I WOULDN'T BE SO CONFI-- **AAAHHHHH!**
SONOVABITCH!
YOU'LL BE LAUGHING OUT THE OTHER SIDE OF THAT UGLY--

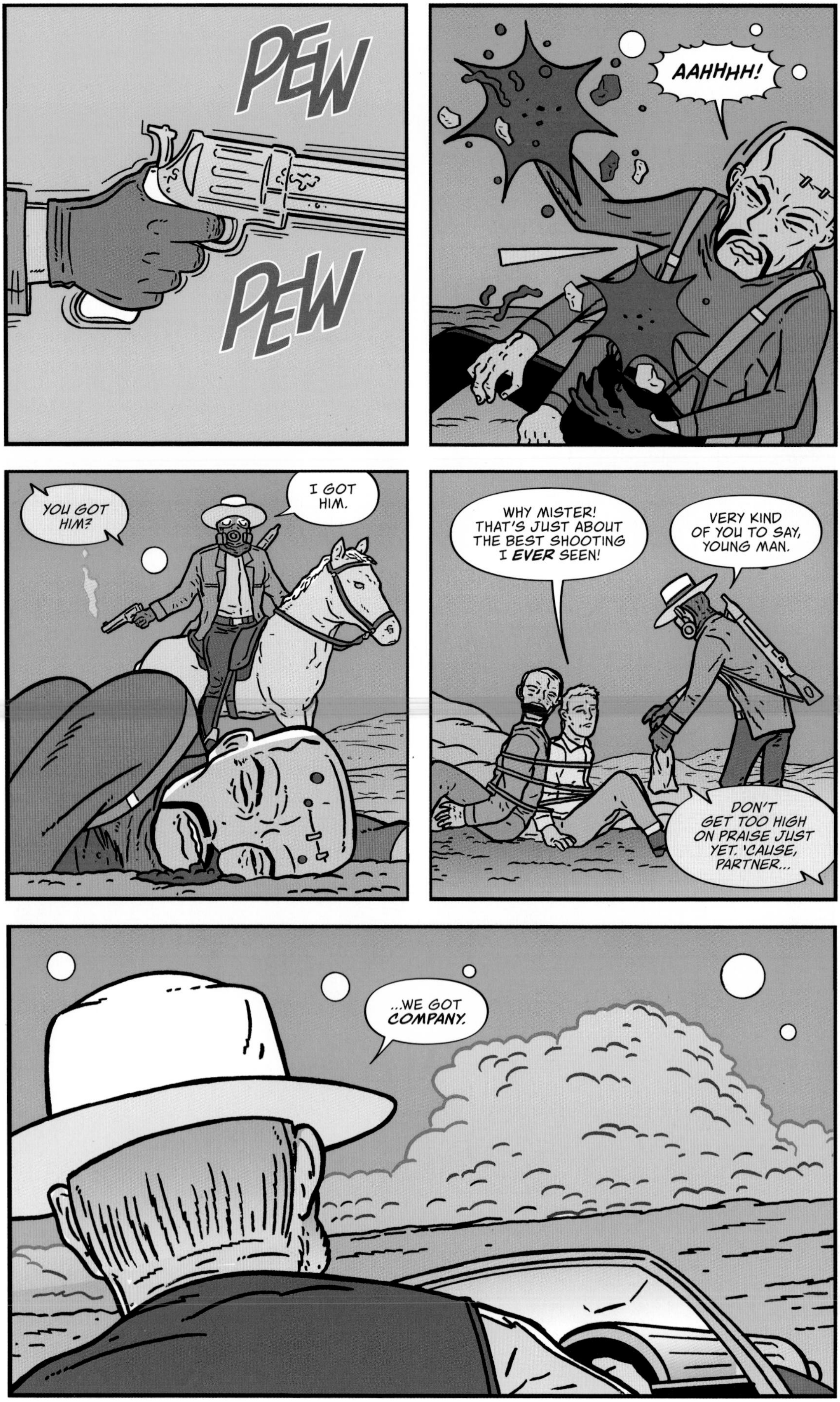
PEW
PEW
AAHHHH!
YOU GOT HIM?
I GOT HIM.
WHY MISTER! THAT'S JUST ABOUT THE BEST SHOOTING I EVER SEEN!
VERY KIND OF YOU TO SAY, YOUNG MAN.
DON'T GET TOO HIGH ON PRAISE JUST YET. 'CAUSE, PARTNER...
...WE GOT COMPANY.

GOOD MORNING, MR. DENNY. IT IS 8:42 A.M. ON DAY 28,607 OF THE NEW AGE.

HEAD OF YOUR OBSERVATION TEAM, GARNA WESK, HAS REQUESTED A MEETING WITH YOU.

SET FOR 10 A.M.

MEETING SET WITH GARNA WESK FOR 10 A.M.

LITTLE BOY OUTPOST REPORTS INCREASED UNREST AMONGST SETTLERS IN THEIR AREA. REQUEST TO USE INCREASED FORCE.

REQUEST GRANTED.

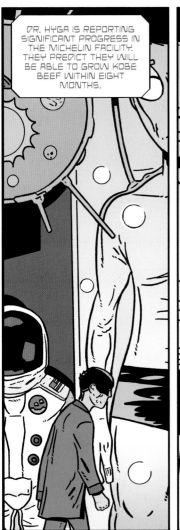

DR. HYGA IS REPORTING SIGNIFICANT PROGRESS IN THE MICHELIN FACILITY. THEY PREDICT THEY WILL BE ABLE TO GROW KOBE BEEF WITHIN EIGHT MONTHS.

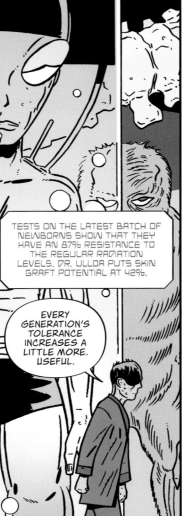

TESTS ON THE LATEST BATCH OF NEWBORNS SHOW THAT THEY HAVE AN 87% RESISTANCE TO THE REGULAR RADIATION LEVELS. DR. ULLOA PUTS SKIN GRAFT POTENTIAL AT 42%.

EVERY GENERATION'S TOLERANCE INCREASES A LITTLE MORE. USEFUL.

WARNING AREA 51 NO TRESPASSING

LEAD ENGINEER TYPHO HAS FORWARDED FOOTAGE OF THE OPERATION FÜHRER EXCAVATION PROJECT THAT HE BELIEVES YOU WILL FIND INTERESTING.

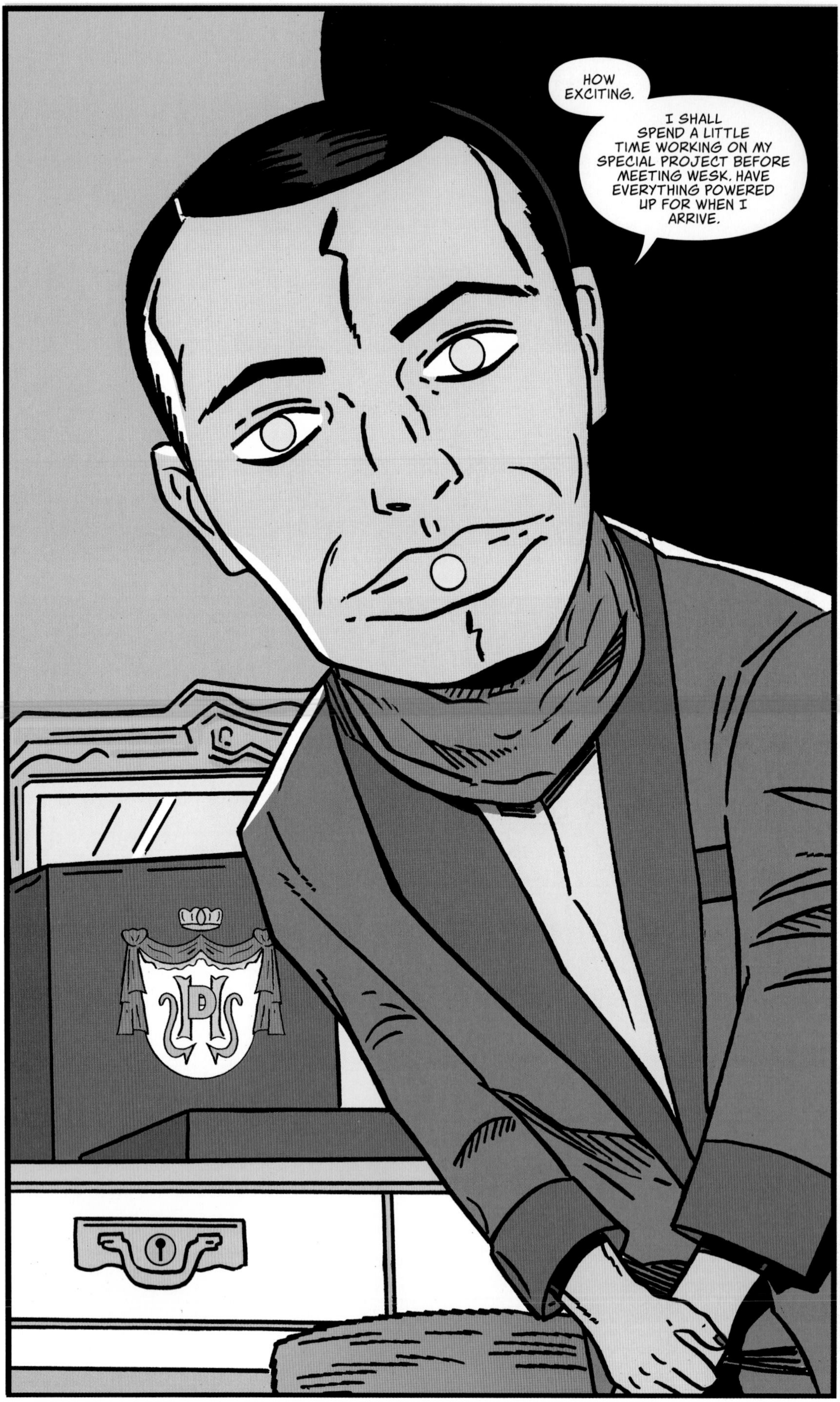
HOW EXCITING.
I SHALL SPEND A LITTLE TIME WORKING ON MY SPECIAL PROJECT BEFORE MEETING WESK. HAVE EVERYTHING POWERED UP FOR WHEN I ARRIVE.

DAMN. LOOKS LIKE THE REST OF THE GRIP GANG. WE MUST HAVE CAUGHT THEM AT THEIR RENDEZVOUS POINT.
THINK THEY'RE THE FORGIVING TYPES?
'BOUT AS MUCH AS YOU CAN TAP DANCE.
GOT A **PLAN,** PARTNER?
LOOKS LIKE THEY'RE HEADED STRAIGHT FOR ME. SO WE MAY HAVE GOT LUCKY AND THEY DON'T KNOW YOU'RE OUT THERE.
WAIT FOR THEM TO PASS AND THEN COME UP BEHIND THEM AND **UNLEASH** "BETSY." IDEALLY WITHOUT **HITTING** ANY OF US.
I CAN PICK OFF ANY YOU MISS.
I WANT YOU TO GO TAKE COVER IN YONDER RIDGE, ANGIE, OK? I'LL WHISTLE WHEN THE COAST IS CLEAR.
NNNHHHHHN.
THAT'S VERY **BRAVE** OF YOU, BUT I'LL BE FINE.
OK, GOPHER. I'D SAY THEY'RE 'BOUT 15 SECONDS FROM MY RANGE. HAPPY SHOOTIN'.
COVER YOUR EARS, SON.
YOU TOO, MARSHAL.

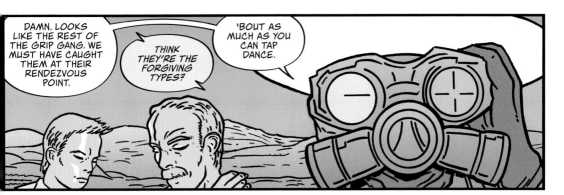

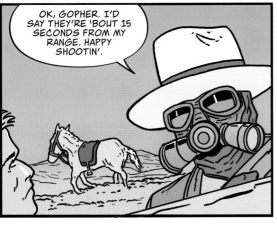

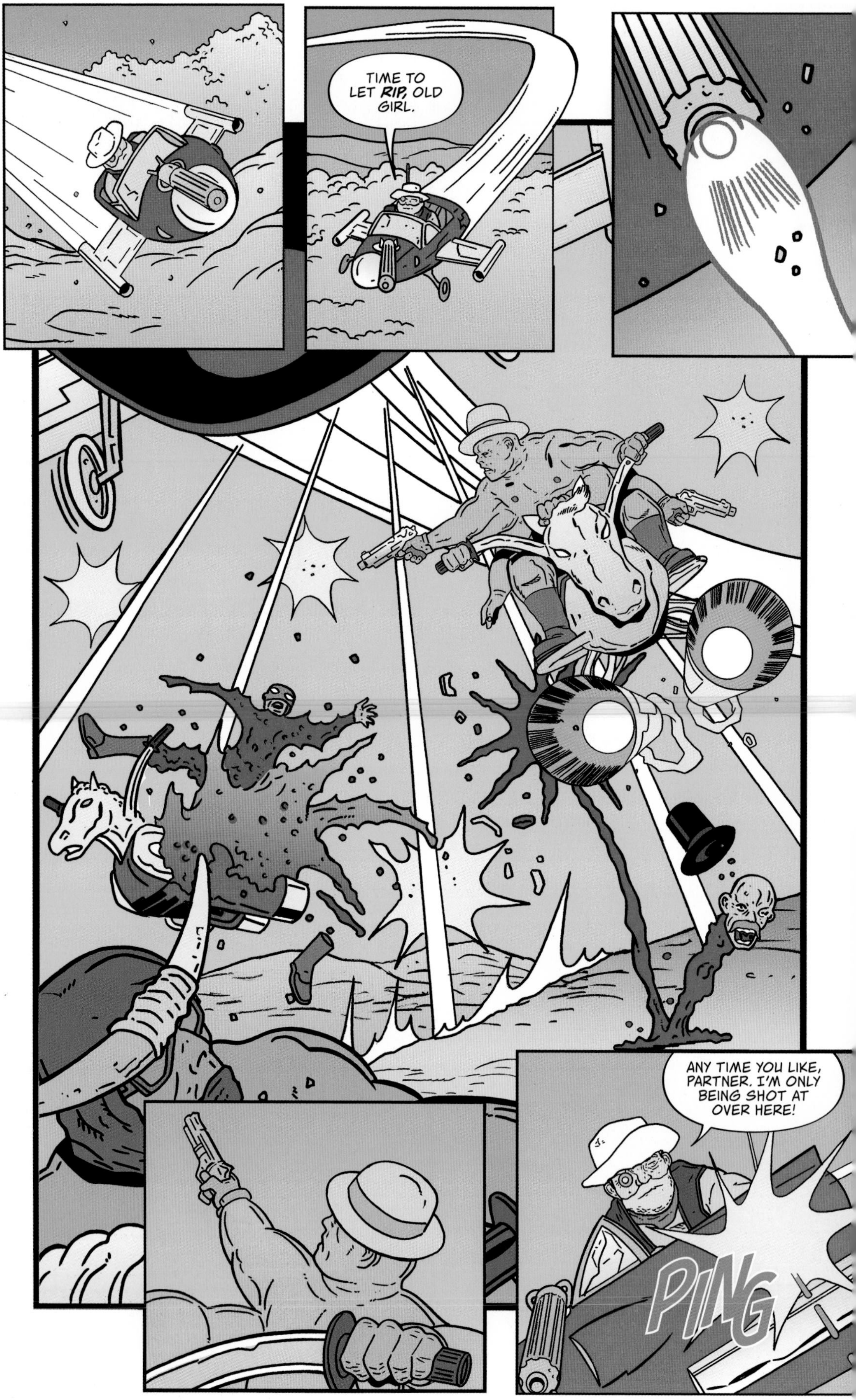
TIME TO LET RIP, OLD GIRL.
ANY TIME YOU LIKE, PARTNER. I'M ONLY BEING SHOT AT OVER HERE!
PING

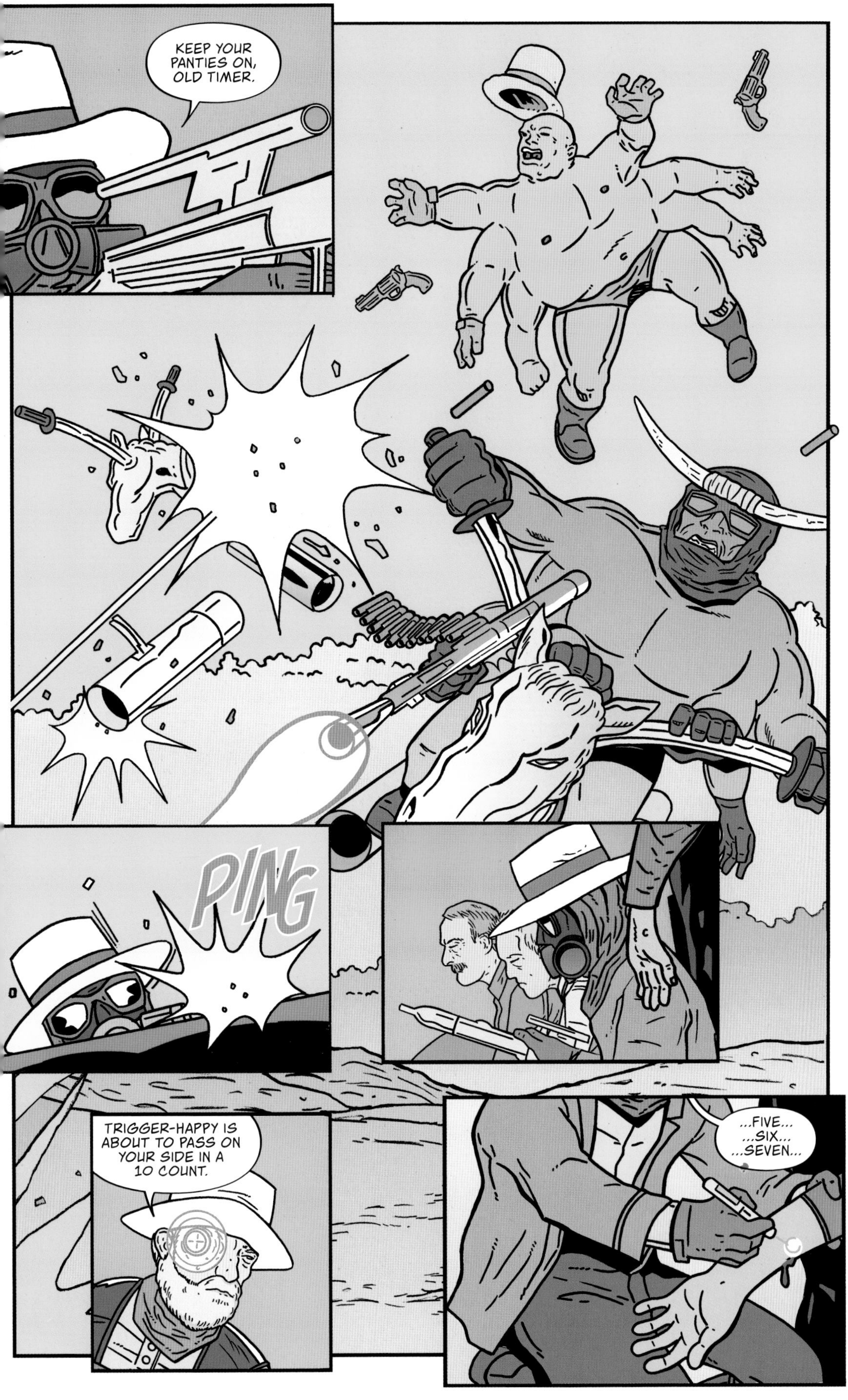
KEEP YOUR PANTIES ON, OLD TIMER.
PING
TRIGGER-HAPPY IS ABOUT TO PASS ON YOUR SIDE IN A 10 COUNT.
...FIVE... ...SIX... ...SEVEN...

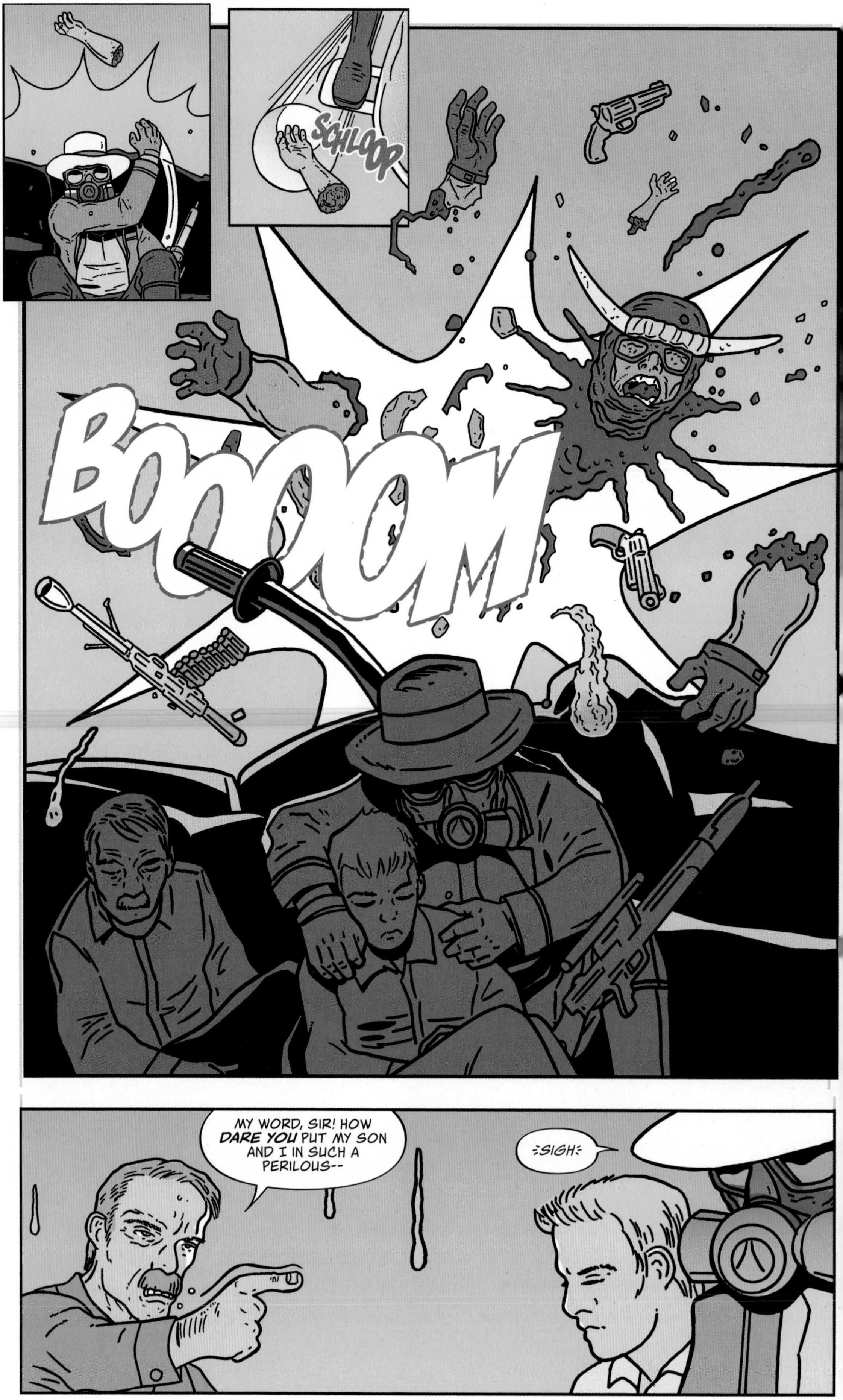
SCHLOOP
BOOOOM
MY WORD, SIR! HOW DARE YOU PUT MY SON AND I IN SUCH A PERILOUS--
SIGH

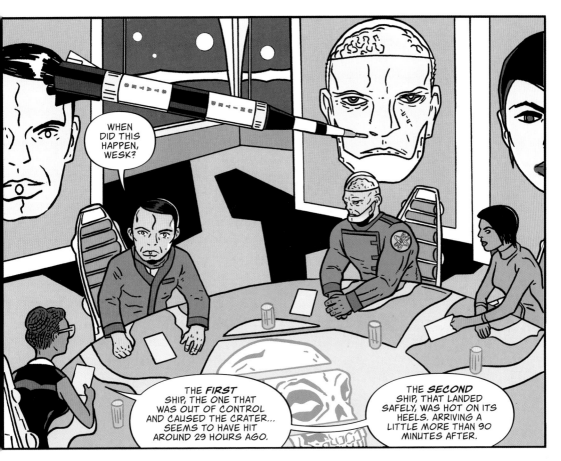

WHEN DID THIS HAPPEN, WESK?

THE *FIRST* SHIP, THE ONE THAT WAS OUT OF CONTROL AND CAUSED THE CRATER... SEEMS TO HAVE HIT AROUND 29 HOURS AGO.

THE *SECOND* SHIP, THAT LANDED SAFELY, WAS HOT ON ITS HEELS. ARRIVING A LITTLE MORE THAN 90 MINUTES AFTER.

SO WHY AM I JUST HEARING ABOUT THIS NOW?

OFF-WORLD VISITORS, METEORITES, UNMANNED UNITS--THE NUMBER OF ALERTS WE'RE RECEIVING RECENTLY ARE OFF THE CHARTS.

AN INCREASE OF 320% FROM TWO YEARS AGO.

WHEREAS A VISITOR FROM THE STARS USED TO BE NEWSWORTHY, NOW IT'S JUST A TUESDAY.

IT'S...*uh*...A LOT OF DATA TO RUN THROUGH, IS WHAT I MEAN. IF WE JUST HAD A BIT MORE--

HERE WE GO! WHO HAD *12 MINUTES* BEFORE WESK WENT LOOKING FOR *MORE* FUNDING?

YOU *KNOW* HOW MUCH SPACE MY TEAM HAS TO MONITOR.

"COLONEL"! WHAT ARE YOU EVEN COLONEL OF? WE'VE NO ARMY. YOU'RE HEAD OF SECURITY. COLONEL INGERBERG. WHAT A JOKE.

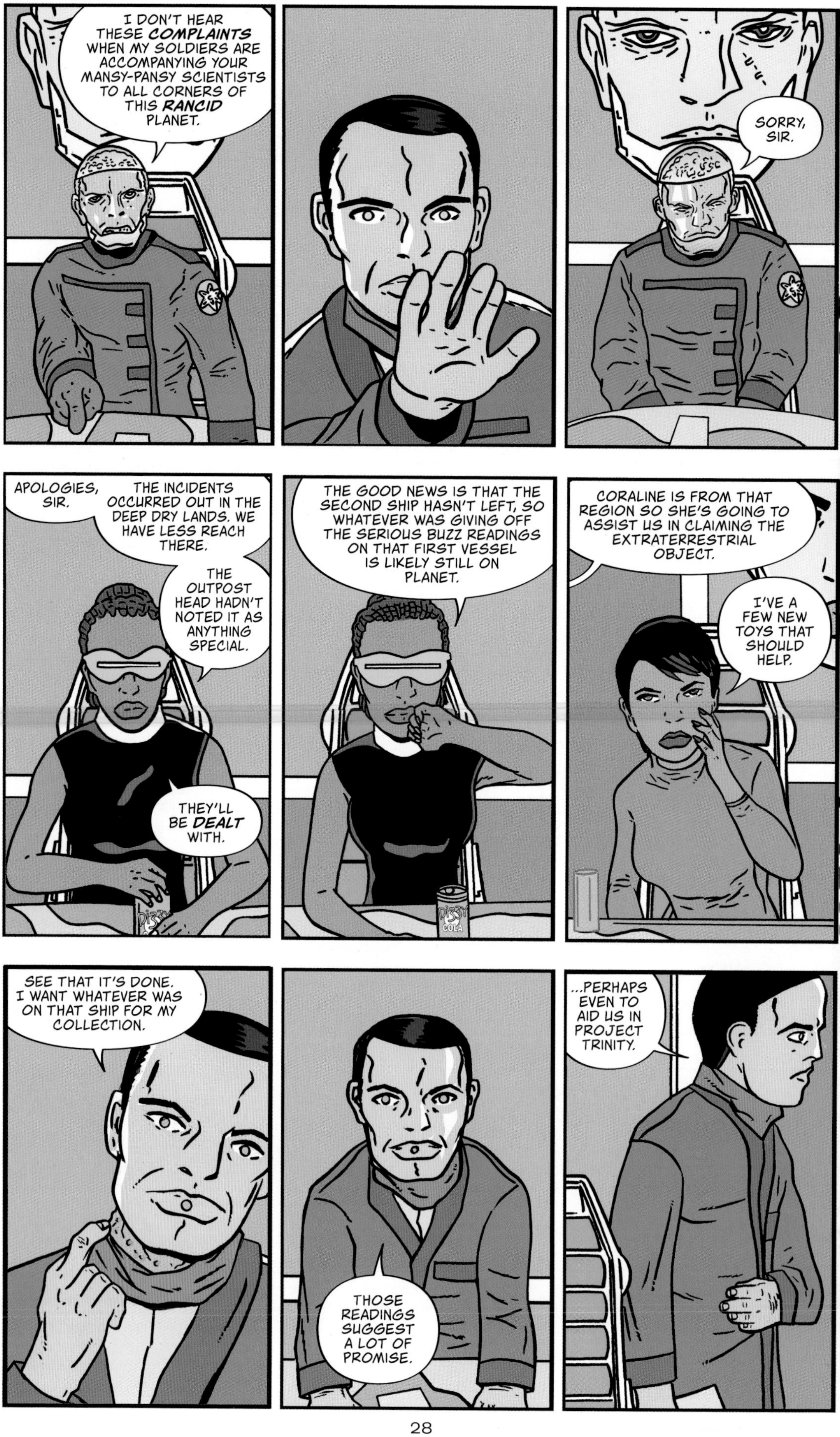
I DON'T HEAR THESE **COMPLAINTS** WHEN MY SOLDIERS ARE ACCOMPANYING YOUR MANSY-PANSY SCIENTISTS TO ALL CORNERS OF THIS **RANCID** PLANET.
SORRY, SIR.
APOLOGIES, SIR.
THE INCIDENTS OCCURRED OUT IN THE DEEP DRY LANDS. WE HAVE LESS REACH THERE.
THE OUTPOST HEAD HADN'T NOTED IT AS ANYTHING SPECIAL.
THEY'LL BE **DEALT** WITH.
THE GOOD NEWS IS THAT THE SECOND SHIP HASN'T LEFT, SO WHATEVER WAS GIVING OFF THE SERIOUS BUZZ READINGS ON THAT FIRST VESSEL IS LIKELY STILL ON PLANET.
CORALINE IS FROM THAT REGION SO SHE'S GOING TO ASSIST US IN CLAIMING THE EXTRATERRESTRIAL OBJECT.
I'VE A FEW NEW TOYS THAT SHOULD HELP.
SEE THAT IT'S DONE. I WANT WHATEVER WAS ON THAT SHIP FOR MY COLLECTION.
THOSE READINGS SUGGEST A LOT OF PROMISE.
...PERHAPS EVEN TO AID US IN PROJECT TRINITY.

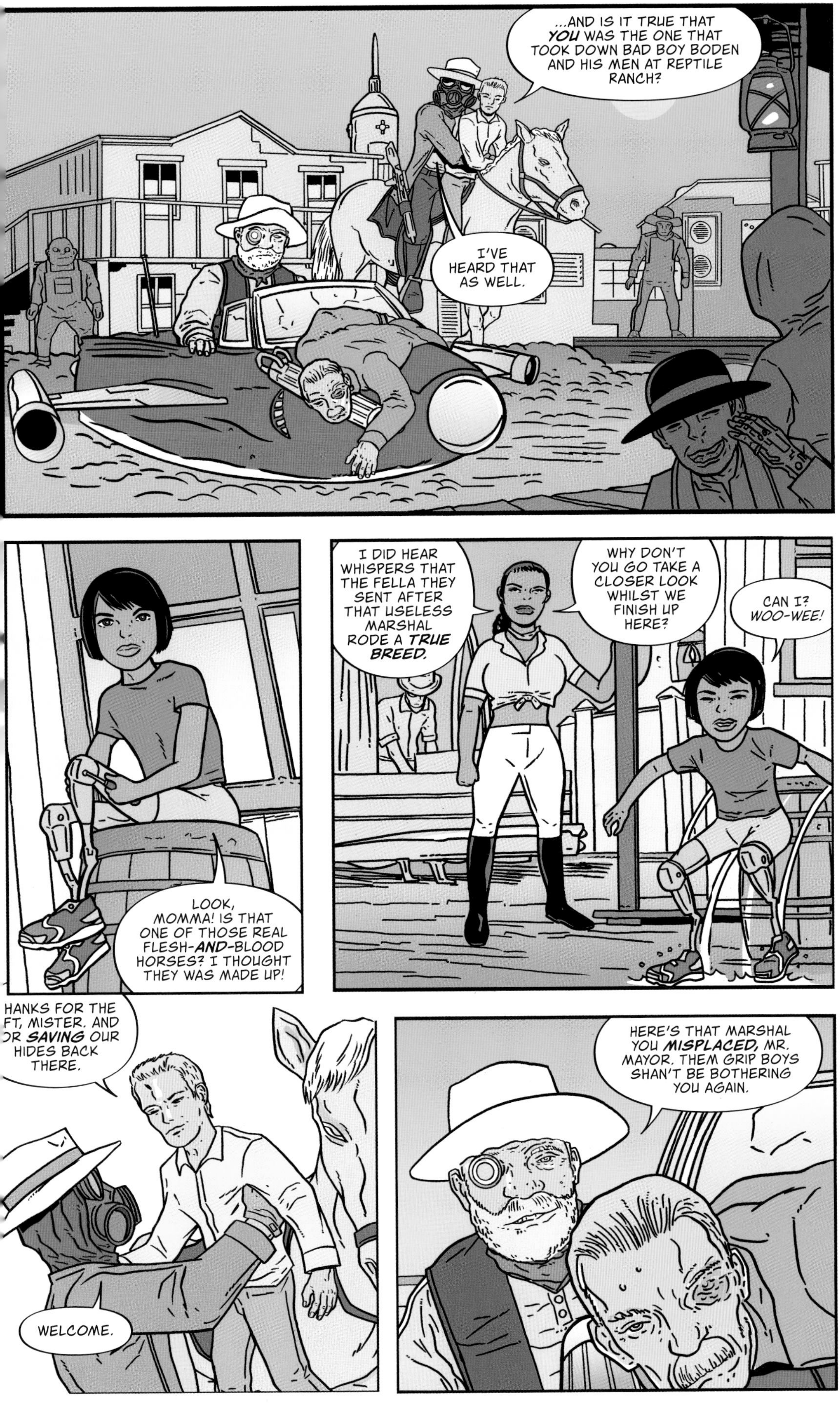
...AND IS IT TRUE THAT YOU WAS THE ONE THAT TOOK DOWN BAD BOY BODEN AND HIS MEN AT REPTILE RANCH?
I'VE HEARD THAT AS WELL.
LOOK, MOMMA! IS THAT ONE OF THOSE REAL FLESH-AND-BLOOD HORSES? I THOUGHT THEY WAS MADE UP!
I DID HEAR WHISPERS THAT THE FELLA THEY SENT AFTER THAT USELESS MARSHAL RODE A TRUE BREED.
WHY DON'T YOU GO TAKE A CLOSER LOOK WHILST WE FINISH UP HERE?
CAN I? WOO-WEE!
HANKS FOR THE FT, MISTER. AND OR SAVING OUR HIDES BACK THERE.
WELCOME.
HERE'S THAT MARSHAL YOU MISPLACED, MR. MAYOR. THEM GRIP BOYS SHAN'T BE BOTHERING YOU AGAIN.

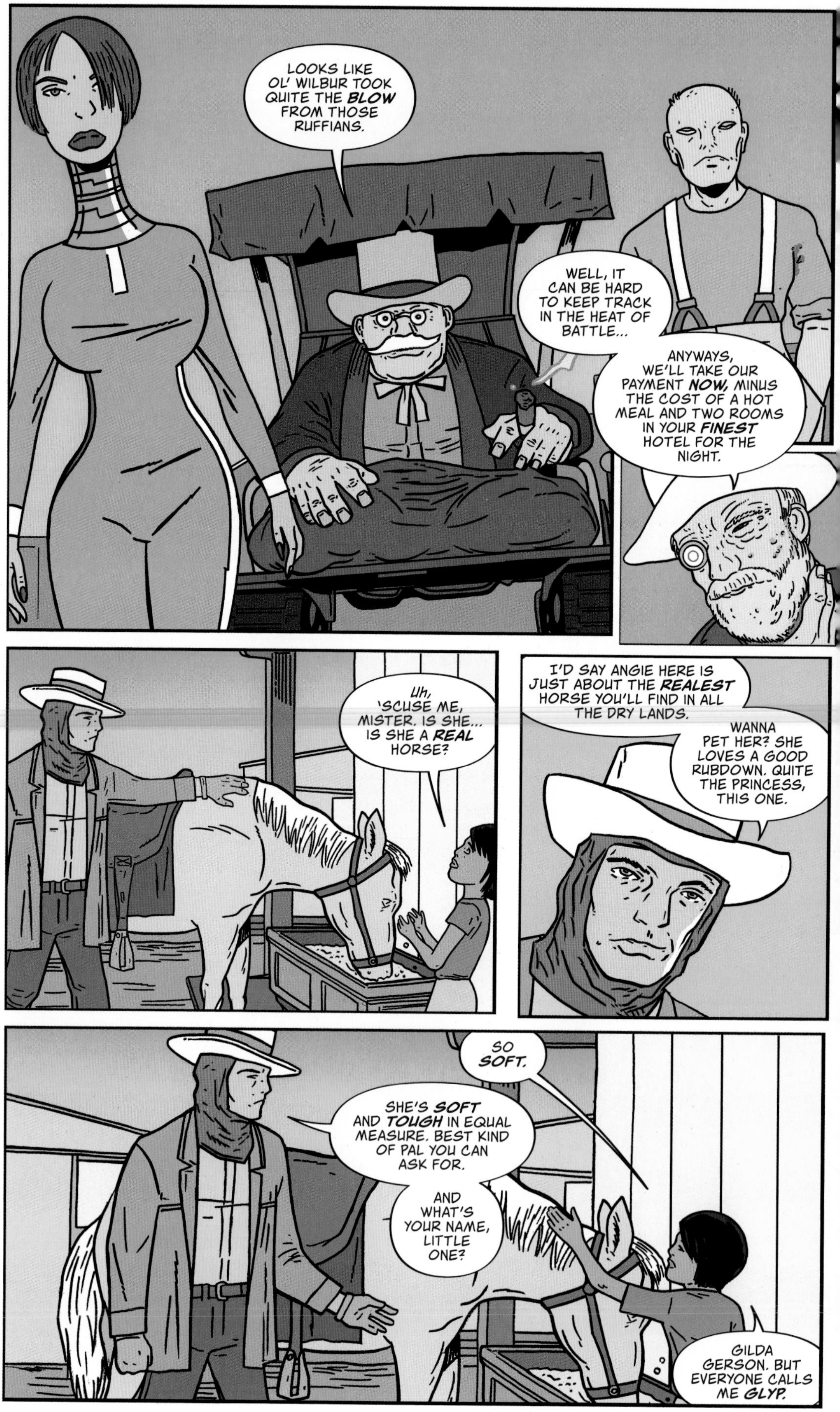
LOOKS LIKE OL' WILBUR TOOK QUITE THE BLOW FROM THOSE RUFFIANS.
WELL, IT CAN BE HARD TO KEEP TRACK IN THE HEAT OF BATTLE...
ANYWAYS, WE'LL TAKE OUR PAYMENT NOW, MINUS THE COST OF A HOT MEAL AND TWO ROOMS IN YOUR FINEST HOTEL FOR THE NIGHT.
UH, 'SCUSE ME, MISTER. IS SHE... IS SHE A REAL HORSE?
I'D SAY ANGIE HERE IS JUST ABOUT THE REALEST HORSE YOU'LL FIND IN ALL THE DRY LANDS.
WANNA PET HER? SHE LOVES A GOOD RUBDOWN. QUITE THE PRINCESS, THIS ONE.
SO SOFT.
SHE'S SOFT AND TOUGH IN EQUAL MEASURE. BEST KIND OF PAL YOU CAN ASK FOR.
AND WHAT'S YOUR NAME, LITTLE ONE?
GILDA GERSON. BUT EVERYONE CALLS ME GLYP.

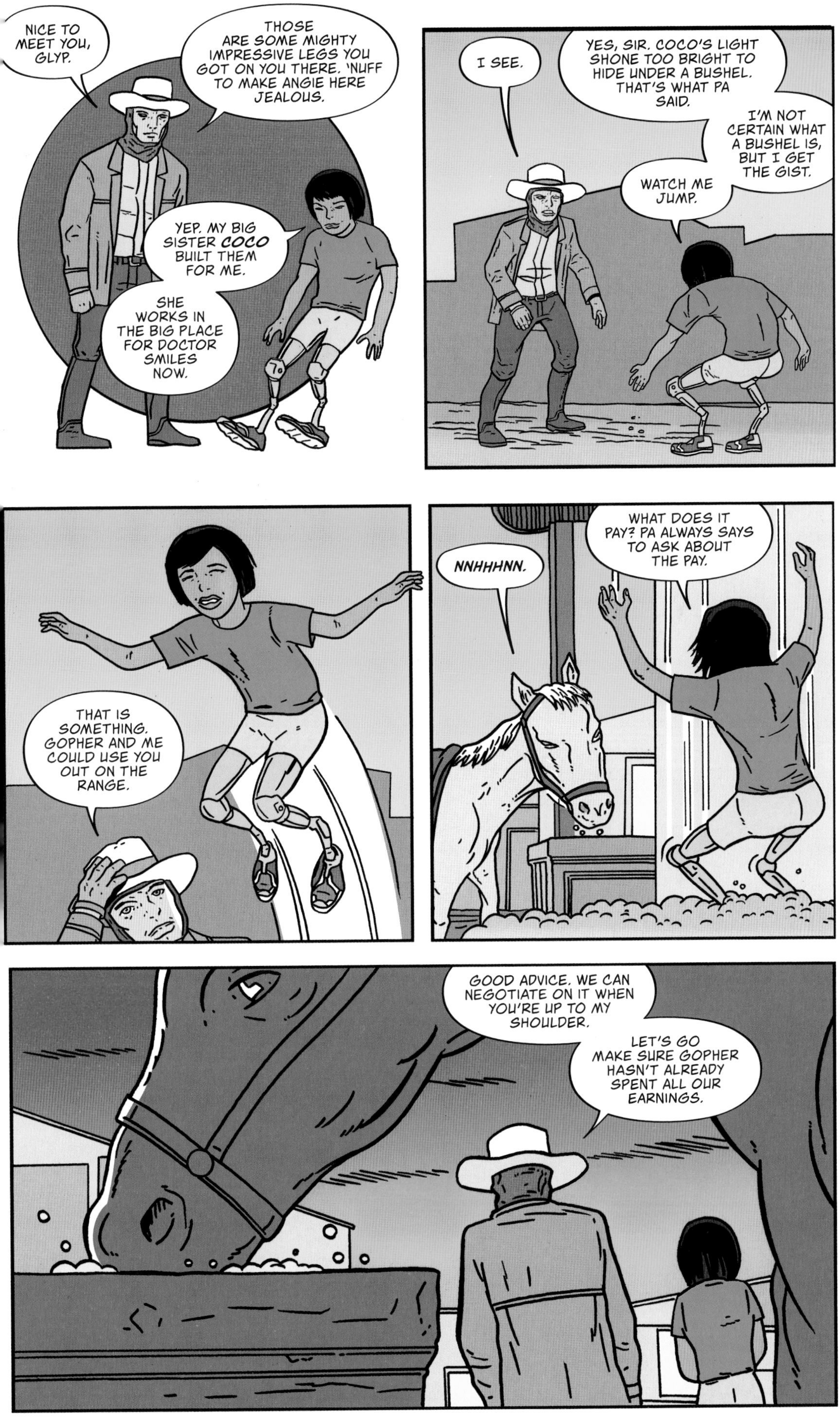
NICE TO MEET YOU, GLYP.
THOSE ARE SOME MIGHTY IMPRESSIVE LEGS YOU GOT ON YOU THERE. 'NUFF TO MAKE ANGIE HERE JEALOUS.
YEP. MY BIG SISTER **COCO** BUILT THEM FOR ME.
SHE WORKS IN THE BIG PLACE FOR DOCTOR SMILES NOW.
I SEE.
YES, SIR. COCO'S LIGHT SHONE TOO BRIGHT TO HIDE UNDER A BUSHEL. THAT'S WHAT PA SAID.
I'M NOT CERTAIN WHAT A BUSHEL IS, BUT I GET THE GIST.
WATCH ME JUMP.
THAT IS SOMETHING. GOPHER AND ME COULD USE YOU OUT ON THE RANGE.
NNHHHNN.
WHAT DOES IT PAY? PA ALWAYS SAYS TO ASK ABOUT THE PAY.
GOOD ADVICE. WE CAN NEGOTIATE ON IT WHEN YOU'RE UP TO MY SHOULDER.
LET'S GO MAKE SURE GOPHER HASN'T ALREADY SPENT ALL OUR EARNINGS.

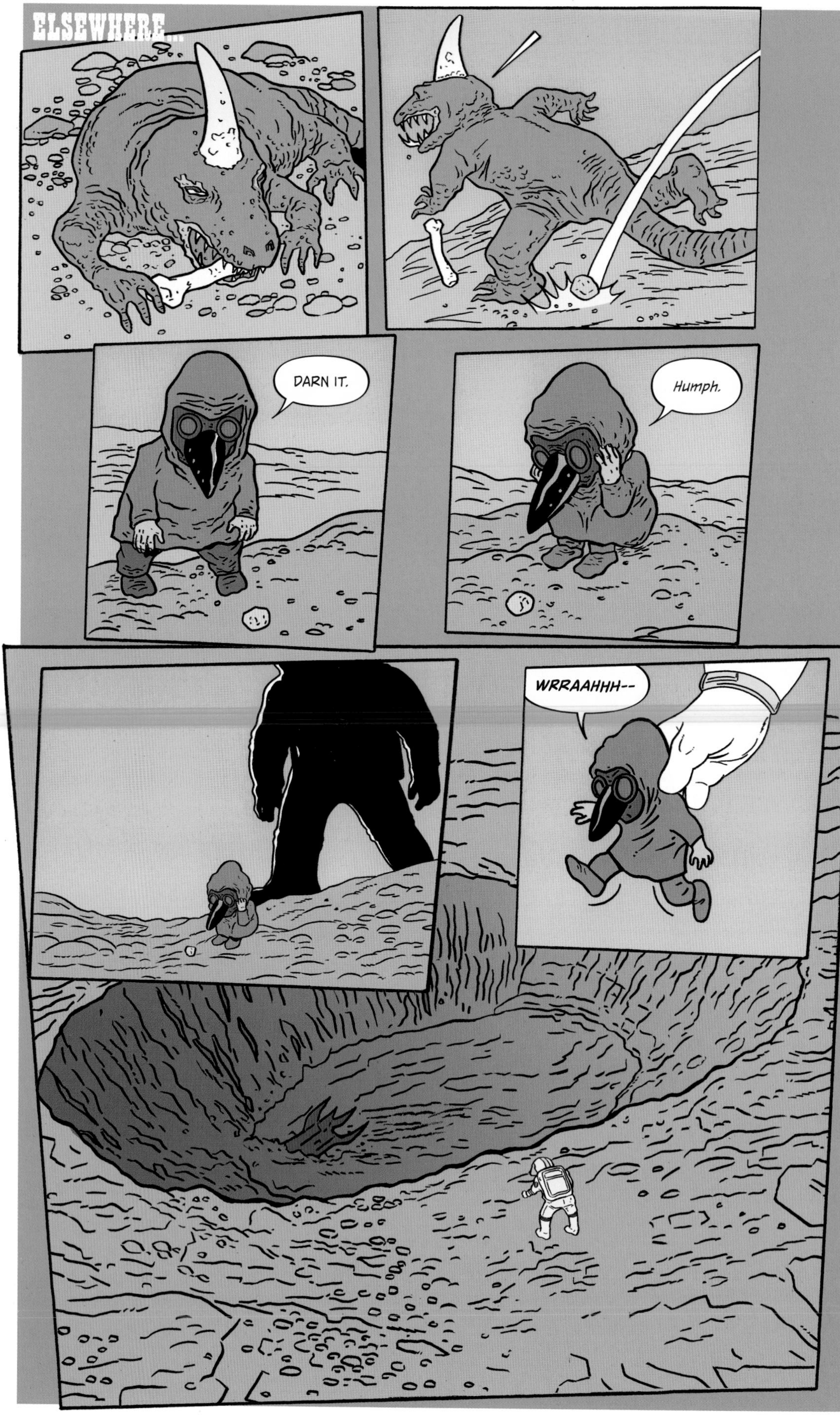
ELSEWHERE...
DARN IT.
Humph.
WRRAAHHH--

THE OLD GIRL THOUGHT HE HAD THREE LEGS!

THREE DAMN LEGS!

AHAHAHAHA!

I DON'T NEVER GET TIRED OF THAT ONE, PARTNER.

YOU SURE DON'T.

WIPE YOUR MOUTH. SEEMS WE GOT COMPANY.

SORRY TO DISTURB YOU FINE GENTLEMEN IN YOUR LIBATIONS.

DON'T KNOW ABOUT GENTLEMEN, BUT WE CERTAINLY *LIBATE!* HOW CAN WE HELP YOU PAIR?

MY NAME IS HUMBERTO GERSON, AND YOU SEE, OUR FAMILY, MINE AND MY WIFE, LUCIA HERE. I BELIEVE YOU MET OUR YOUNG DAUGHTER EARLIER. GLYP. GILDA.

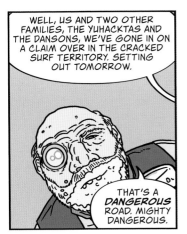

WELL, US AND TWO OTHER FAMILIES, THE YUHACKTAS AND THE DANSONS, WE'VE GONE IN ON A CLAIM OVER IN THE CRACKED SURF TERRITORY. SETTING OUT TOMORROW.

THAT'S A *DANGEROUS* ROAD. MIGHTY DANGEROUS.

PRECISELY. WHICH IS WHY WE WANT TO ACQUIRE THE SERVICES OF YOU *FINE MEN* TO ACCOMPANY US ON OUR JOURNEY. SCARE OFF ANY WOULD-BE *OPPORTUNISTS.*

WHEN YOU SETTING OFF?

"WE MEAN TO LEAVE AT FIRST LIGHT."

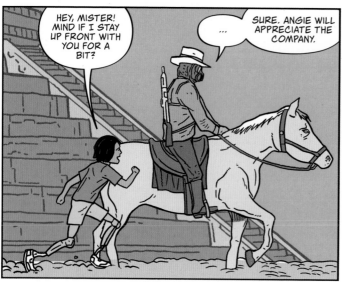

HEY, MISTER! MIND IF I STAY UP FRONT WITH YOU FOR A BIT?

... SURE. ANGIE WILL APPRECIATE THE COMPANY.

SO ANGIE DON'T GET SICK FROM THE *FALLOUT RAINS* OR NOTHING?

NOPE. SHE'S 100% IMMUNE.

AND YOU?

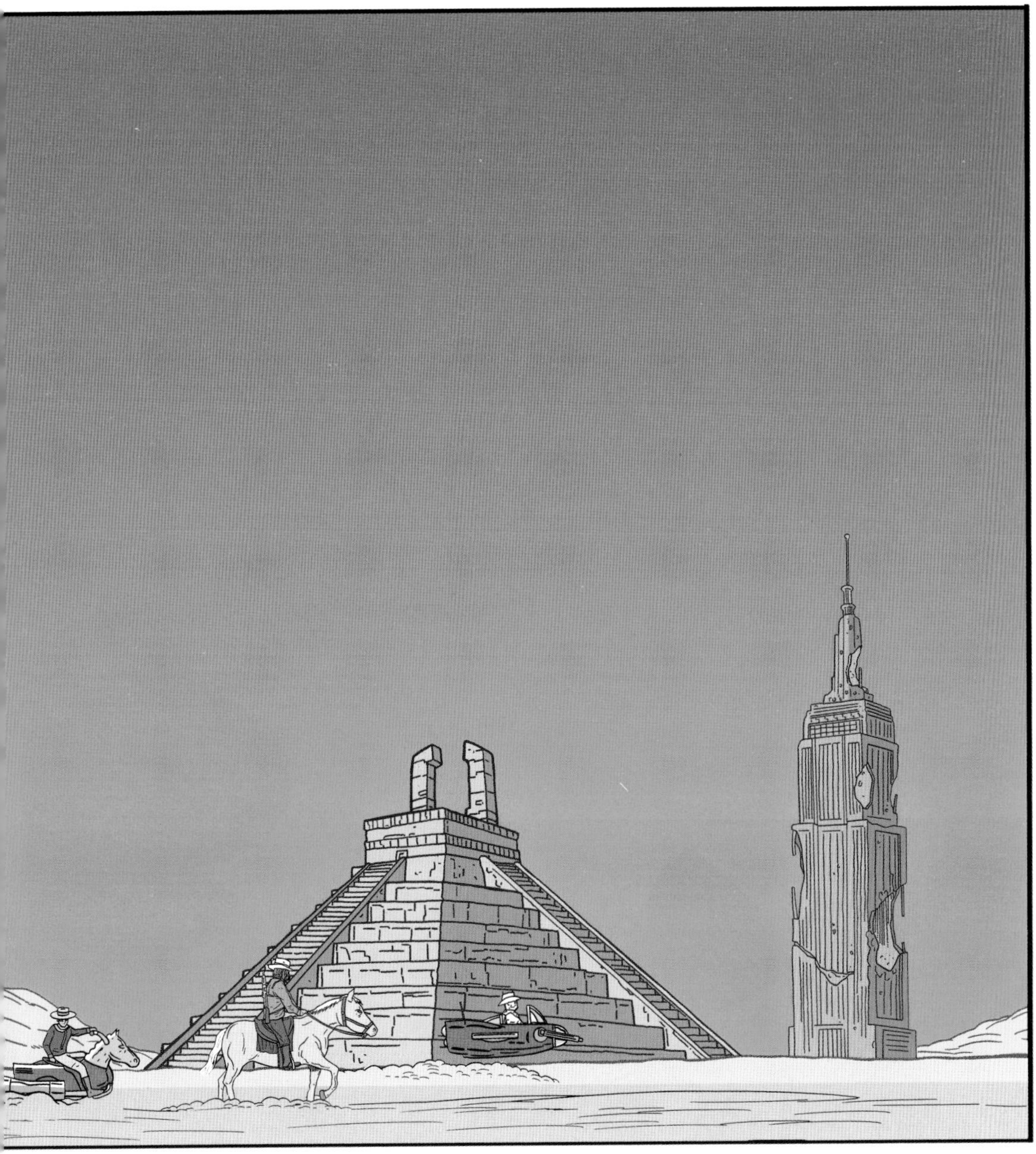

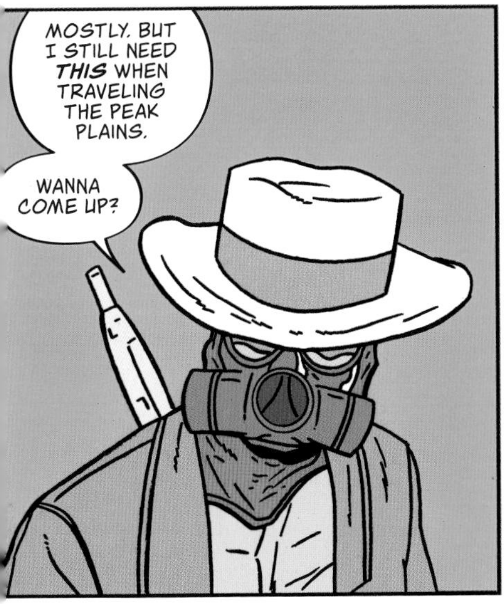
MOSTLY. BUT I STILL NEED **THIS** WHEN TRAVELING THE PEAK PLAINS.
WANNA COME UP?

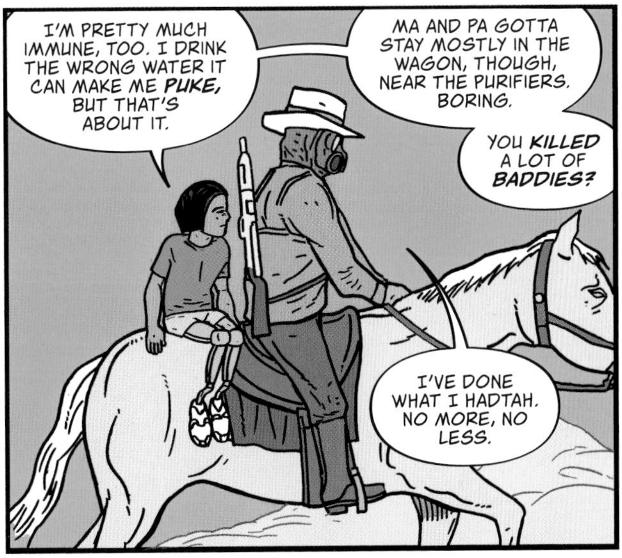
I'M PRETTY MUCH IMMUNE, TOO. I DRINK THE WRONG WATER IT CAN MAKE ME **PUKE,** BUT THAT'S ABOUT IT.
MA AND PA GOTTA STAY MOSTLY IN THE WAGON, THOUGH, NEAR THE PURIFIERS. BORING.
YOU **KILLED** A LOT OF **BADDIES?**
I'VE DONE WHAT I HADTAH. NO MORE, NO LESS.

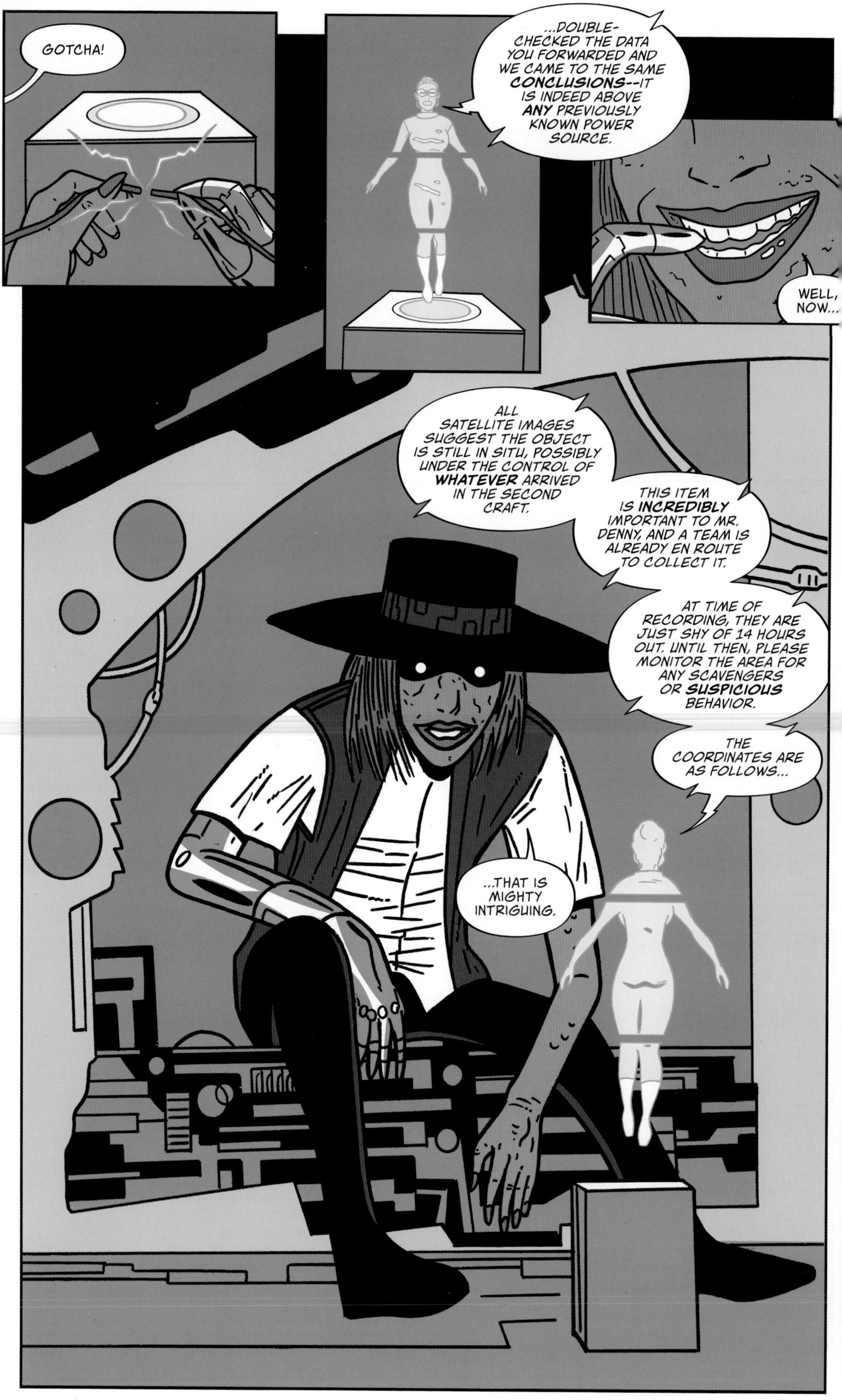
GOTCHA!
...DOUBLE-CHECKED THE DATA YOU FORWARDED AND WE CAME TO THE SAME **CONCLUSIONS**--IT IS INDEED ABOVE **ANY** PREVIOUSLY KNOWN POWER SOURCE.
WELL, NOW...
ALL SATELLITE IMAGES SUGGEST THE OBJECT IS STILL IN SITU, POSSIBLY UNDER THE CONTROL OF **WHATEVER** ARRIVED IN THE SECOND CRAFT.
THIS ITEM IS **INCREDIBLY** IMPORTANT TO MR. DENNY, AND A TEAM IS ALREADY EN ROUTE TO COLLECT IT.
AT TIME OF RECORDING, THEY ARE JUST SHY OF 14 HOURS OUT. UNTIL THEN, PLEASE MONITOR THE AREA FOR ANY SCAVENGERS OR **SUSPICIOUS** BEHAVIOR.
THE COORDINATES ARE AS FOLLOWS...
...THAT IS MIGHTY INTRIGUING.

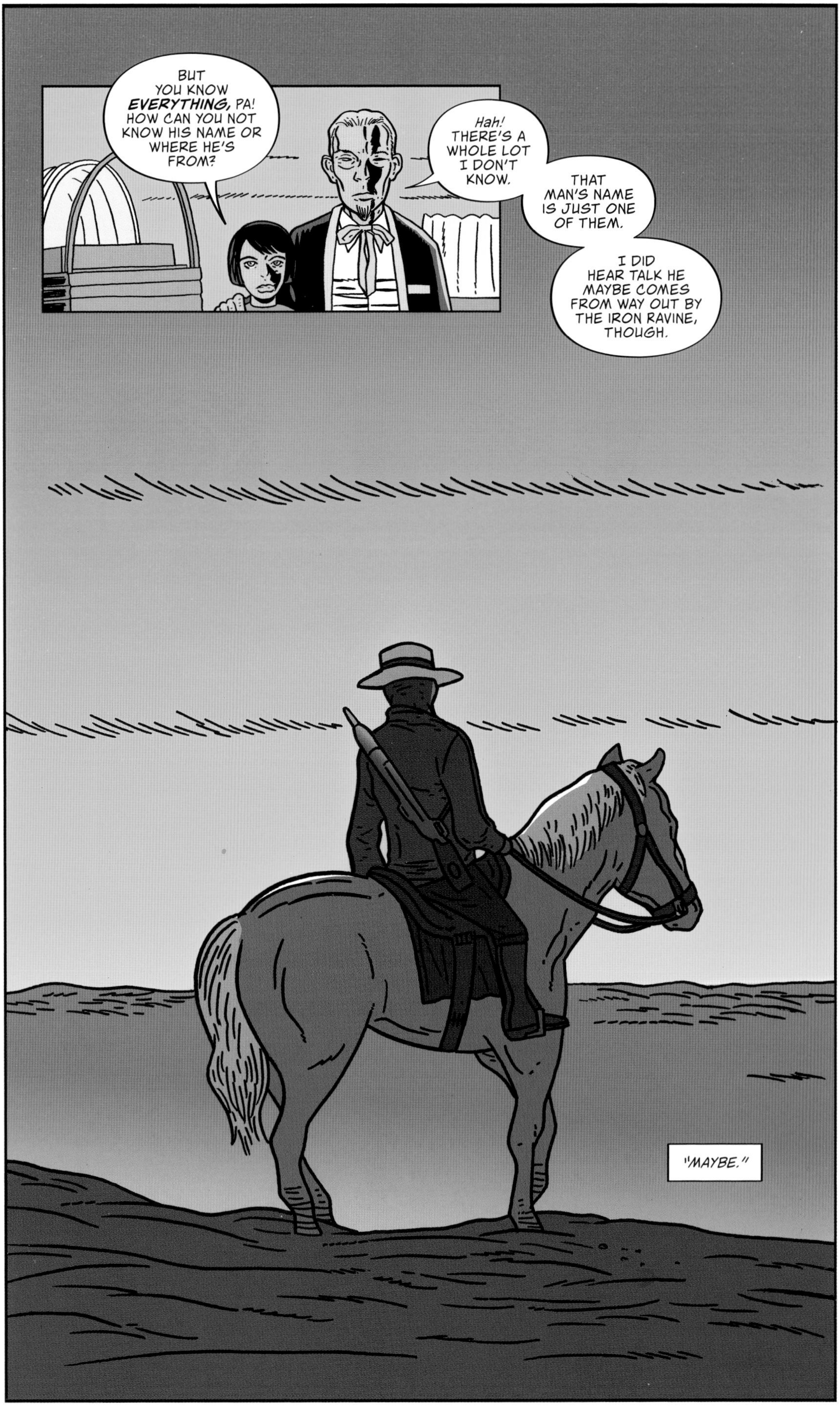

BUT YOU KNOW **EVERYTHING,** PA! HOW CAN YOU NOT KNOW HIS NAME OR WHERE HE'S FROM?
Hah! THERE'S A WHOLE LOT I DON'T KNOW.
THAT MAN'S NAME IS JUST ONE OF THEM.
I DID HEAR TALK HE MAYBE COMES FROM WAY OUT BY THE IRON RAVINE, THOUGH.
"MAYBE."

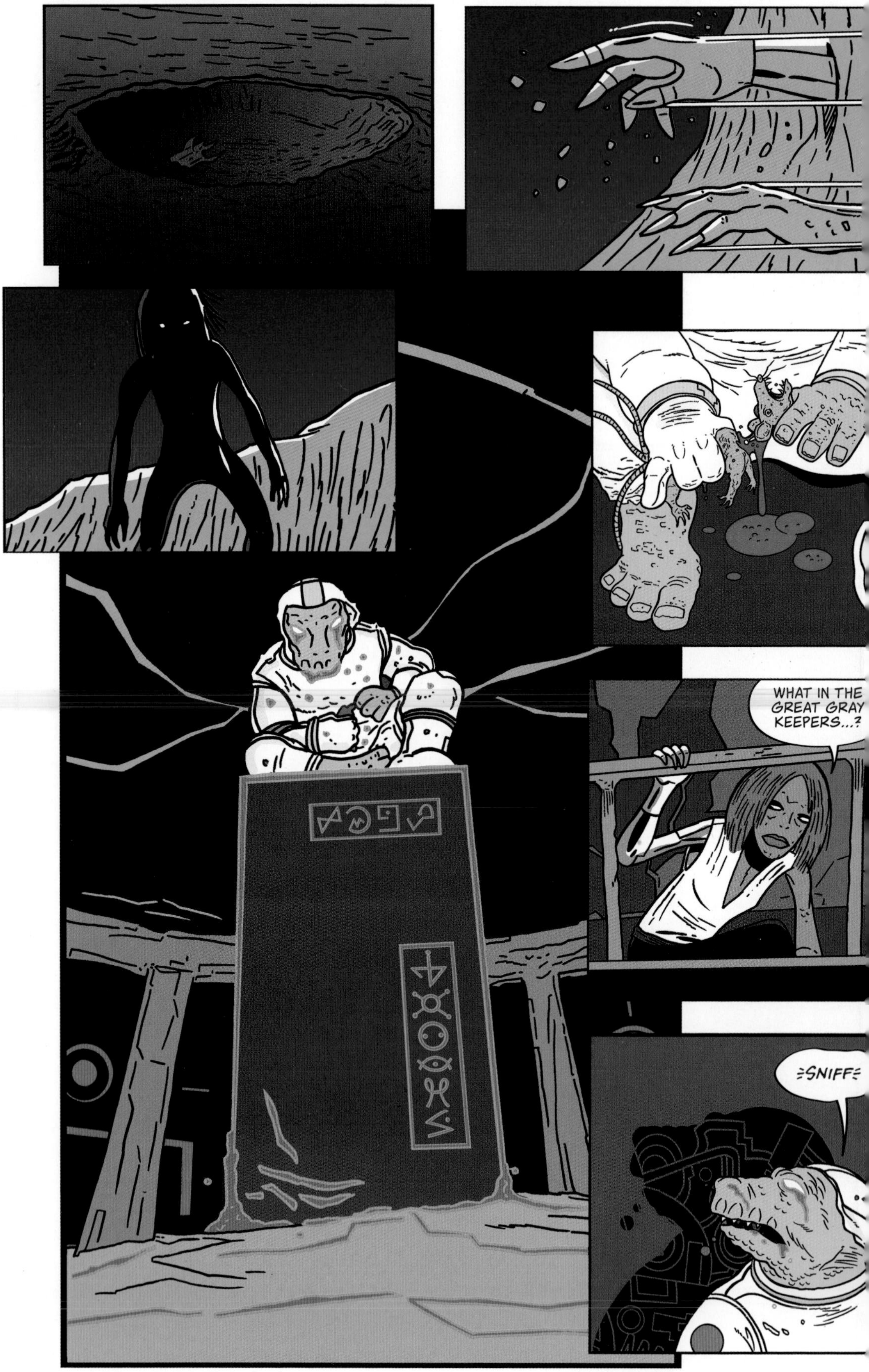
WHAT IN THE GREAT GRAY KEEPERS...?
≡SNIFF≡

THUMP!

HMM?

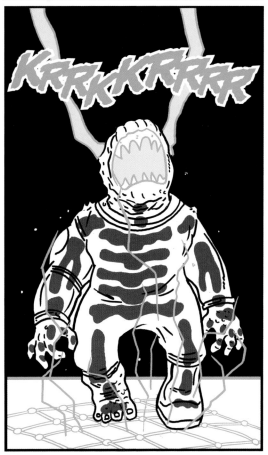

KRRKKRRRR

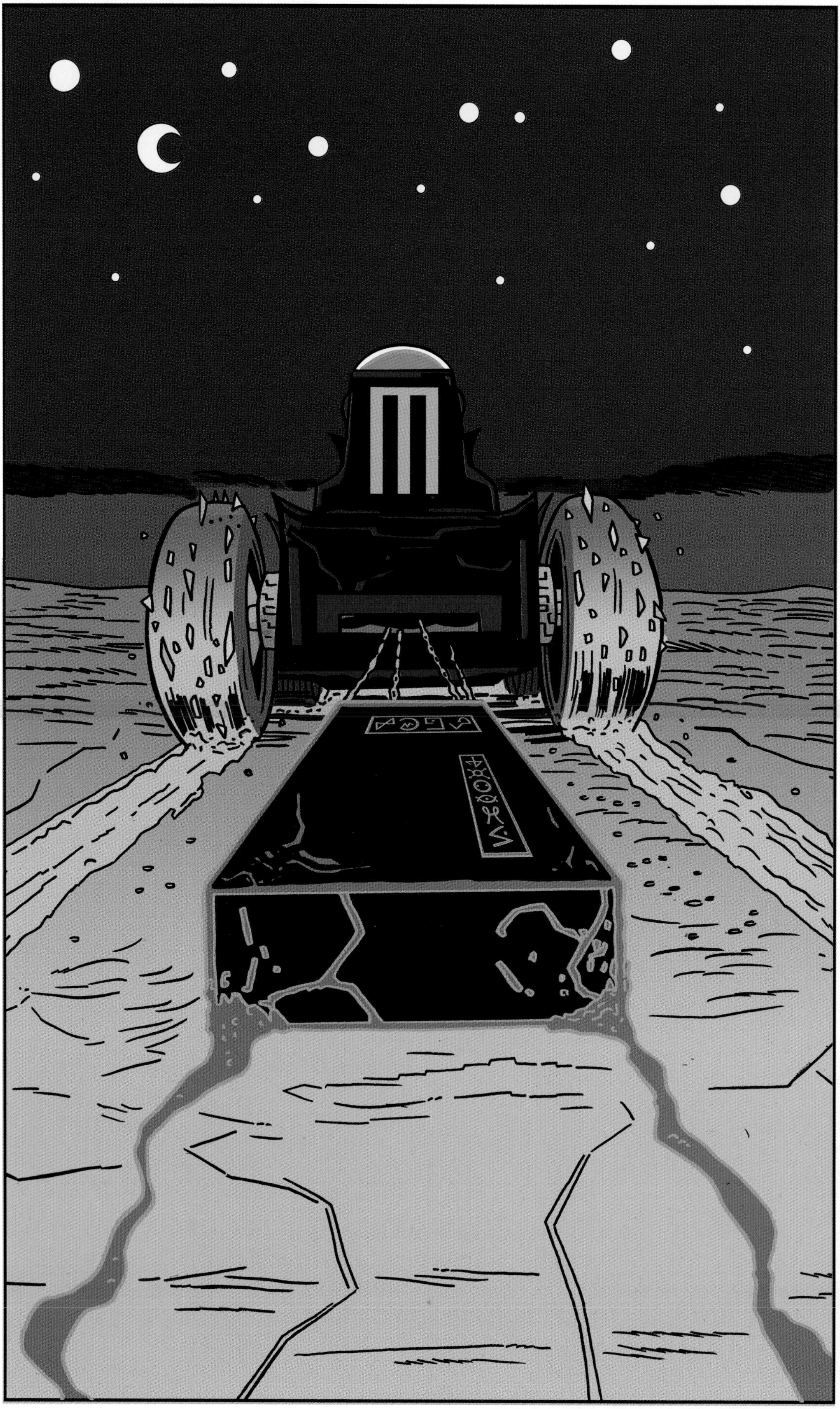

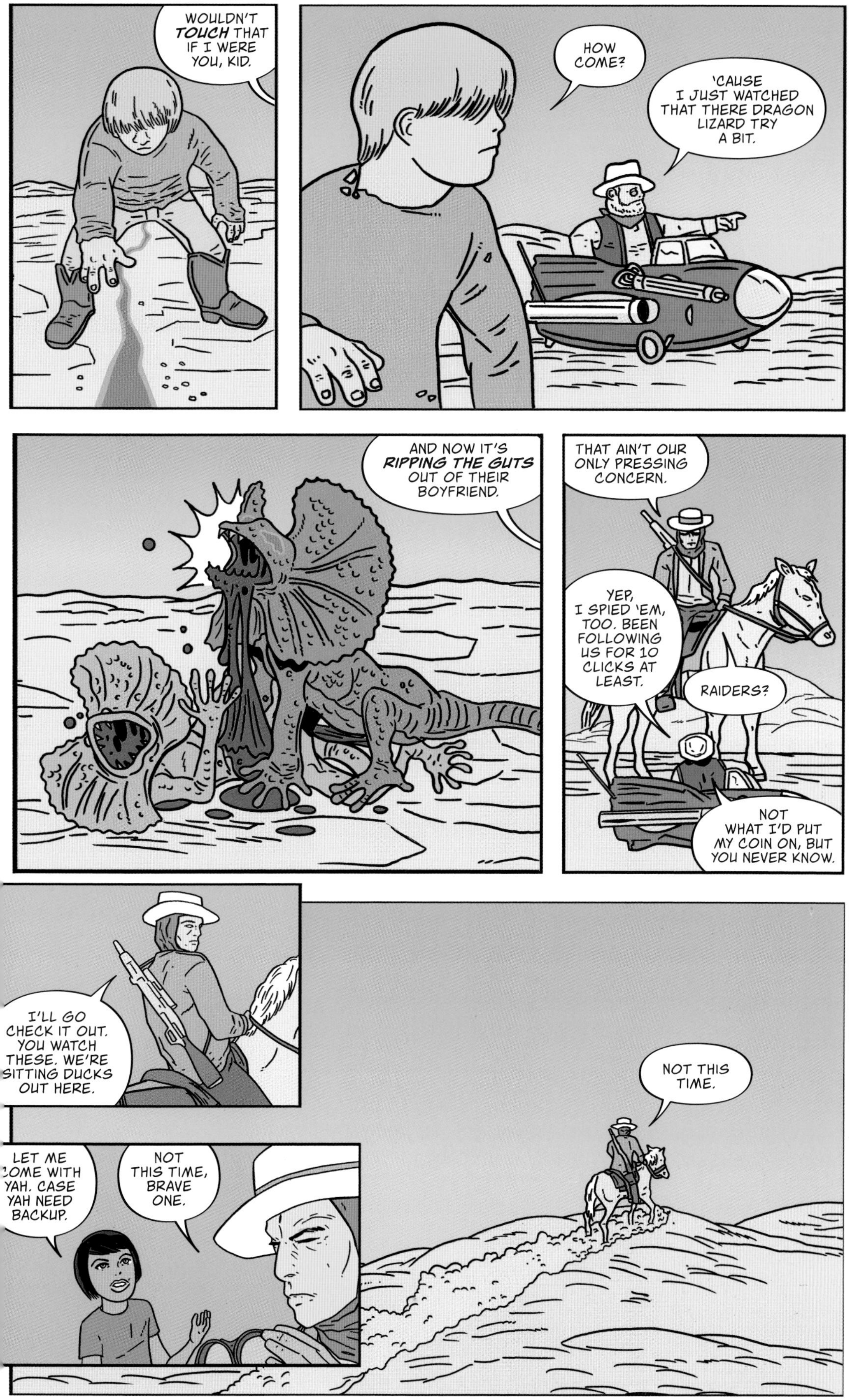

WOULDN'T **TOUCH** THAT IF I WERE YOU, KID.
HOW COME?
'CAUSE I JUST WATCHED THAT THERE DRAGON LIZARD TRY A BIT.
AND NOW IT'S **RIPPING THE GUTS** OUT OF THEIR BOYFRIEND.
THAT AIN'T OUR ONLY PRESSING CONCERN.
YEP, I SPIED 'EM, TOO. BEEN FOLLOWING US FOR 10 CLICKS AT LEAST.
RAIDERS?
NOT WHAT I'D PUT MY COIN ON, BUT YOU NEVER KNOW.
I'LL GO CHECK IT OUT. YOU WATCH THESE. WE'RE SITTING DUCKS OUT HERE.
LET ME COME WITH YAH. CASE YAH NEED BACKUP.
NOT THIS TIME, BRAVE ONE.
NOT THIS TIME.

BUT HOW CAN IT BE GONE WITHOUT YOU SEEING *ANYTHING?*

IT SEEMS SURVEILLANCE... uh...WENT DOWN SOMETIME LAST NIGHT--NO IDEA HOW--AND WELL, WHEN IT CAME BACK, THERE WERE...uh...TRACKS LEADING AWAY FROM THE CRATER.

BIG ONES.

"THAT OBJECT HAD TO WEIGH 10 TONS.

"HOW COULD SOMEONE SNEAK IT AWAY?"

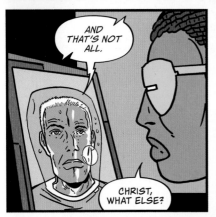

AND THAT'S NOT ALL.

CHRIST, WHAT ELSE?

"FOLLOWING THEIR DISCOVERY OF THE MISSING ITEM...uh...

"IT SEEMS THE TEAM TURNED THEIR WEAPONS...uh...ON THEMSELVES."

"YOU'VE GOT TO BE KIDDIN' ME?"

"ALL FLATLINERS, OPS LEAD WESK."

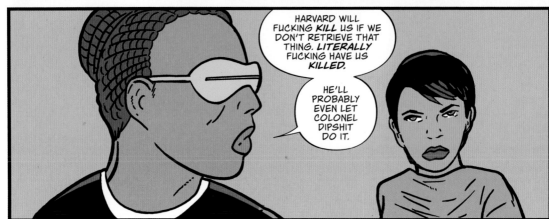

HARVARD WILL FUCKING *KILL* US IF WE DON'T RETRIEVE THAT THING. *LITERALLY* FUCKING HAVE US *KILLED.*

HE'LL PROBABLY EVEN LET COLONEL DIPSHIT DO IT.

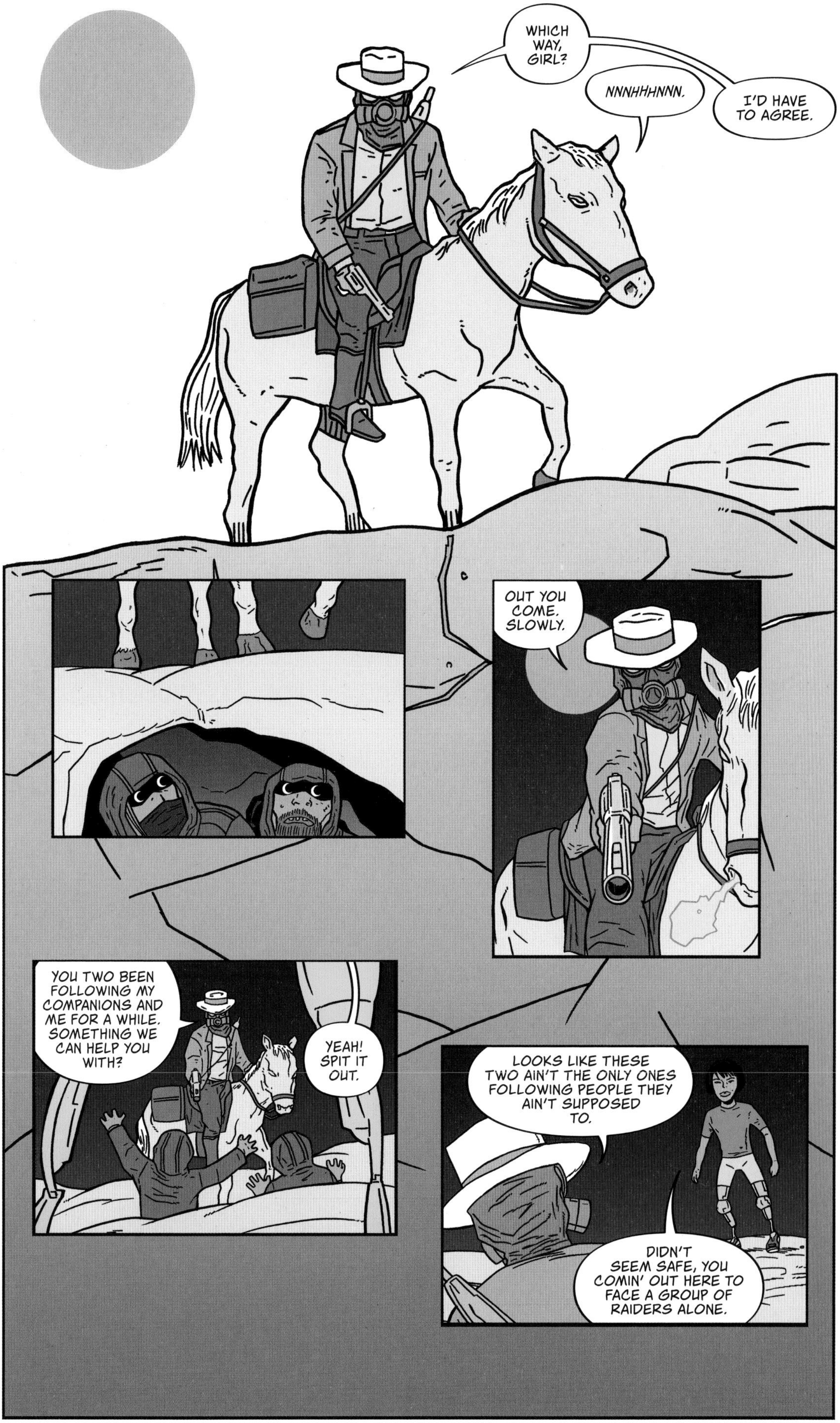
WHICH WAY, GIRL?
NNNHHHNNN.
I'D HAVE TO AGREE.
OUT YOU COME. SLOWLY.
YOU TWO BEEN FOLLOWING MY COMPANIONS AND ME FOR A WHILE. SOMETHING WE CAN HELP YOU WITH?
YEAH! SPIT IT OUT.
LOOKS LIKE THESE TWO AIN'T THE ONLY ONES FOLLOWING PEOPLE THEY AIN'T SUPPOSED TO.
DIDN'T SEEM SAFE, YOU COMIN' OUT HERE TO FACE A GROUP OF RAIDERS ALONE.

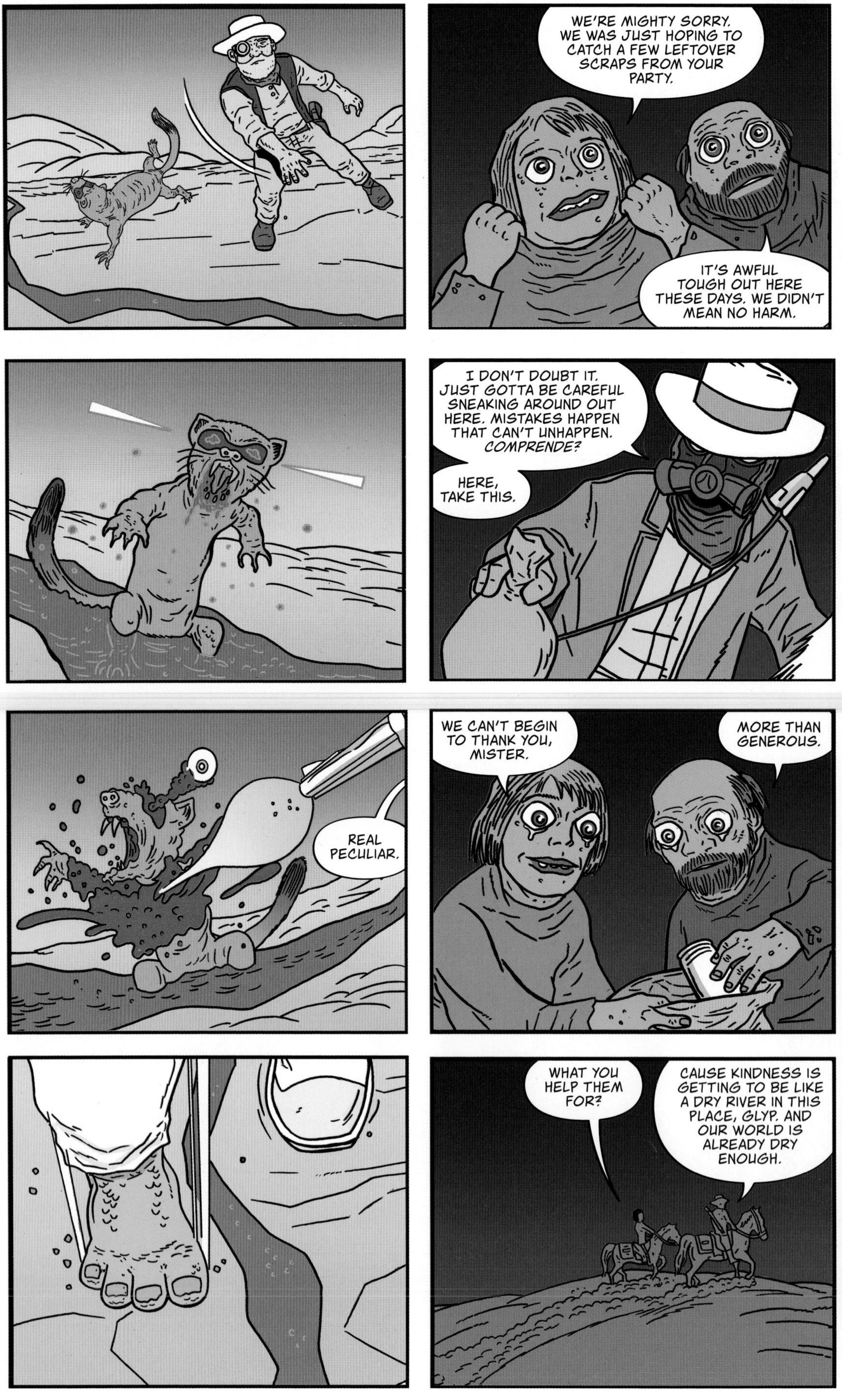
WE'RE MIGHTY SORRY. WE WAS JUST HOPING TO CATCH A FEW LEFTOVER SCRAPS FROM YOUR PARTY.
IT'S AWFUL TOUGH OUT HERE THESE DAYS. WE DIDN'T MEAN NO HARM.
I DON'T DOUBT IT. JUST GOTTA BE CAREFUL SNEAKING AROUND OUT HERE. MISTAKES HAPPEN THAT CAN'T UNHAPPEN. *COMPRENDE?*
HERE, TAKE THIS.
REAL PECULIAR.
WE CAN'T BEGIN TO THANK YOU, MISTER.
MORE THAN GENEROUS.
WHAT YOU HELP THEM FOR?
CAUSE KINDNESS IS GETTING TO BE LIKE A DRY RIVER IN THIS PLACE, GLYP. AND OUR WORLD IS ALREADY DRY ENOUGH.

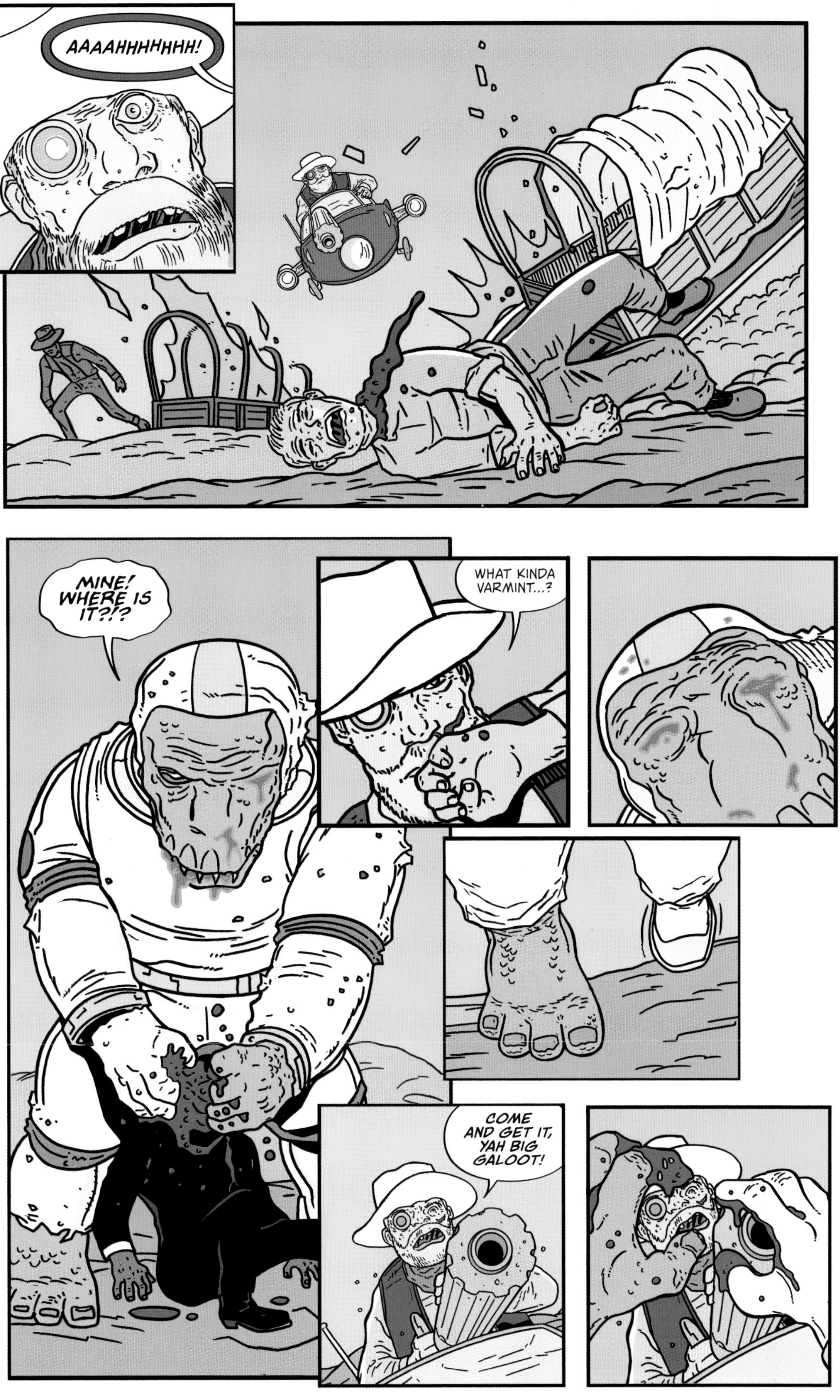
AAAAHHHHHHH!
MINE! WHERE IS IT?!?
WHAT KINDA VARMINT...?
COME AND GET IT, YAH BIG GALOOT!

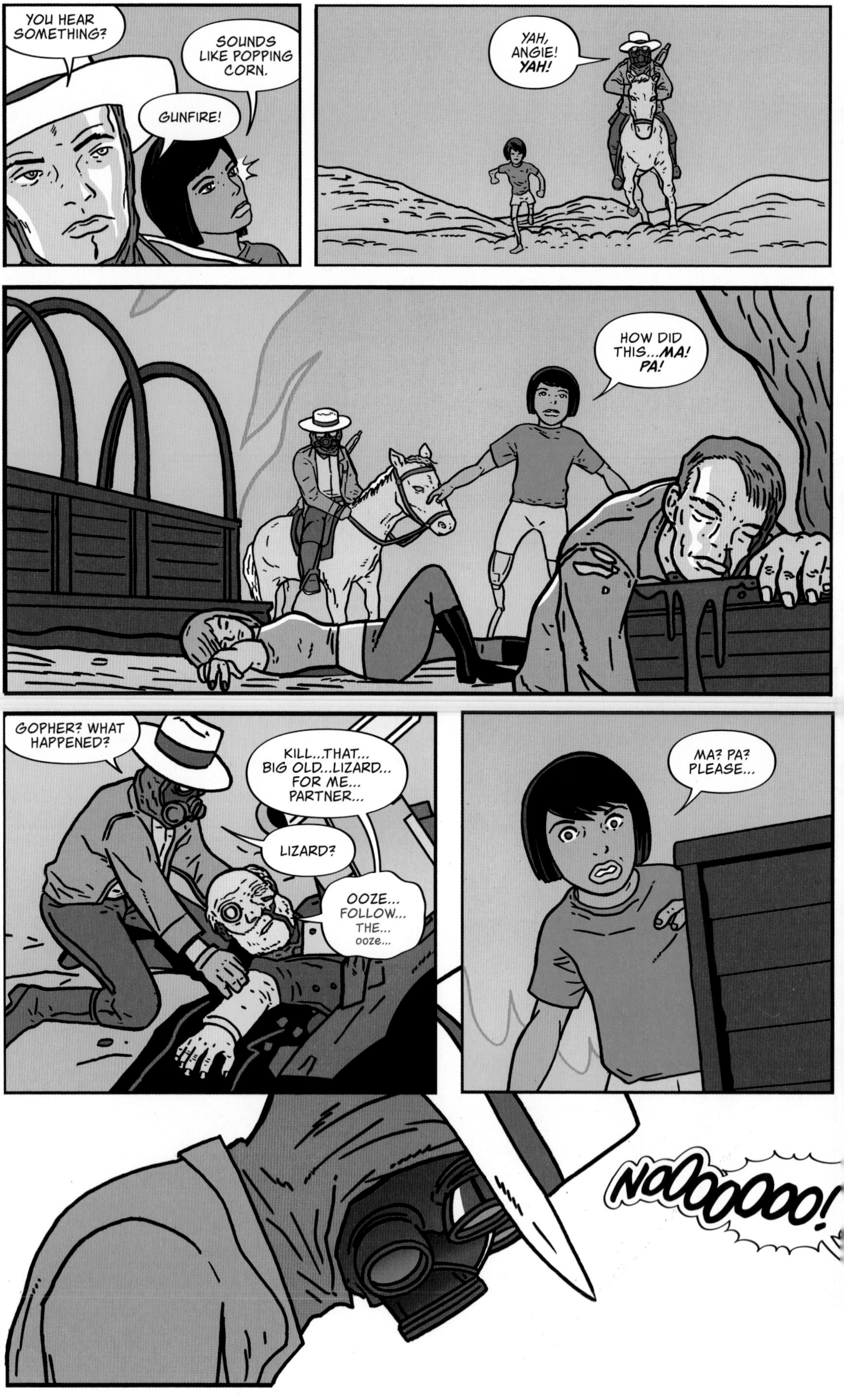
YOU HEAR SOMETHING?
SOUNDS LIKE POPPING CORN.
GUNFIRE!
YAH, ANGIE! YAH!
HOW DID THIS...MA! PA!
GOPHER? WHAT HAPPENED?
KILL...THAT... BIG OLD...LIZARD... FOR ME... PARTNER...
LIZARD?
OOZE... FOLLOW... THE... ooze...
MA? PA? PLEASE...
NOOOOOOO!

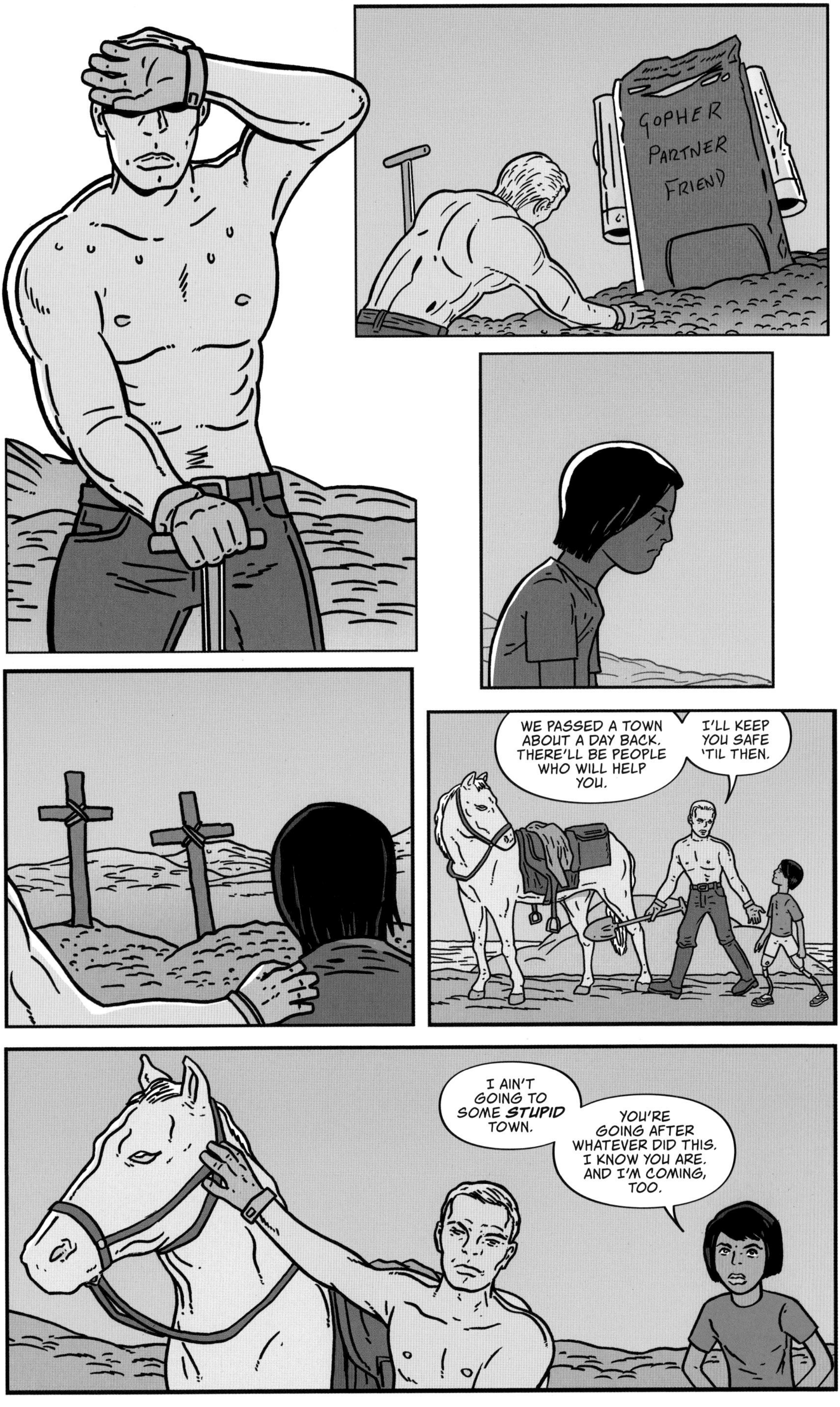
GOPHER
PARTNER
FRIEND
WE PASSED A TOWN ABOUT A DAY BACK. THERE'LL BE PEOPLE WHO WILL HELP YOU.
I'LL KEEP YOU SAFE 'TIL THEN.
I AIN'T GOING TO SOME STUPID TOWN.
YOU'RE GOING AFTER WHATEVER DID THIS. I KNOW YOU ARE. AND I'M COMING, TOO.

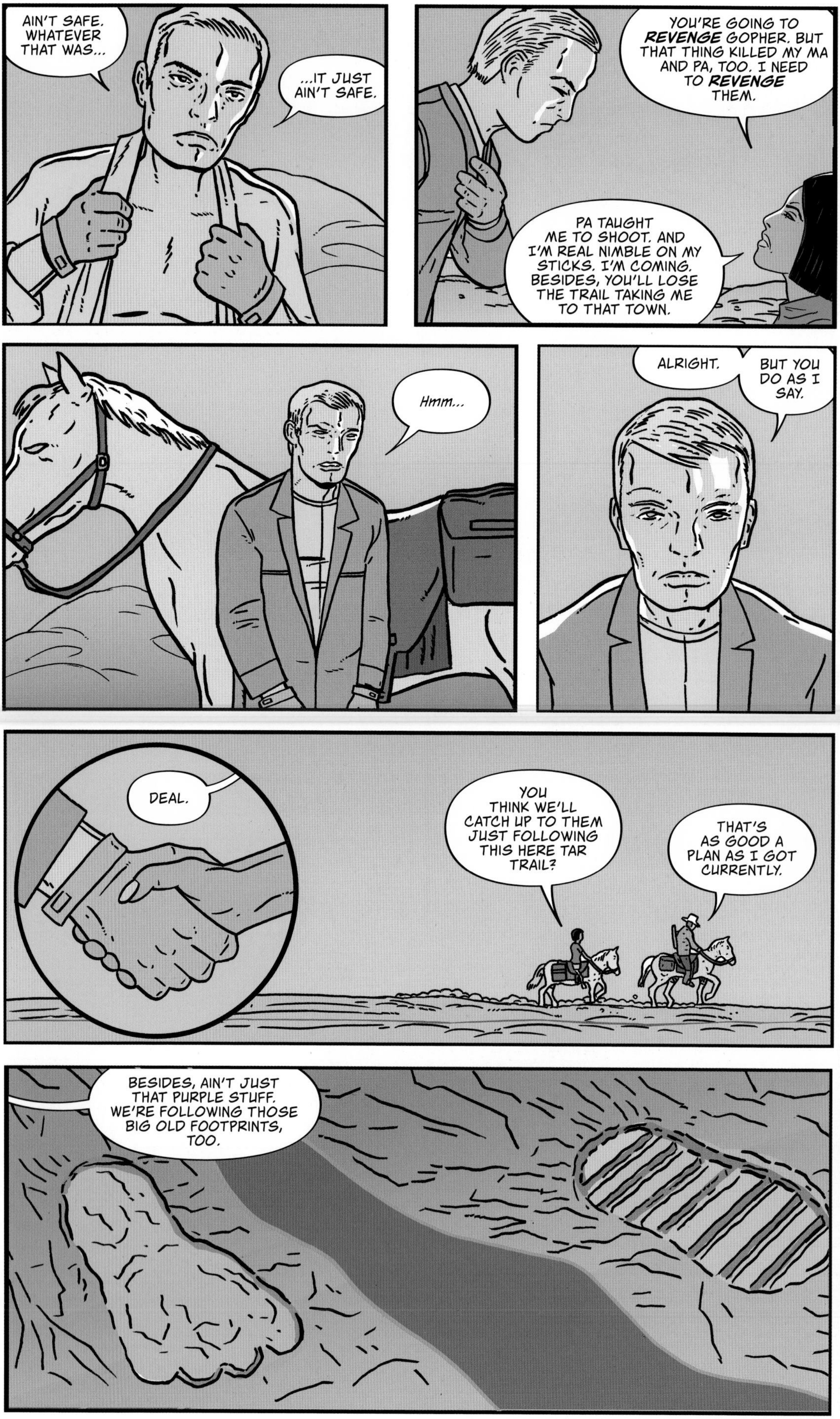
AIN'T SAFE. WHATEVER THAT WAS...
...IT JUST AIN'T SAFE.
YOU'RE GOING TO **REVENGE** GOPHER. BUT THAT THING KILLED MY MA AND PA, TOO. I NEED TO **REVENGE** THEM.
PA TAUGHT ME TO SHOOT. AND I'M REAL NIMBLE ON MY STICKS. I'M COMING. BESIDES, YOU'LL LOSE THE TRAIL TAKING ME TO THAT TOWN.
Hmm...
ALRIGHT.
BUT YOU DO AS I SAY.
DEAL.
YOU THINK WE'LL CATCH UP TO THEM JUST FOLLOWING THIS HERE TAR TRAIL?
THAT'S AS GOOD A PLAN AS I GOT CURRENTLY.
BESIDES, AIN'T JUST THAT PURPLE STUFF. WE'RE FOLLOWING THOSE BIG OLD FOOTPRINTS, TOO.

THINK WE BEST SET UP CAMP FOR THE NIGHT.
YOU SEE THAT?
SURE DID. AND LOOK. IT'S COMIN' BACK AROUND.
GET DOWN!

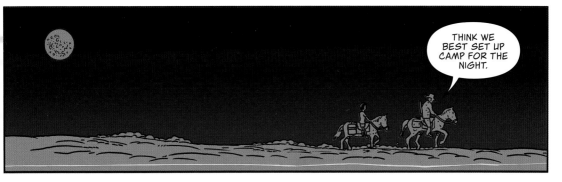

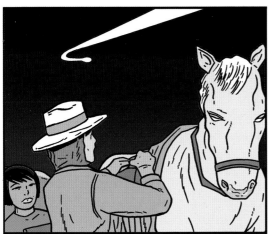

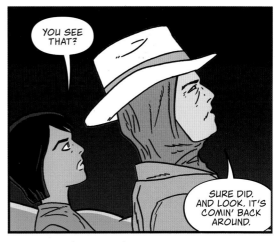

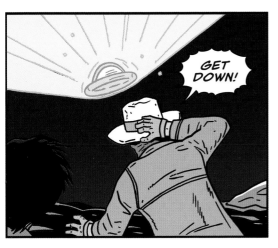

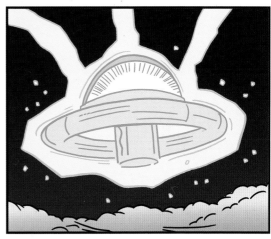

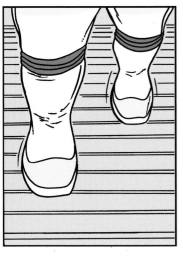

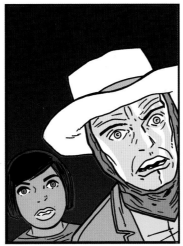

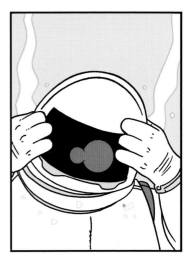

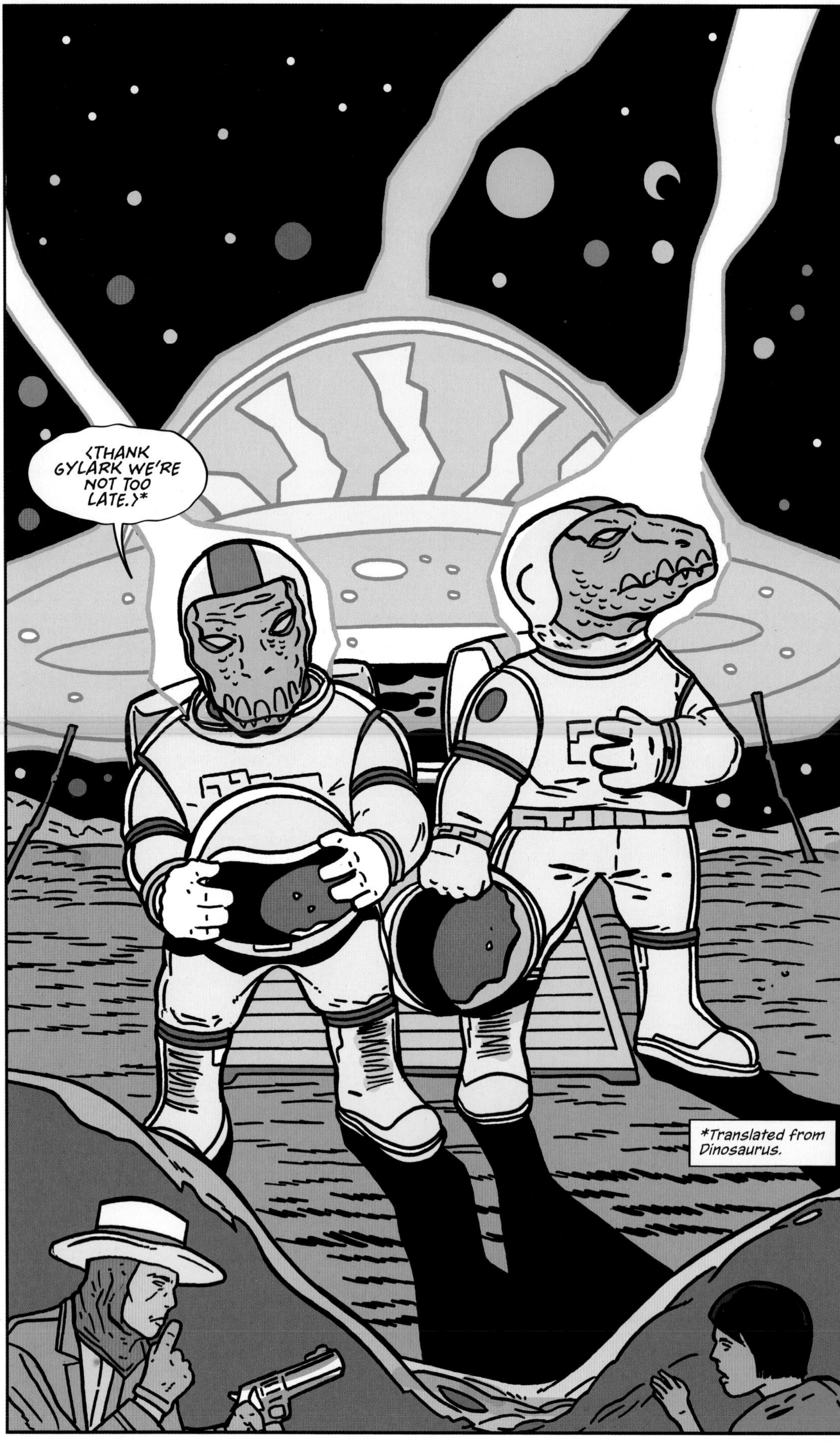
<THANK GYLARK WE'RE NOT TOO LATE.>*
*Translated from Dinosaurus.

CHAPTER TWO

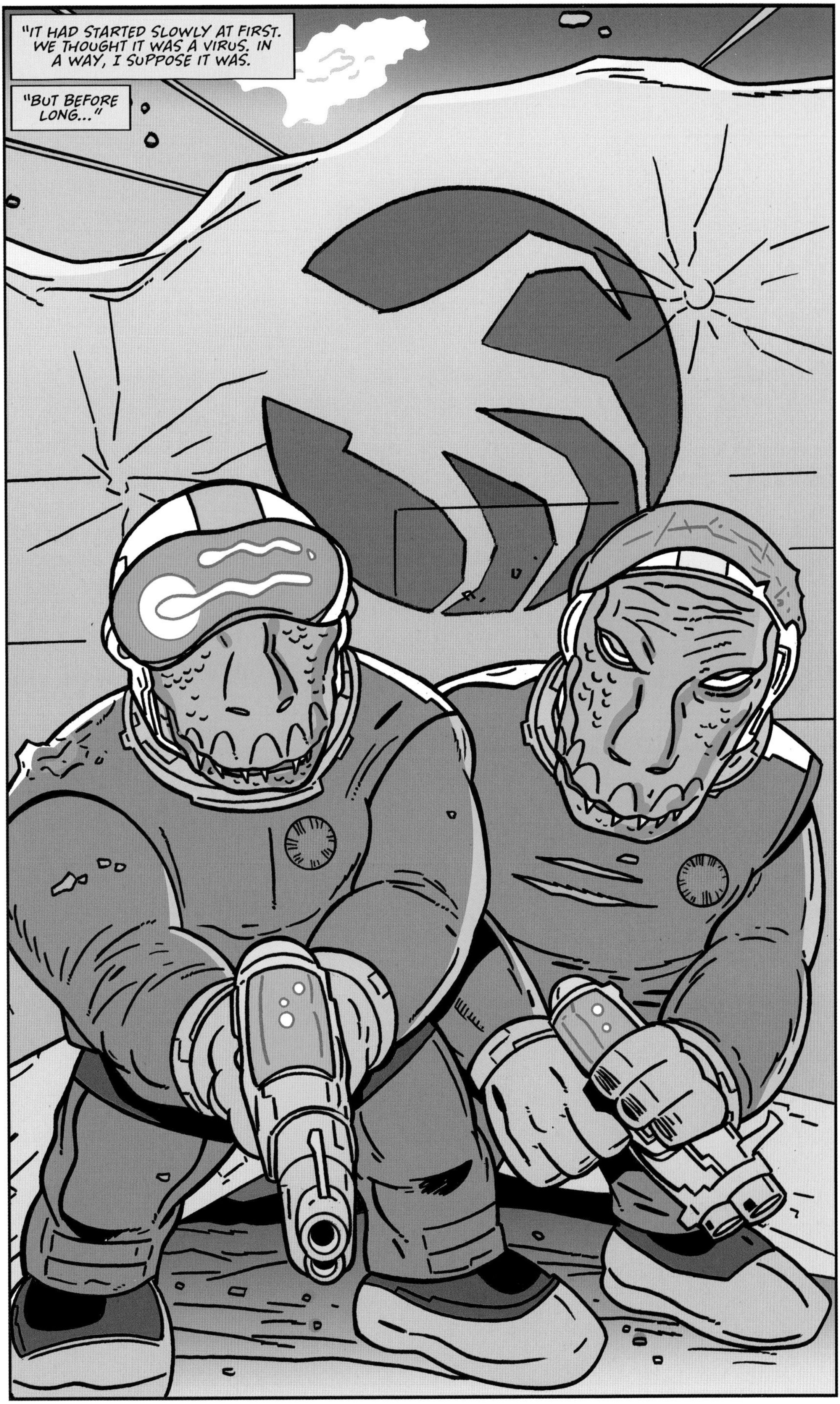
"IT HAD STARTED SLOWLY AT FIRST. WE THOUGHT IT WAS A VIRUS. IN A WAY, I SUPPOSE IT WAS.
"BUT BEFORE LONG..."

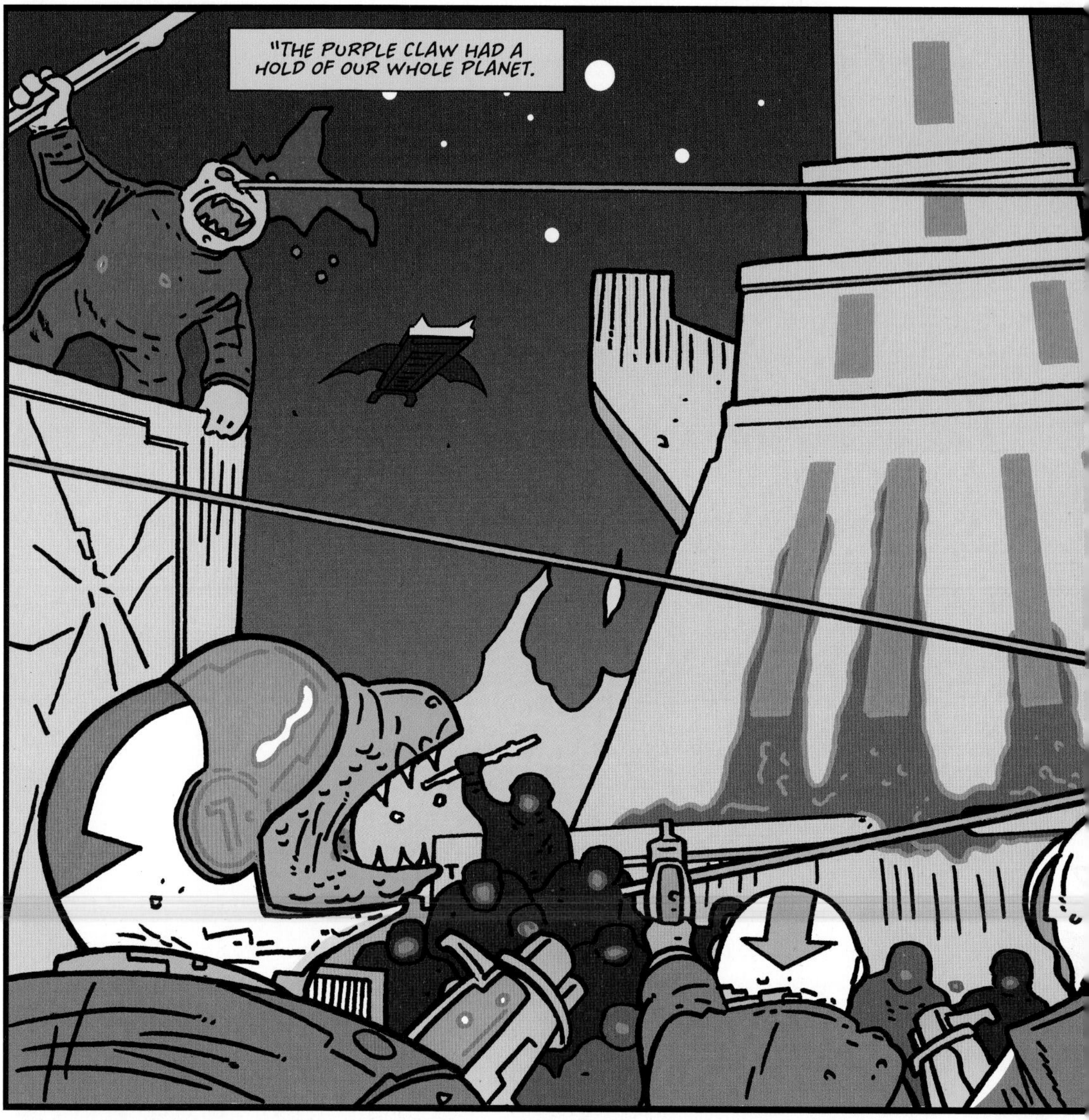
"THE PURPLE CLAW HAD A HOLD OF OUR WHOLE PLANET.
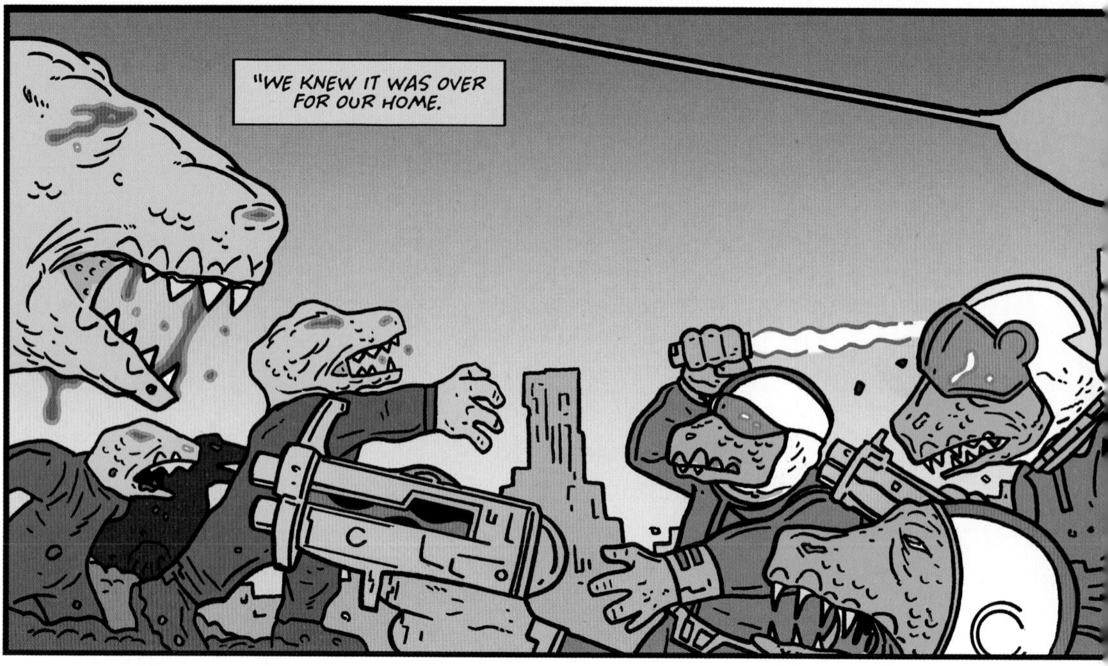
"WE KNEW IT WAS OVER FOR OUR HOME.

"WE, THE DINAMMI, WERE A SMALL POPULATION, BUT LONG-LIVED. THAT MAKES US PATIENT. BUT ALSO CURIOUS.

"PERHAPS OUR LEADERS BELIEVED THEY COULD CONTROL THE CREATURE. STUDY IT. LEARN FROM IT.

"WHATEVER THEIR REASONS, IT WAS OUR DOOM.

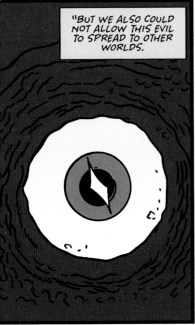

"BUT WE ALSO COULD NOT ALLOW THIS EVIL TO SPREAD TO OTHER WORLDS.

"TO CONTINUE TO FEED ON THE SUFFERING OF CIVILIZATIONS."

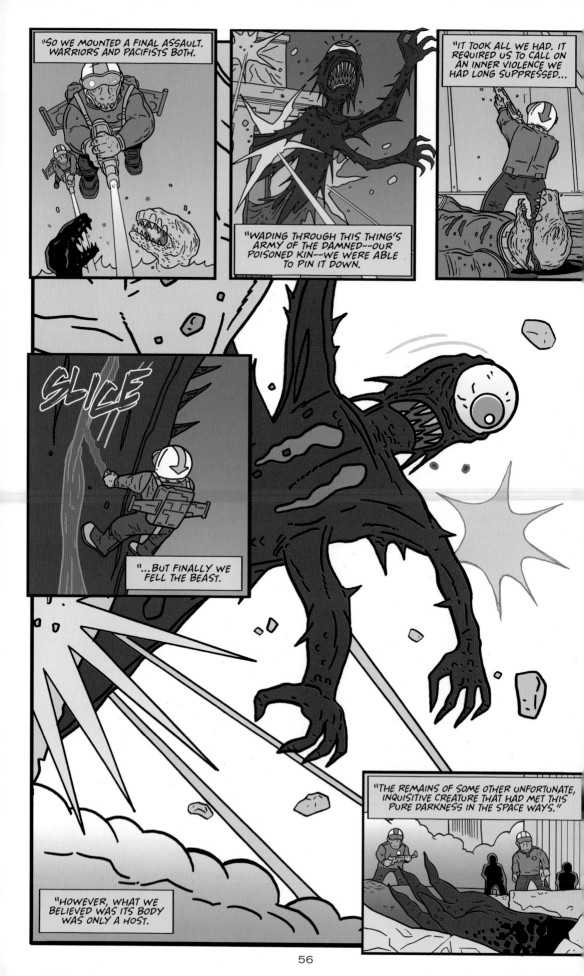

"SO WE MOUNTED A FINAL ASSAULT. WARRIORS AND PACIFISTS BOTH.

"IT TOOK ALL WE HAD. IT REQUIRED US TO CALL ON AN INNER VIOLENCE WE HAD LONG SUPPRESSED...

"WADING THROUGH THIS THING'S ARMY OF THE DAMNED--OUR POISONED KIN--WE WERE ABLE TO PIN IT DOWN.

SLICE

"...BUT FINALLY WE FELL THE BEAST.

"HOWEVER, WHAT WE BELIEVED WAS ITS BODY WAS ONLY A HOST.

"THE REMAINS OF SOME OTHER UNFORTUNATE, INQUISITIVE CREATURE THAT HAD MET THIS PURE DARKNESS IN THE SPACE WAYS."

"MY SILENT FRIEND HERE, QUEK, THEORIZED THAT IT WAS SOME OLD GOD WHICH HAD SOUGHT OUT POWER..."

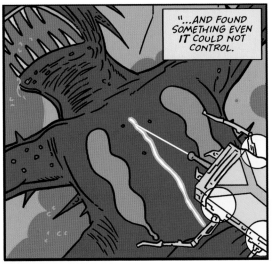

"...AND FOUND SOMETHING EVEN *IT* COULD NOT CONTROL."

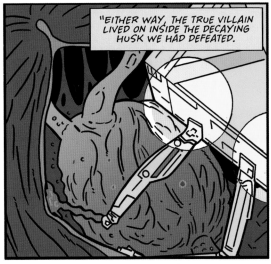

"EITHER WAY, THE TRUE VILLAIN LIVED ON INSIDE THE DECAYING HUSK WE HAD DEFEATED."

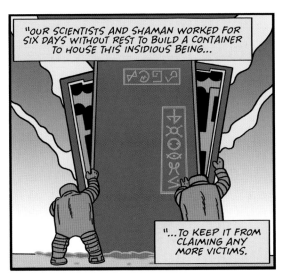

"OUR SCIENTISTS AND SHAMAN WORKED FOR SIX DAYS WITHOUT REST TO BUILD A CONTAINER TO HOUSE THIS INSIDIOUS BEING..."

"...TO KEEP IT FROM CLAIMING ANY MORE VICTIMS."

"IT WAS DECIDED THAT TO PROTECT THE WIDER UNIVERSE, IT MUST BE SENT INTO A MAIN SEQUENCE STAR.

"YOUR SUN."

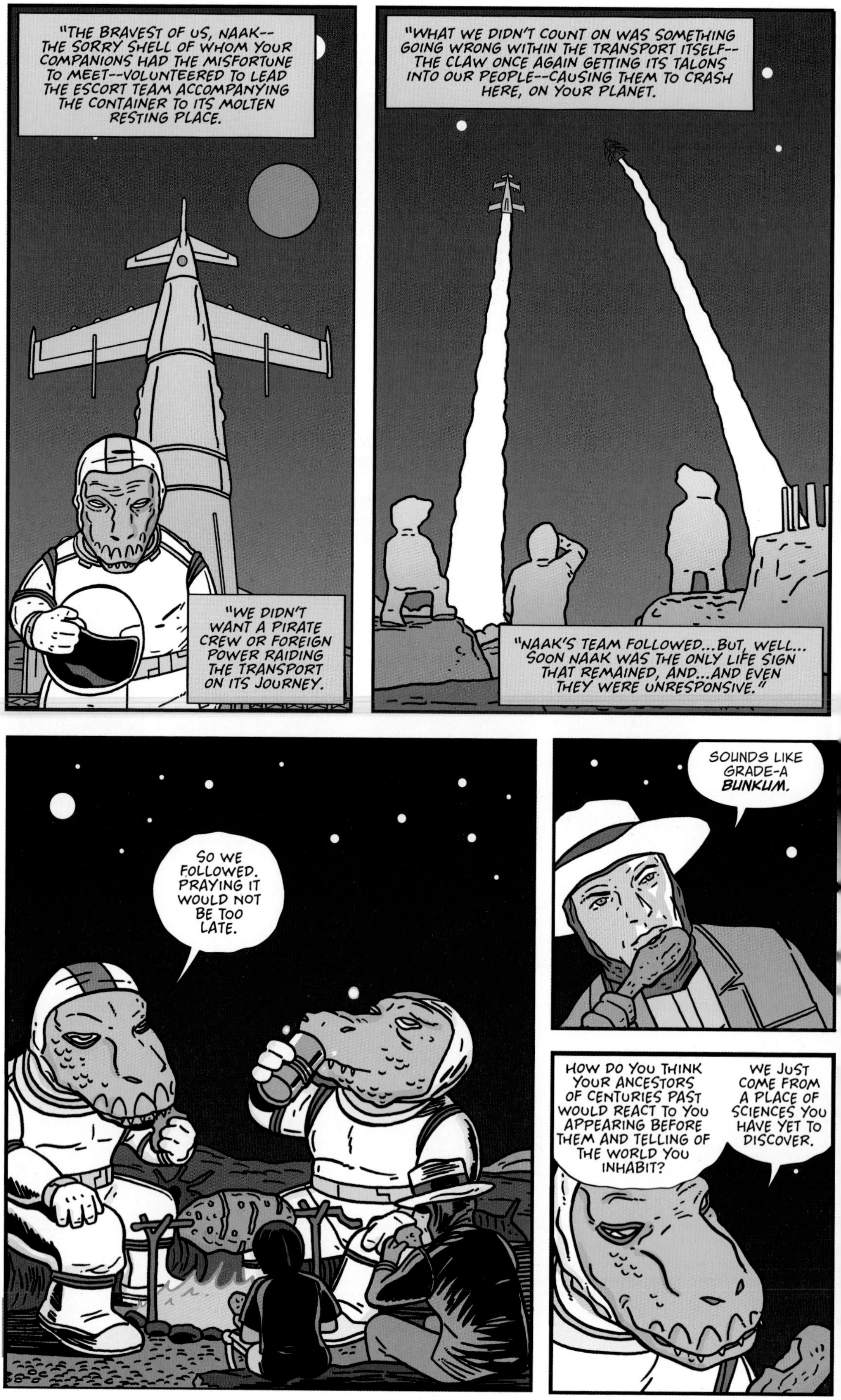
"THE BRAVEST OF US, NAAK-- THE SORRY SHELL OF WHOM YOUR COMPANIONS HAD THE MISFORTUNE TO MEET--VOLUNTEERED TO LEAD THE ESCORT TEAM ACCOMPANYING THE CONTAINER TO ITS MOLTEN RESTING PLACE.
"WE DIDN'T WANT A PIRATE CREW OR FOREIGN POWER RAIDING THE TRANSPORT ON ITS JOURNEY.
"WHAT WE DIDN'T COUNT ON WAS SOMETHING GOING WRONG WITHIN THE TRANSPORT ITSELF-- THE CLAW ONCE AGAIN GETTING ITS TALONS INTO OUR PEOPLE--CAUSING THEM TO CRASH HERE, ON YOUR PLANET.
"NAAK'S TEAM FOLLOWED...BUT, WELL... SOON NAAK WAS THE ONLY LIFE SIGN THAT REMAINED, AND...AND EVEN THEY WERE UNRESPONSIVE."
SO WE FOLLOWED. PRAYING IT WOULD NOT BE TOO LATE.
SOUNDS LIKE GRADE-A BUNKUM.
HOW DO YOU THINK YOUR ANCESTORS OF CENTURIES PAST WOULD REACT TO YOU APPEARING BEFORE THEM AND TELLING OF THE WORLD YOU INHABIT?
WE JUST COME FROM A PLACE OF SCIENCES YOU HAVE YET TO DISCOVER.

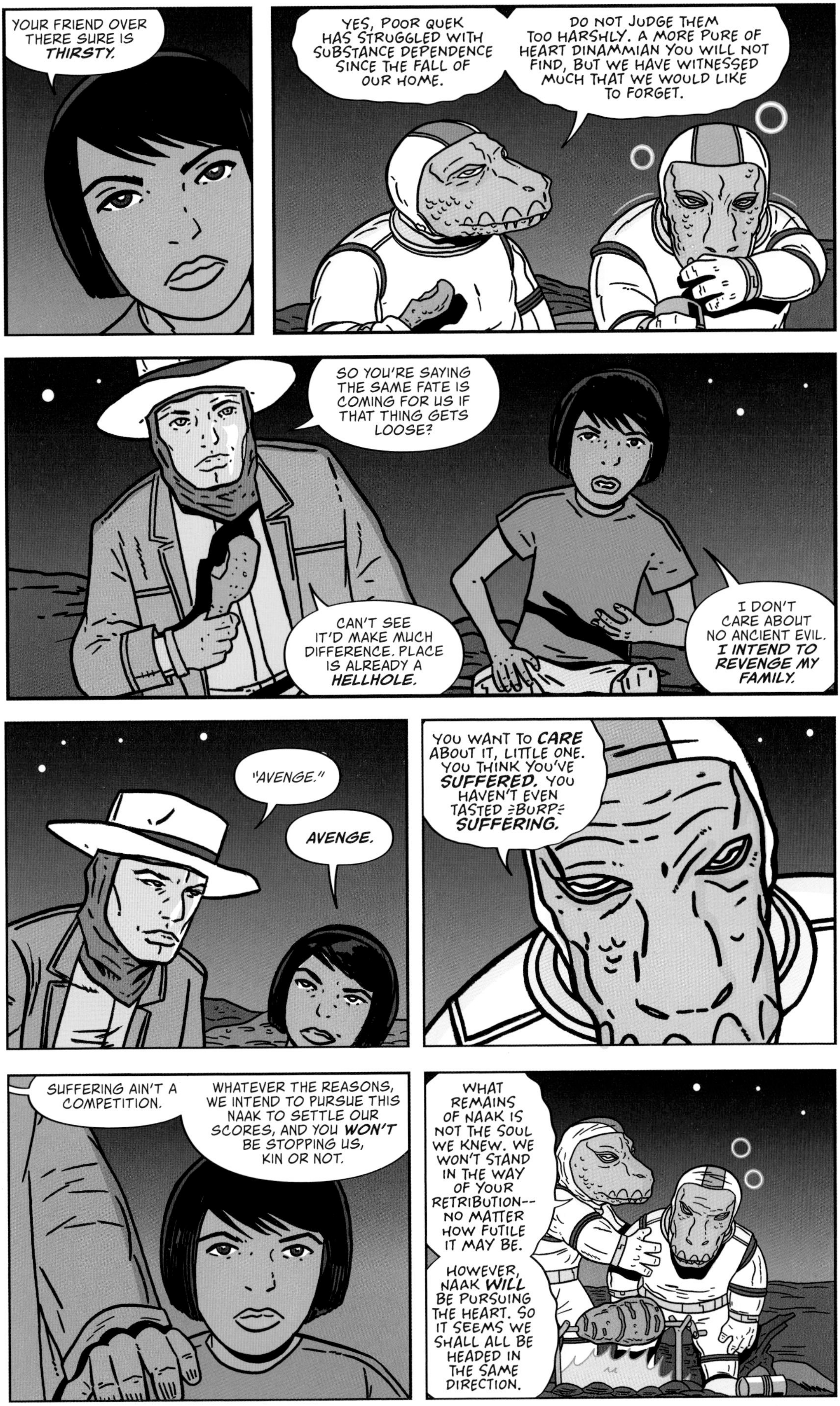
YOUR FRIEND OVER THERE SURE IS THIRSTY.
YES, POOR QUEK HAS STRUGGLED WITH SUBSTANCE DEPENDENCE SINCE THE FALL OF OUR HOME.
DO NOT JUDGE THEM TOO HARSHLY. A MORE PURE OF HEART DINAMMIAN YOU WILL NOT FIND, BUT WE HAVE WITNESSED MUCH THAT WE WOULD LIKE TO FORGET.
SO YOU'RE SAYING THE SAME FATE IS COMING FOR US IF THAT THING GETS LOOSE?
CAN'T SEE IT'D MAKE MUCH DIFFERENCE. PLACE IS ALREADY A HELLHOLE.
I DON'T CARE ABOUT NO ANCIENT EVIL. I INTEND TO REVENGE MY FAMILY.
"AVENGE."
AVENGE.
YOU WANT TO CARE ABOUT IT, LITTLE ONE. YOU THINK YOU'VE SUFFERED. YOU HAVEN'T EVEN TASTED =BURP= SUFFERING.
SUFFERING AIN'T A COMPETITION.
WHATEVER THE REASONS, WE INTEND TO PURSUE THIS NAAK TO SETTLE OUR SCORES, AND YOU WON'T BE STOPPING US, KIN OR NOT.
WHAT REMAINS OF NAAK IS NOT THE SOUL WE KNEW. WE WON'T STAND IN THE WAY OF YOUR RETRIBUTION-- NO MATTER HOW FUTILE IT MAY BE.
HOWEVER, NAAK WILL BE PURSUING THE HEART. SO IT SEEMS WE SHALL ALL BE HEADED IN THE SAME DIRECTION.

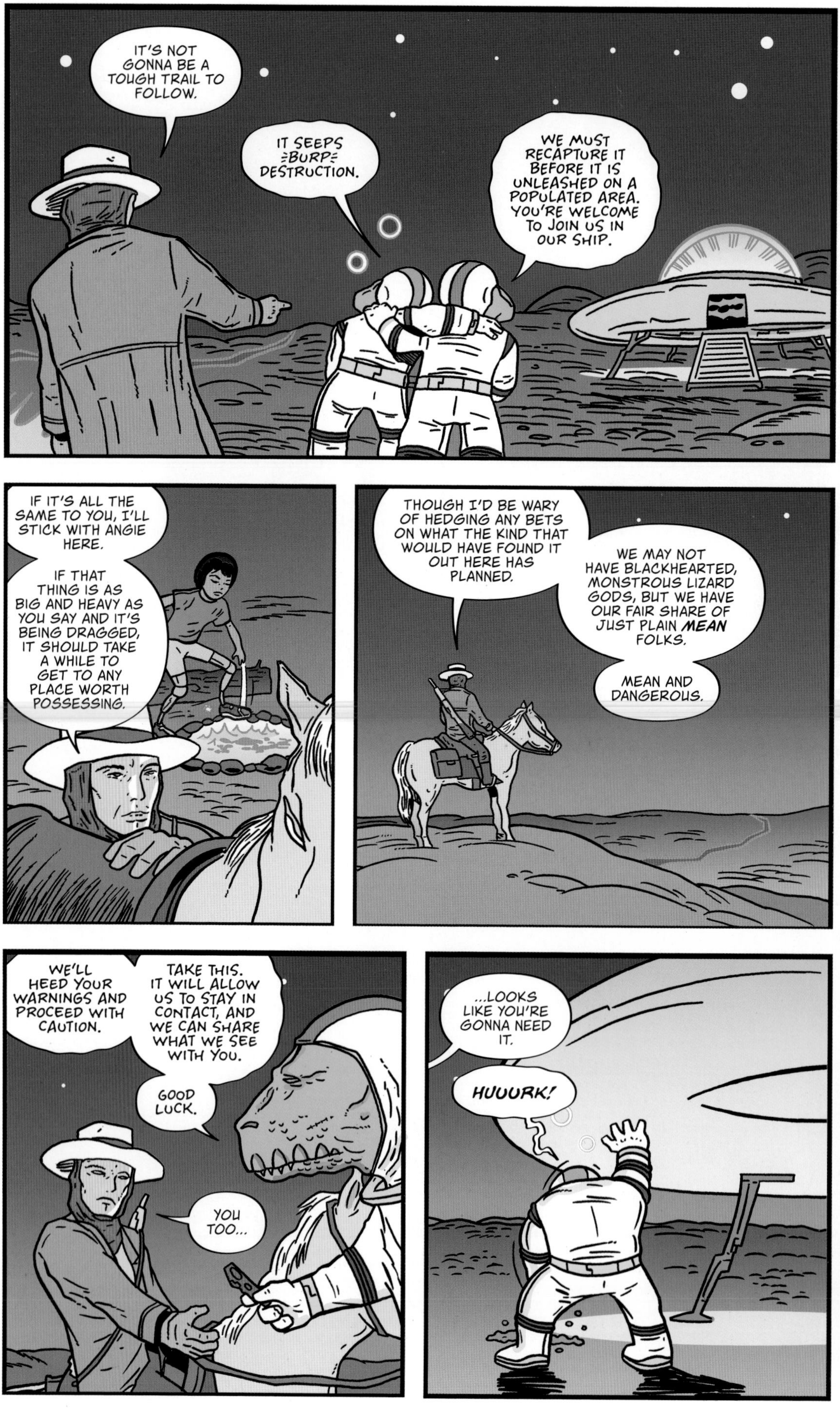
IT'S NOT GONNA BE A TOUGH TRAIL TO FOLLOW.
IT SEEPS =BURP= DESTRUCTION.
WE MUST RECAPTURE IT BEFORE IT IS UNLEASHED ON A POPULATED AREA. YOU'RE WELCOME TO JOIN US IN OUR SHIP.
IF IT'S ALL THE SAME TO YOU, I'LL STICK WITH ANGIE HERE.
IF THAT THING IS AS BIG AND HEAVY AS YOU SAY AND IT'S BEING DRAGGED, IT SHOULD TAKE A WHILE TO GET TO ANY PLACE WORTH POSSESSING.
THOUGH I'D BE WARY OF HEDGING ANY BETS ON WHAT THE KIND THAT WOULD HAVE FOUND IT OUT HERE HAS PLANNED.
WE MAY NOT HAVE BLACKHEARTED, MONSTROUS LIZARD GODS, BUT WE HAVE OUR FAIR SHARE OF JUST PLAIN MEAN FOLKS.
MEAN AND DANGEROUS.
WE'LL HEED YOUR WARNINGS AND PROCEED WITH CAUTION.
TAKE THIS. IT WILL ALLOW US TO STAY IN CONTACT, AND WE CAN SHARE WHAT WE SEE WITH YOU.
GOOD LUCK.
YOU TOO...
...LOOKS LIKE YOU'RE GONNA NEED IT.
HUUURK!

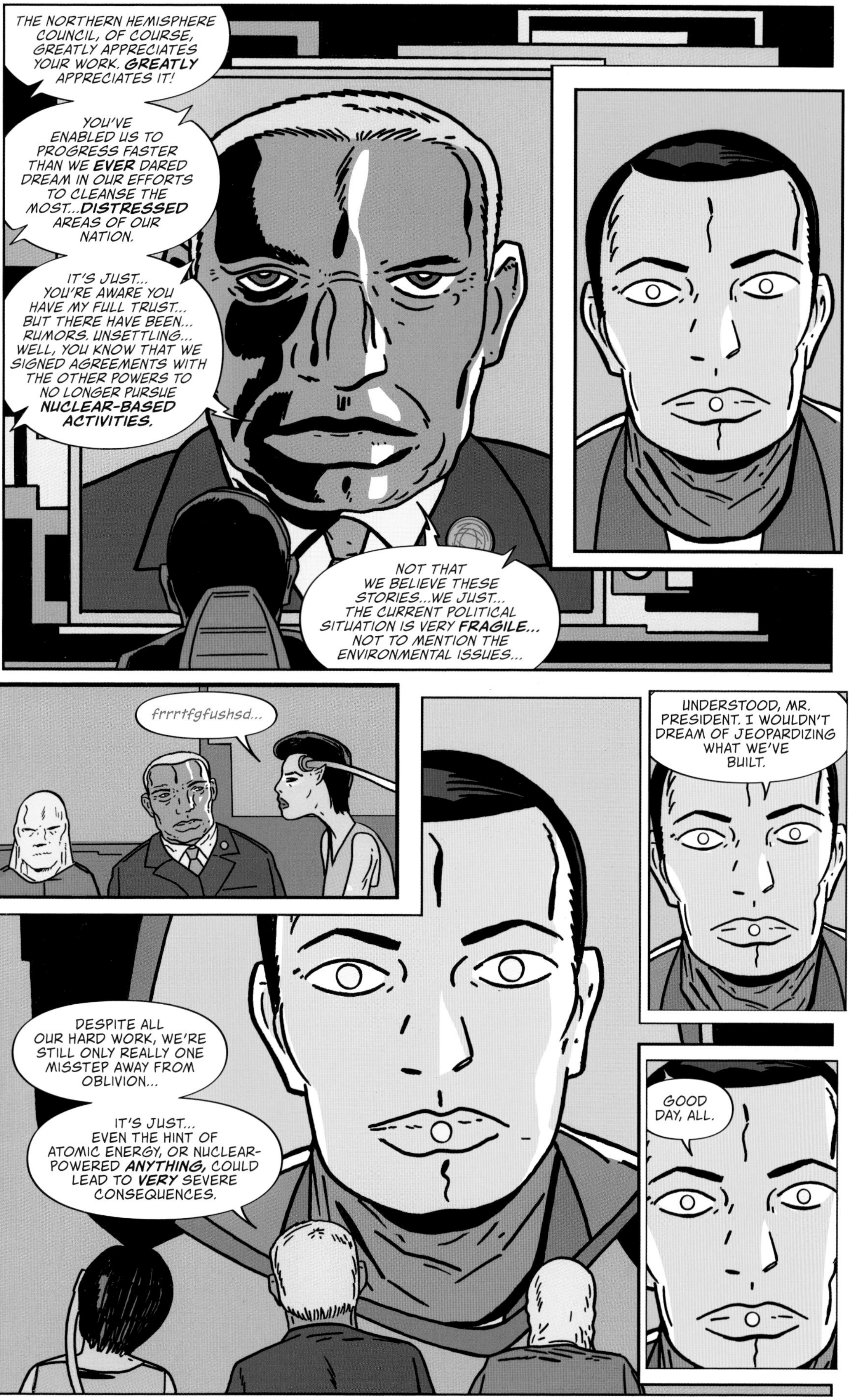
THE NORTHERN HEMISPHERE COUNCIL, OF COURSE, GREATLY APPRECIATES YOUR WORK. GREATLY APPRECIATES IT!
YOU'VE ENABLED US TO PROGRESS FASTER THAN WE EVER DARED DREAM IN OUR EFFORTS TO CLEANSE THE MOST...DISTRESSED AREAS OF OUR NATION.
IT'S JUST... YOU'RE AWARE YOU HAVE MY FULL TRUST... BUT THERE HAVE BEEN... RUMORS. UNSETTLING... WELL, YOU KNOW THAT WE SIGNED AGREEMENTS WITH THE OTHER POWERS TO NO LONGER PURSUE NUCLEAR-BASED ACTIVITIES.
NOT THAT WE BELIEVE THESE STORIES...WE JUST... THE CURRENT POLITICAL SITUATION IS VERY FRAGILE... NOT TO MENTION THE ENVIRONMENTAL ISSUES...
frrrtfgfushsd...
DESPITE ALL OUR HARD WORK, WE'RE STILL ONLY REALLY ONE MISSTEP AWAY FROM OBLIVION...
IT'S JUST... EVEN THE HINT OF ATOMIC ENERGY, OR NUCLEAR-POWERED ANYTHING, COULD LEAD TO VERY SEVERE CONSEQUENCES.
UNDERSTOOD, MR. PRESIDENT. I WOULDN'T DREAM OF JEOPARDIZING WHAT WE'VE BUILT.
GOOD DAY, ALL.

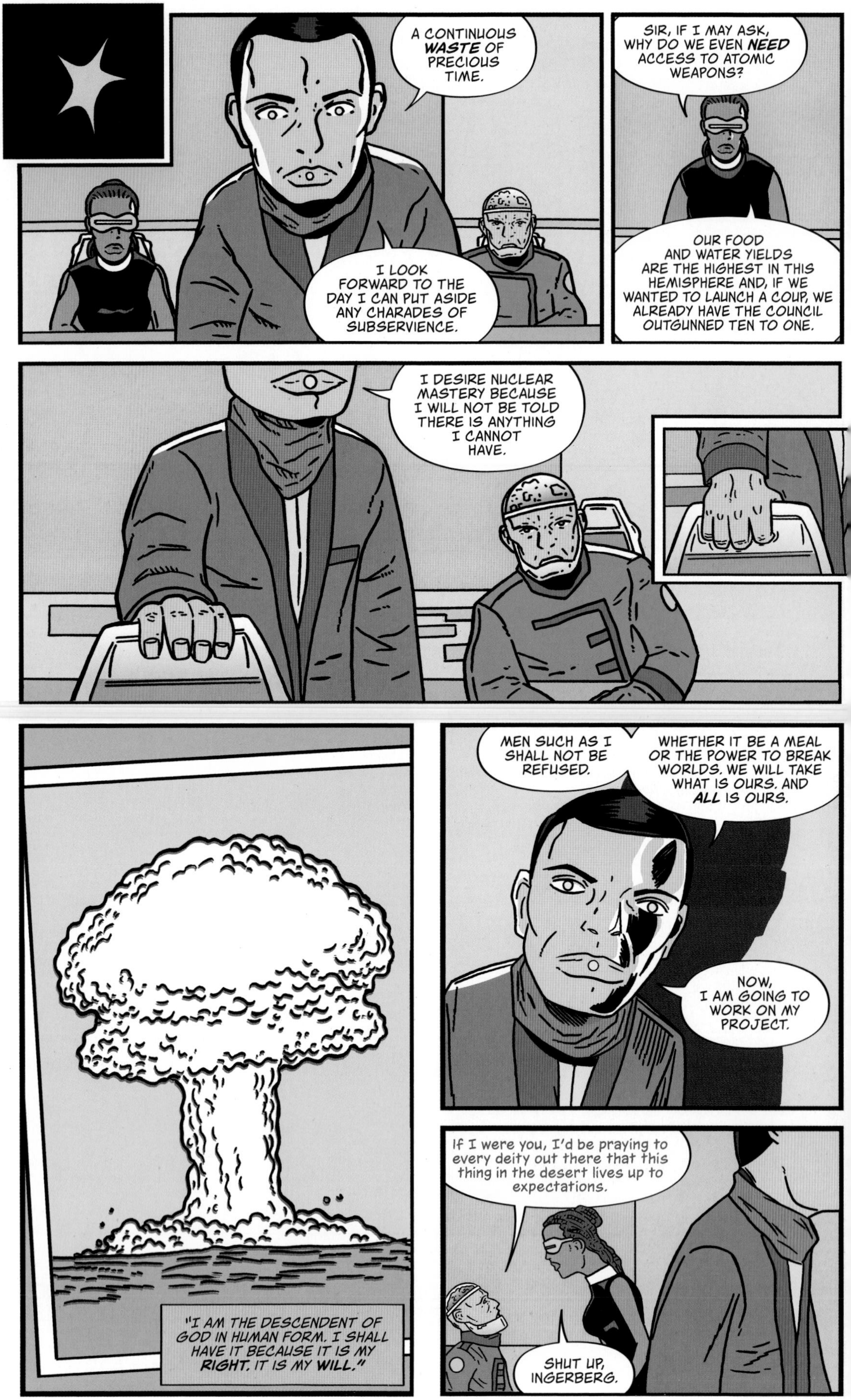
A CONTINUOUS WASTE OF PRECIOUS TIME.
I LOOK FORWARD TO THE DAY I CAN PUT ASIDE ANY CHARADES OF SUBSERVIENCE.
SIR, IF I MAY ASK, WHY DO WE EVEN NEED ACCESS TO ATOMIC WEAPONS?
OUR FOOD AND WATER YIELDS ARE THE HIGHEST IN THIS HEMISPHERE AND, IF WE WANTED TO LAUNCH A COUP, WE ALREADY HAVE THE COUNCIL OUTGUNNED TEN TO ONE.
I DESIRE NUCLEAR MASTERY BECAUSE I WILL NOT BE TOLD THERE IS ANYTHING I CANNOT HAVE.
"I AM THE DESCENDENT OF GOD IN HUMAN FORM. I SHALL HAVE IT BECAUSE IT IS MY RIGHT. IT IS MY WILL."
MEN SUCH AS I SHALL NOT BE REFUSED.
WHETHER IT BE A MEAL OR THE POWER TO BREAK WORLDS. WE WILL TAKE WHAT IS OURS. AND ALL IS OURS.
NOW, I AM GOING TO WORK ON MY PROJECT.
If I were you, I'd be praying to every deity out there that this thing in the desert lives up to expectations.
SHUT UP, INGERBERG.

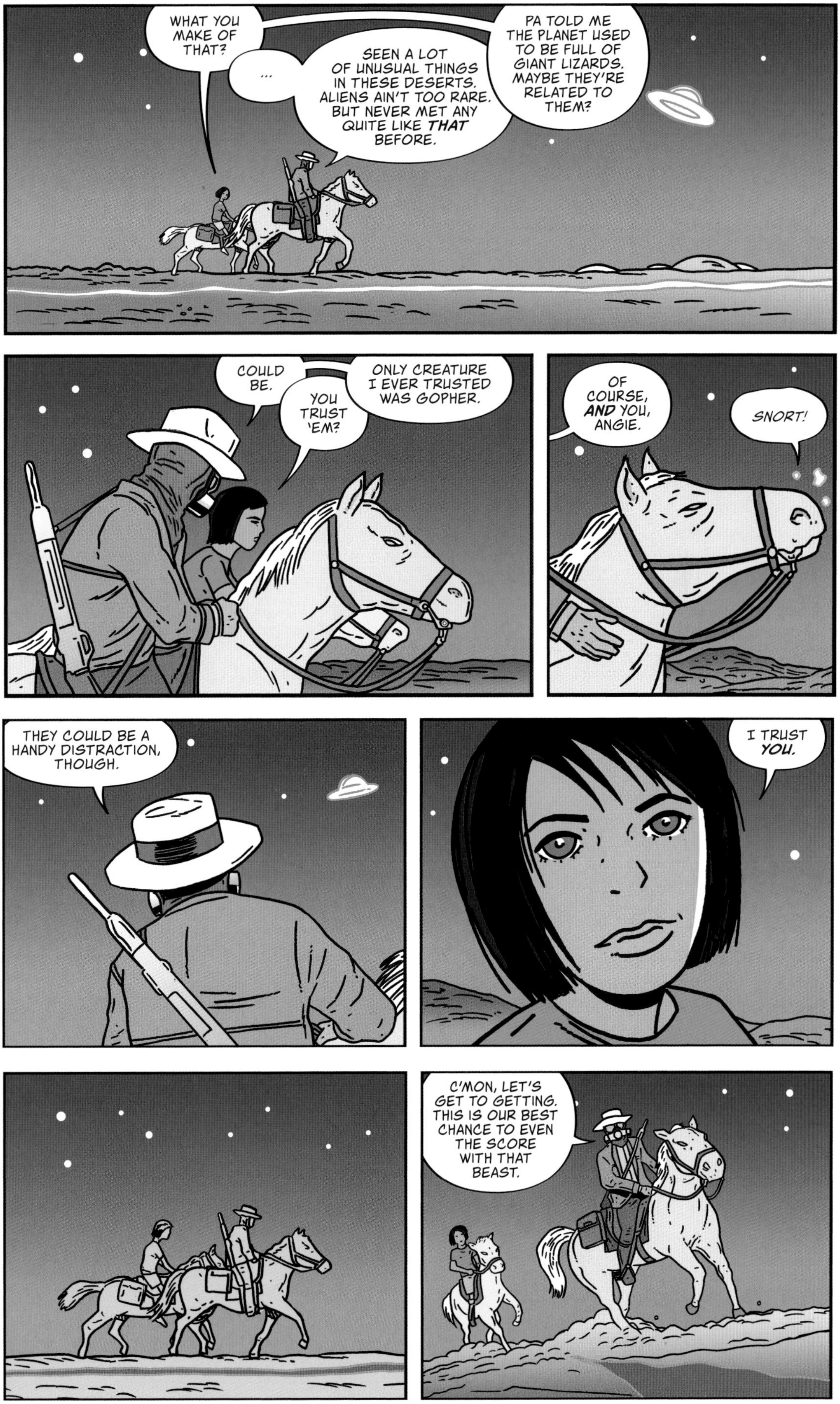
WHAT YOU MAKE OF THAT?
...
SEEN A LOT OF UNUSUAL THINGS IN THESE DESERTS. ALIENS AIN'T TOO RARE. BUT NEVER MET ANY QUITE LIKE ***THAT*** BEFORE.
PA TOLD ME THE PLANET USED TO BE FULL OF GIANT LIZARDS. MAYBE THEY'RE RELATED TO THEM?
COULD BE.
YOU TRUST 'EM?
ONLY CREATURE I EVER TRUSTED WAS GOPHER.
OF COURSE, **AND** YOU, ANGIE.
SNORT!
THEY COULD BE A HANDY DISTRACTION, THOUGH.
I TRUST ***YOU.***
C'MON, LET'S GET TO GETTING. THIS IS OUR BEST CHANCE TO EVEN THE SCORE WITH THAT BEAST.

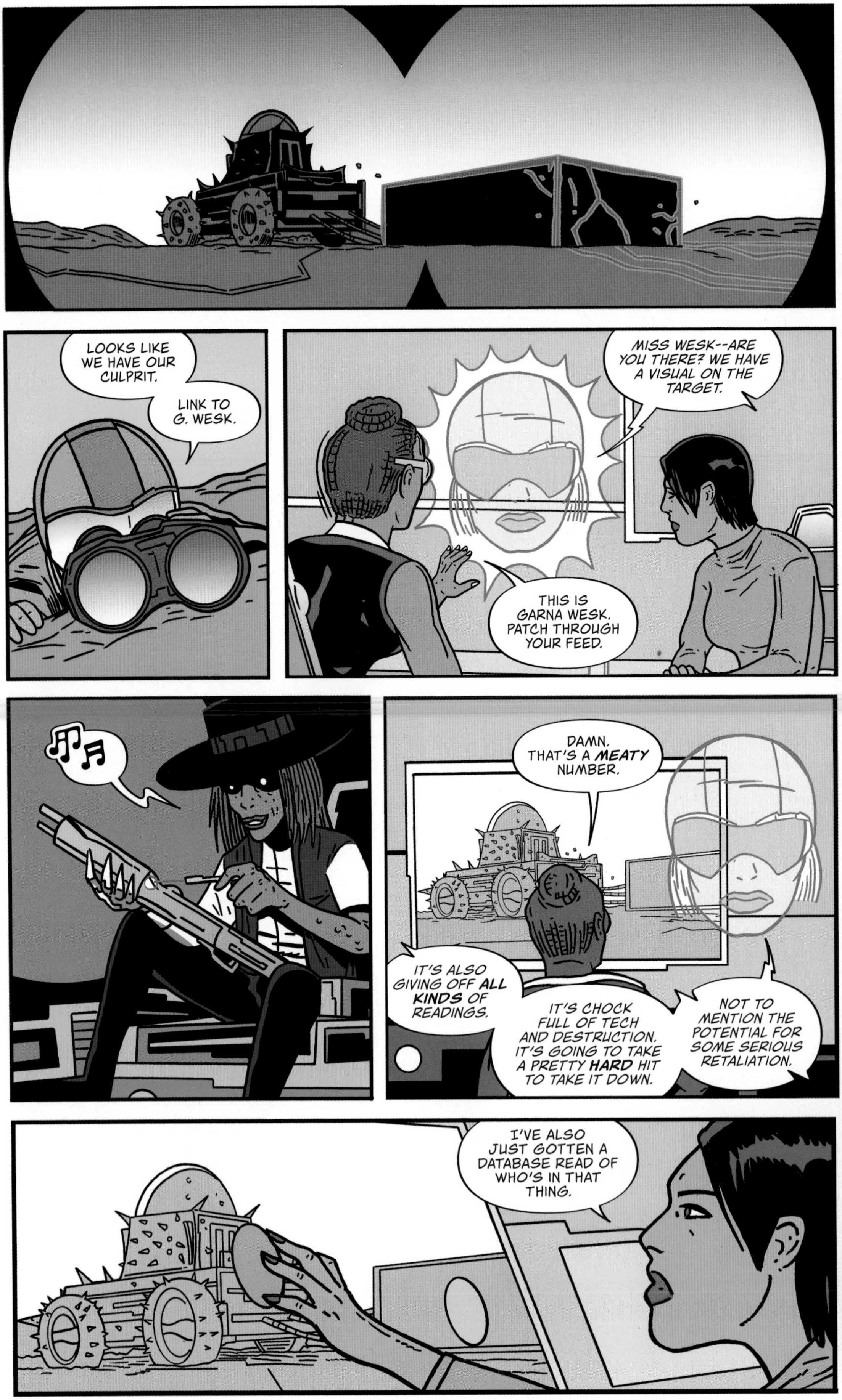
LOOKS LIKE WE HAVE OUR CULPRIT.
LINK TO G. WESK.
MISS WESK--ARE YOU THERE? WE HAVE A VISUAL ON THE TARGET.
THIS IS GARNA WESK. PATCH THROUGH YOUR FEED.
DAMN. THAT'S A MEATY NUMBER.
IT'S ALSO GIVING OFF ALL KINDS OF READINGS.
IT'S CHOCK FULL OF TECH AND DESTRUCTION. IT'S GOING TO TAKE A PRETTY HARD HIT TO TAKE IT DOWN.
NOT TO MENTION THE POTENTIAL FOR SOME SERIOUS RETALIATION.
I'VE ALSO JUST GOTTEN A DATABASE READ OF WHO'S IN THAT THING.

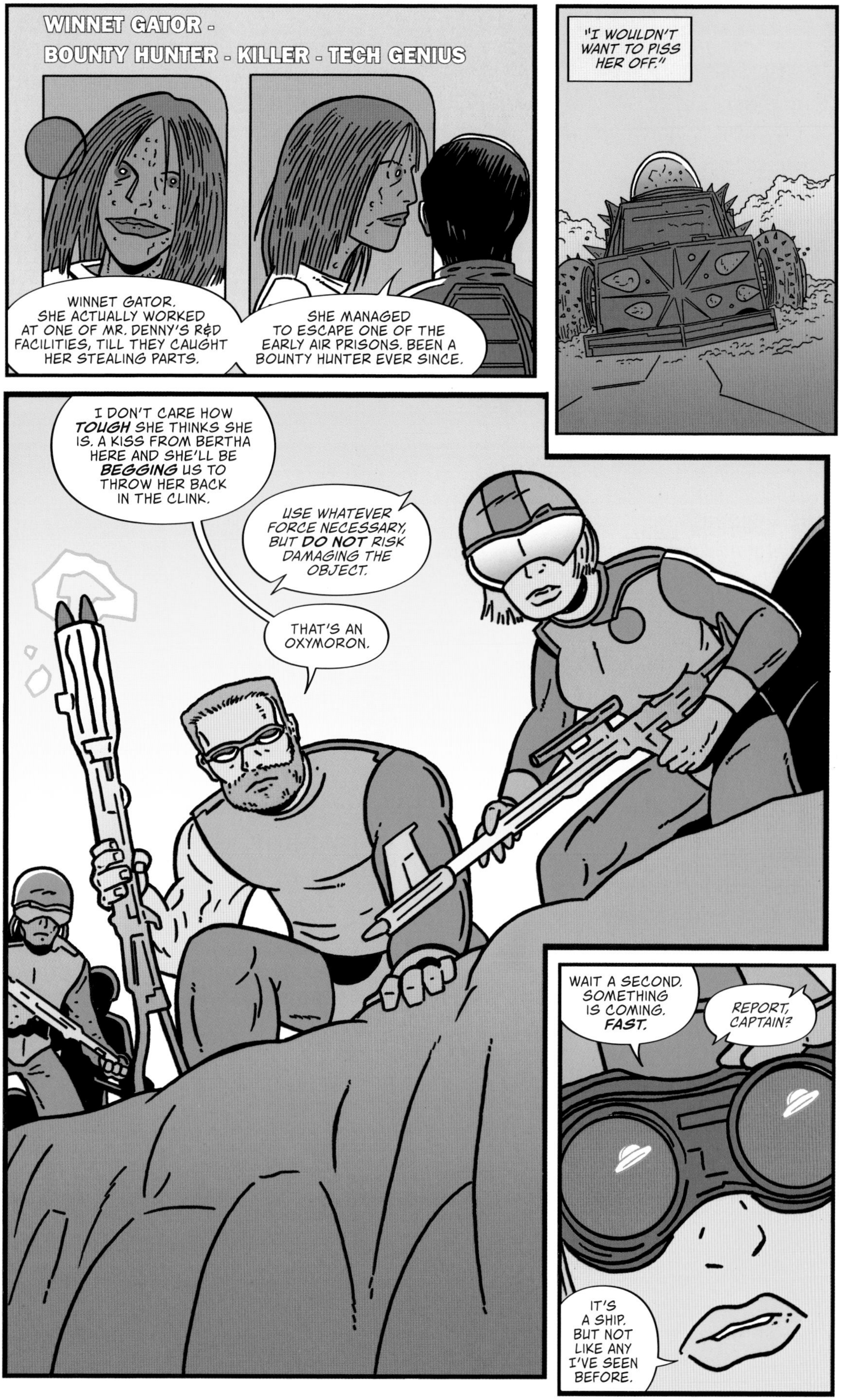
WINNET GATOR -
BOUNTY HUNTER - KILLER - TECH GENIUS
WINNET GATOR. SHE ACTUALLY WORKED AT ONE OF MR. DENNY'S R&D FACILITIES, TILL THEY CAUGHT HER STEALING PARTS.
SHE MANAGED TO ESCAPE ONE OF THE EARLY AIR PRISONS. BEEN A BOUNTY HUNTER EVER SINCE.
"I WOULDN'T WANT TO PISS HER OFF."
I DON'T CARE HOW TOUGH SHE THINKS SHE IS. A KISS FROM BERTHA HERE AND SHE'LL BE BEGGING US TO THROW HER BACK IN THE CLINK.
USE WHATEVER FORCE NECESSARY, BUT DO NOT RISK DAMAGING THE OBJECT.
THAT'S AN OXYMORON.
WAIT A SECOND. SOMETHING IS COMING. FAST.
REPORT, CAPTAIN?
IT'S A SHIP. BUT NOT LIKE ANY I'VE SEEN BEFORE.

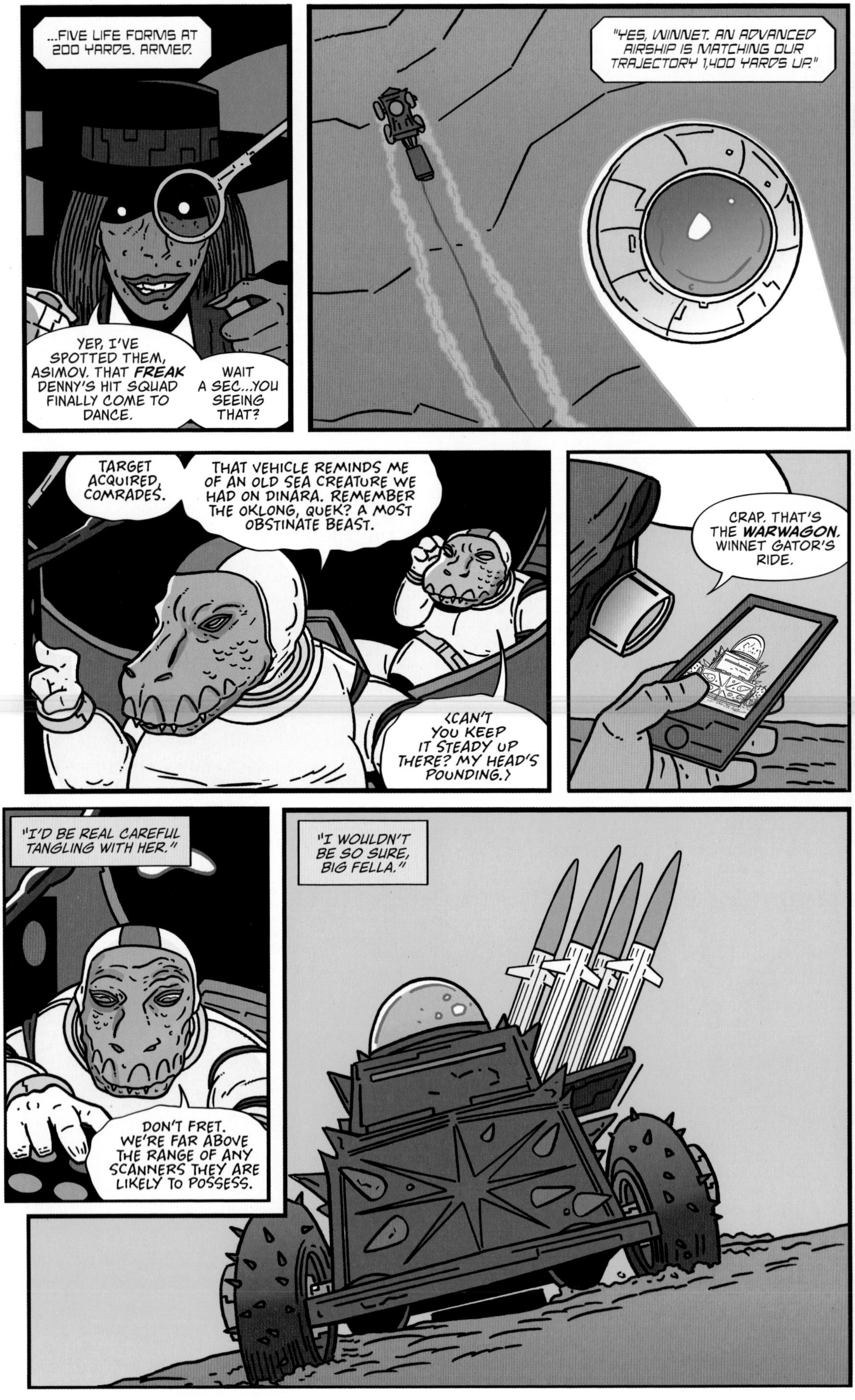
...FIVE LIFE FORMS AT 200 YARDS. ARMED.
YEP, I'VE SPOTTED THEM, ASIMOV. THAT FREAK DENNY'S HIT SQUAD FINALLY COME TO DANCE.
WAIT A SEC...YOU SEEING THAT?
"YES, WINNET. AN ADVANCED AIRSHIP IS MATCHING OUR TRAJECTORY 1,400 YARDS UP."
TARGET ACQUIRED, COMRADES.
THAT VEHICLE REMINDS ME OF AN OLD SEA CREATURE WE HAD ON DINARA. REMEMBER THE OKLONG, QUEK? A MOST OBSTINATE BEAST.
<CAN'T YOU KEEP IT STEADY UP THERE? MY HEAD'S POUNDING.>
CRAP. THAT'S THE WARWAGON. WINNET GATOR'S RIDE.
"I'D BE REAL CAREFUL TANGLING WITH HER."
DON'T FRET. WE'RE FAR ABOVE THE RANGE OF ANY SCANNERS THEY ARE LIKELY TO POSSESS.
"I WOULDN'T BE SO SURE, BIG FELLA."

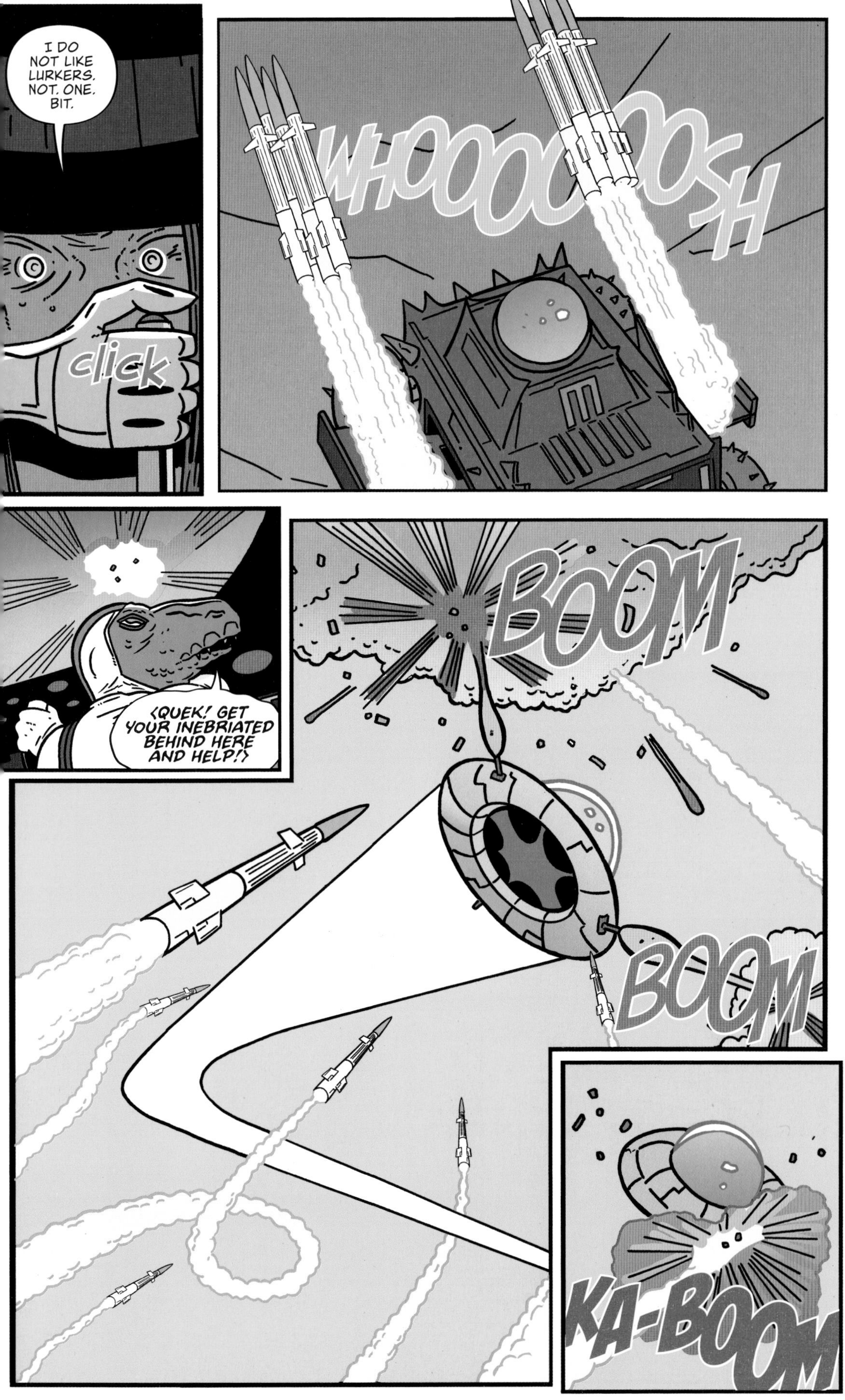

I DO NOT LIKE LURKERS. NOT. ONE. BIT.
click
WHOOOOOOSH
<QUEK! GET YOUR INEBRIATED BEHIND HERE AND HELP!>
BOOM
BOOM
KA-BOOM

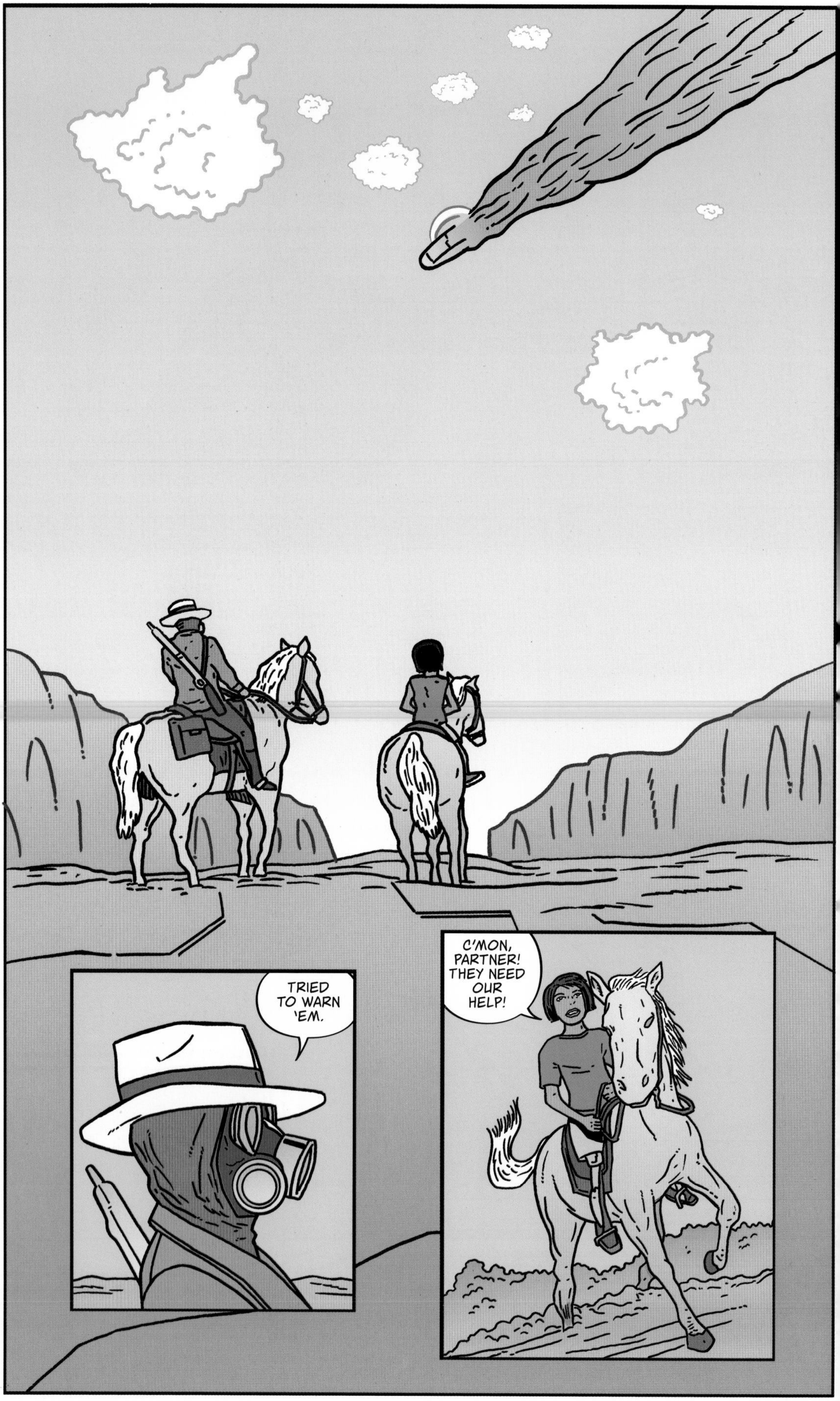
TRIED TO WARN 'EM.
C'MON, PARTNER! THEY NEED OUR HELP!

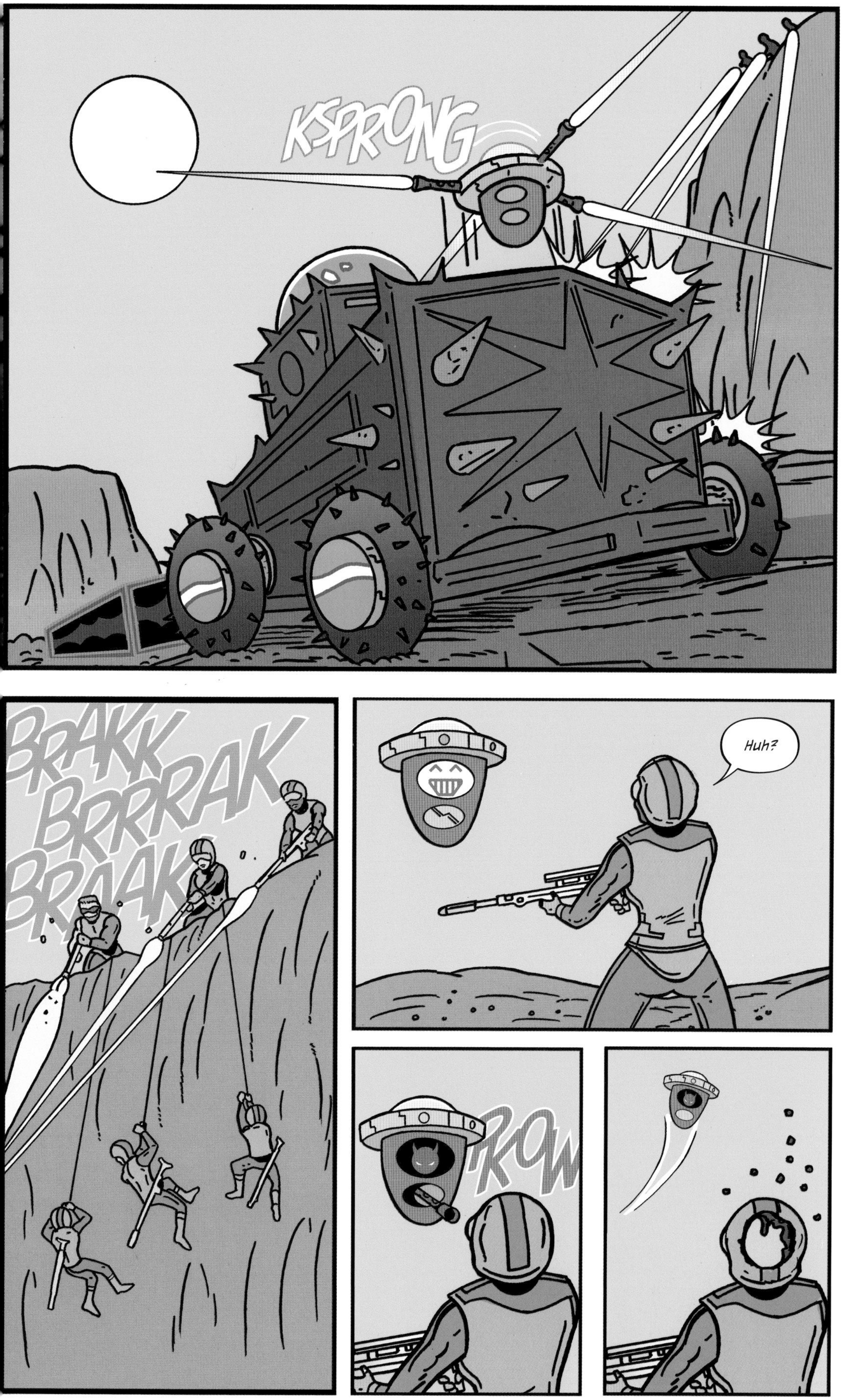
KSPRONG
BRAKK
BRRRAK
BRAAK
Huh?
KROW

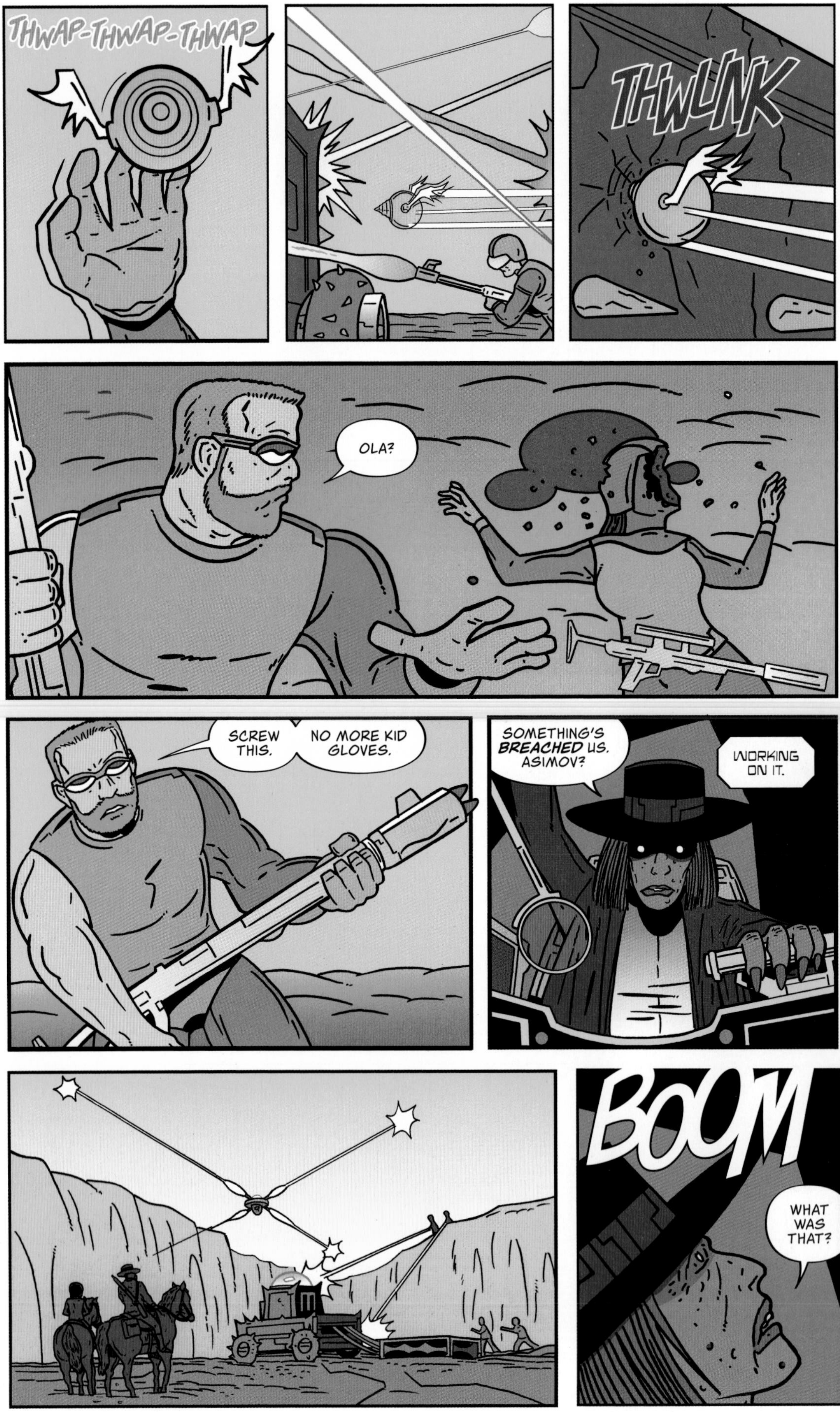
THWAP-THWAP-THWAP
THWUNK
OLA?
SCREW THIS.
NO MORE KID GLOVES.
SOMETHING'S *BREACHED* US. ASIMOV?
WORKING ON IT.
BOOM
WHAT WAS THAT?

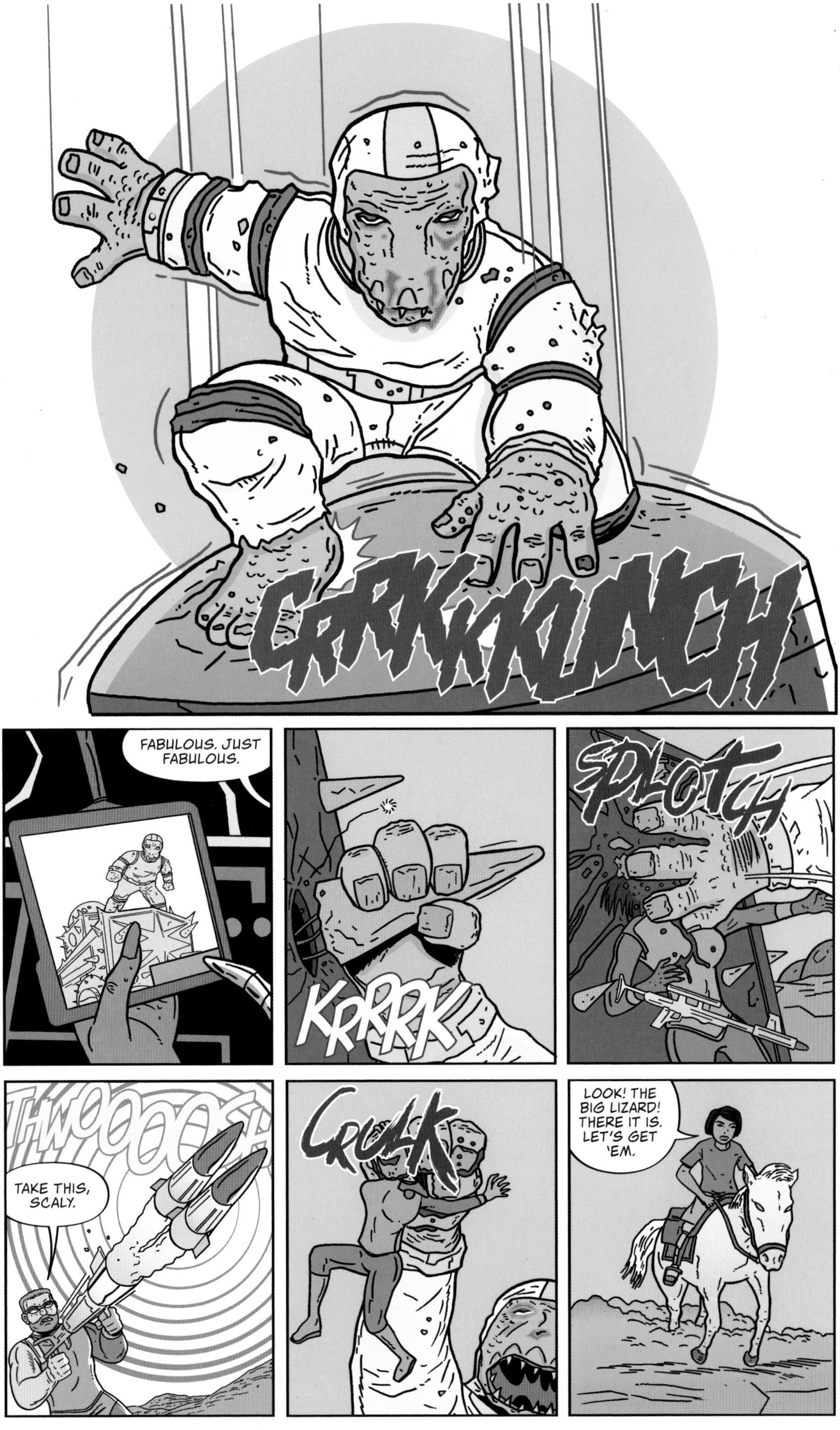
CRRKKKRUNCH
FABULOUS. JUST FABULOUS.
KRRRK
SPLOTCH
THWOOOOSH
TAKE THIS, SCALY.
CRULK
LOOK! THE BIG LIZARD! THERE IT IS. LET'S GET 'EM.

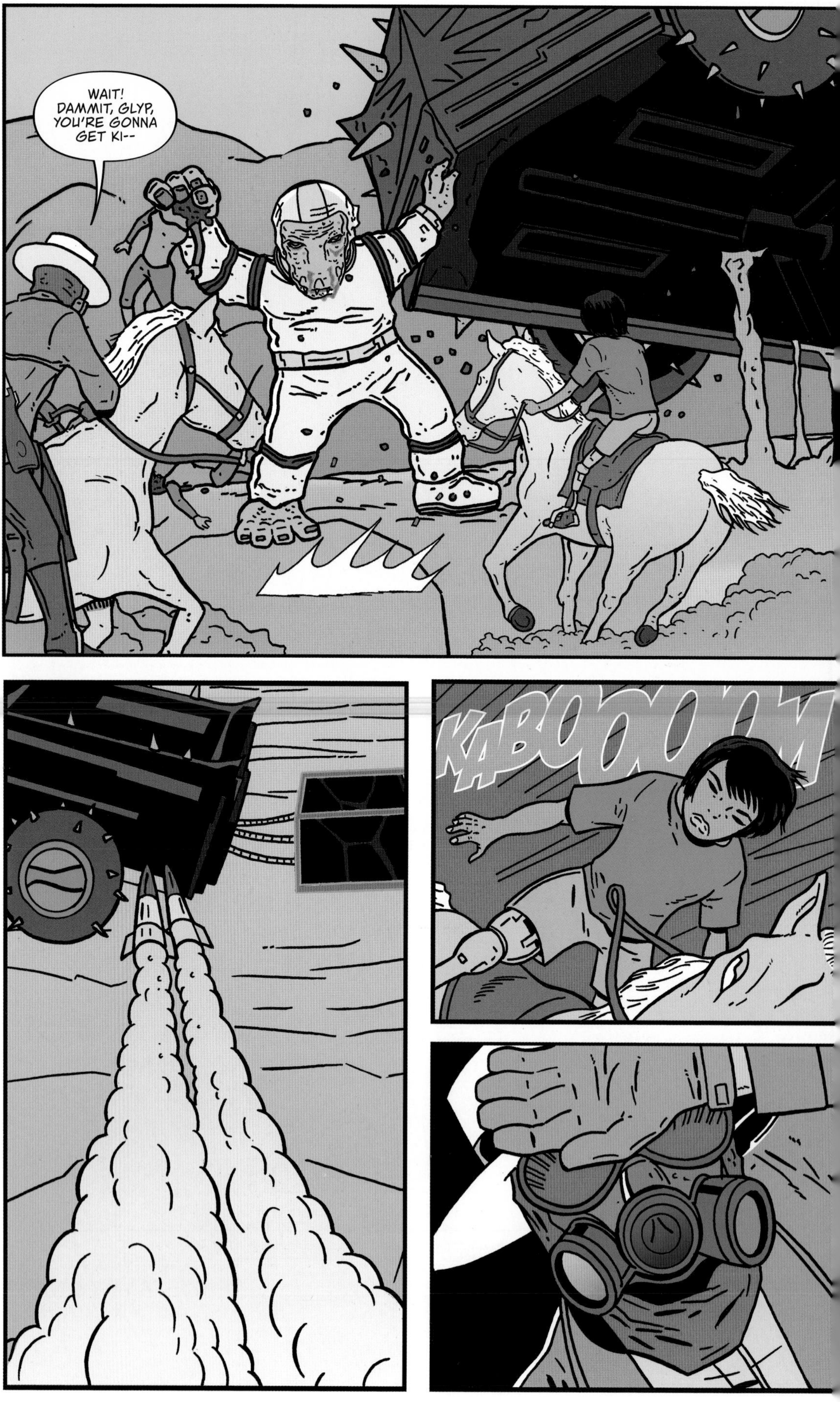
WAIT! DAMMIT, GLYP, YOU'RE GONNA GET KI--
KABOOOOOM

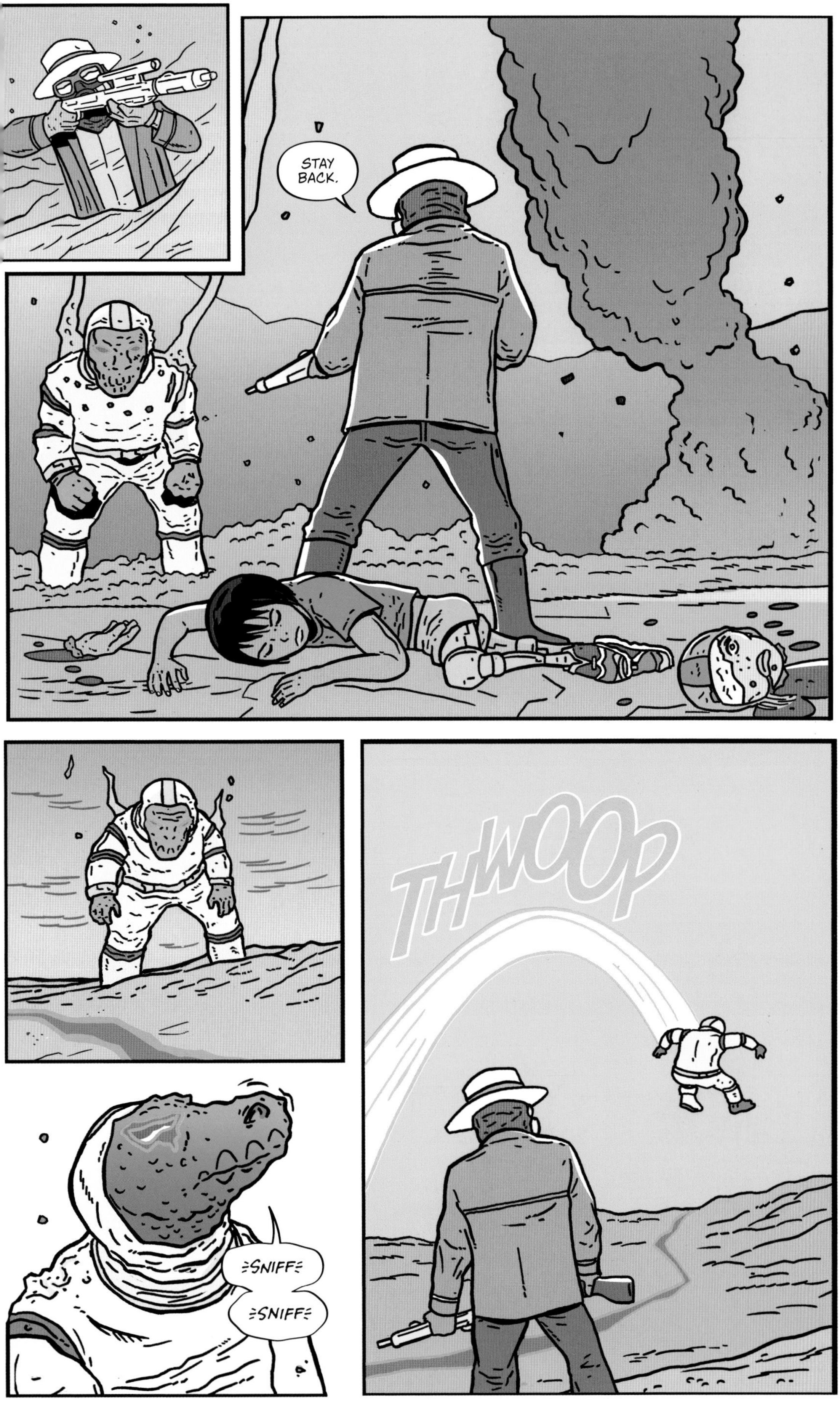
STAY BACK.
THWOOP
=SNIFF=
=SNIFF=

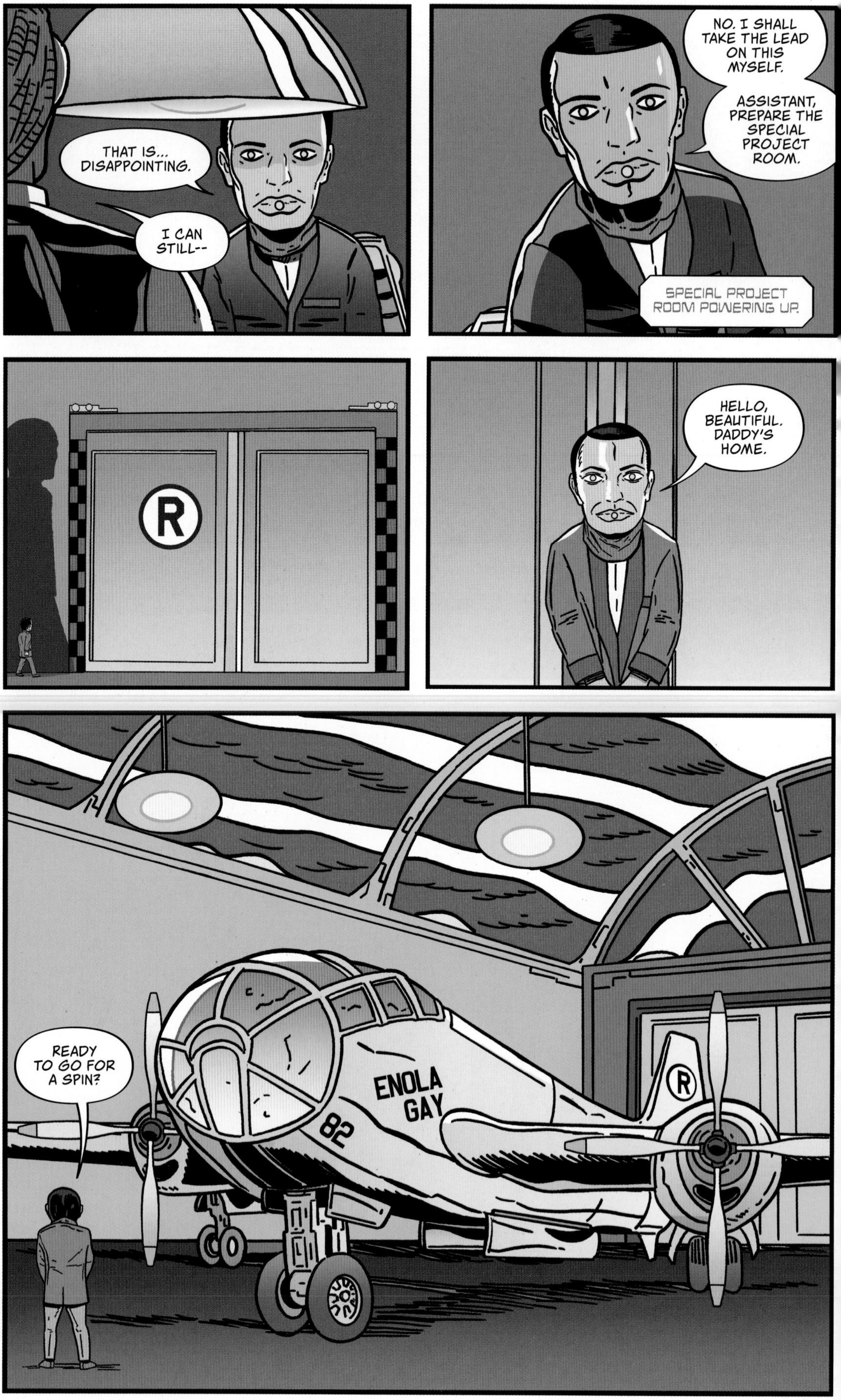
THAT IS... DISAPPOINTING.
I CAN STILL--
NO. I SHALL TAKE THE LEAD ON THIS MYSELF.
ASSISTANT, PREPARE THE SPECIAL PROJECT ROOM.
SPECIAL PROJECT ROOM POWERING UP.
R
HELLO, BEAUTIFUL. DADDY'S HOME.
READY TO GO FOR A SPIN?
ENOLA GAY
82
R

CHAPTER THREE

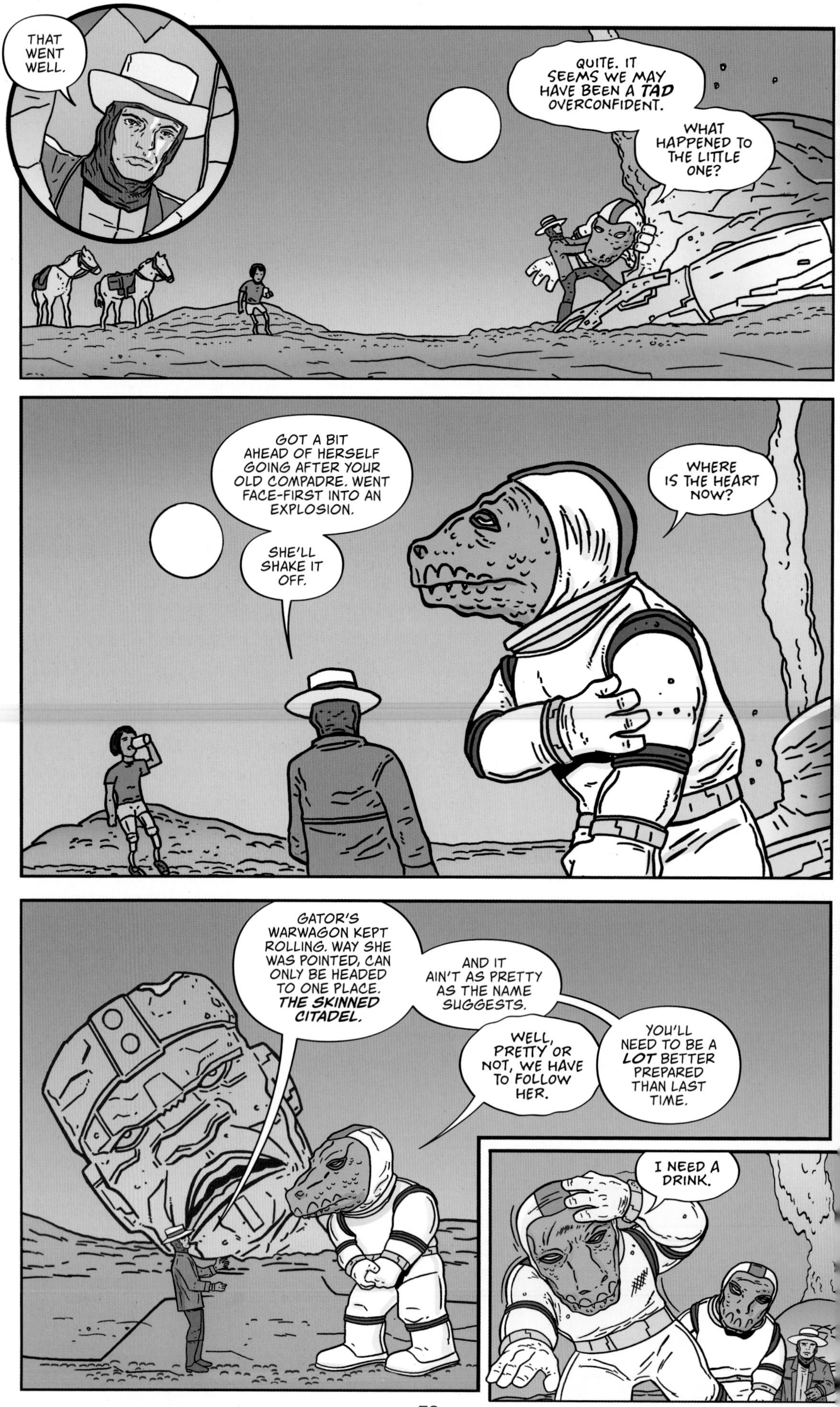
THAT WENT WELL.
QUITE. IT SEEMS WE MAY HAVE BEEN A TAD OVERCONFIDENT.
WHAT HAPPENED TO THE LITTLE ONE?
GOT A BIT AHEAD OF HERSELF GOING AFTER YOUR OLD COMPADRE. WENT FACE-FIRST INTO AN EXPLOSION.
SHE'LL SHAKE IT OFF.
WHERE IS THE HEART NOW?
GATOR'S WARWAGON KEPT ROLLING. WAY SHE WAS POINTED, CAN ONLY BE HEADED TO ONE PLACE. THE SKINNED CITADEL.
AND IT AIN'T AS PRETTY AS THE NAME SUGGESTS.
WELL, PRETTY OR NOT, WE HAVE TO FOLLOW HER.
YOU'LL NEED TO BE A LOT BETTER PREPARED THAN LAST TIME.
I NEED A DRINK.

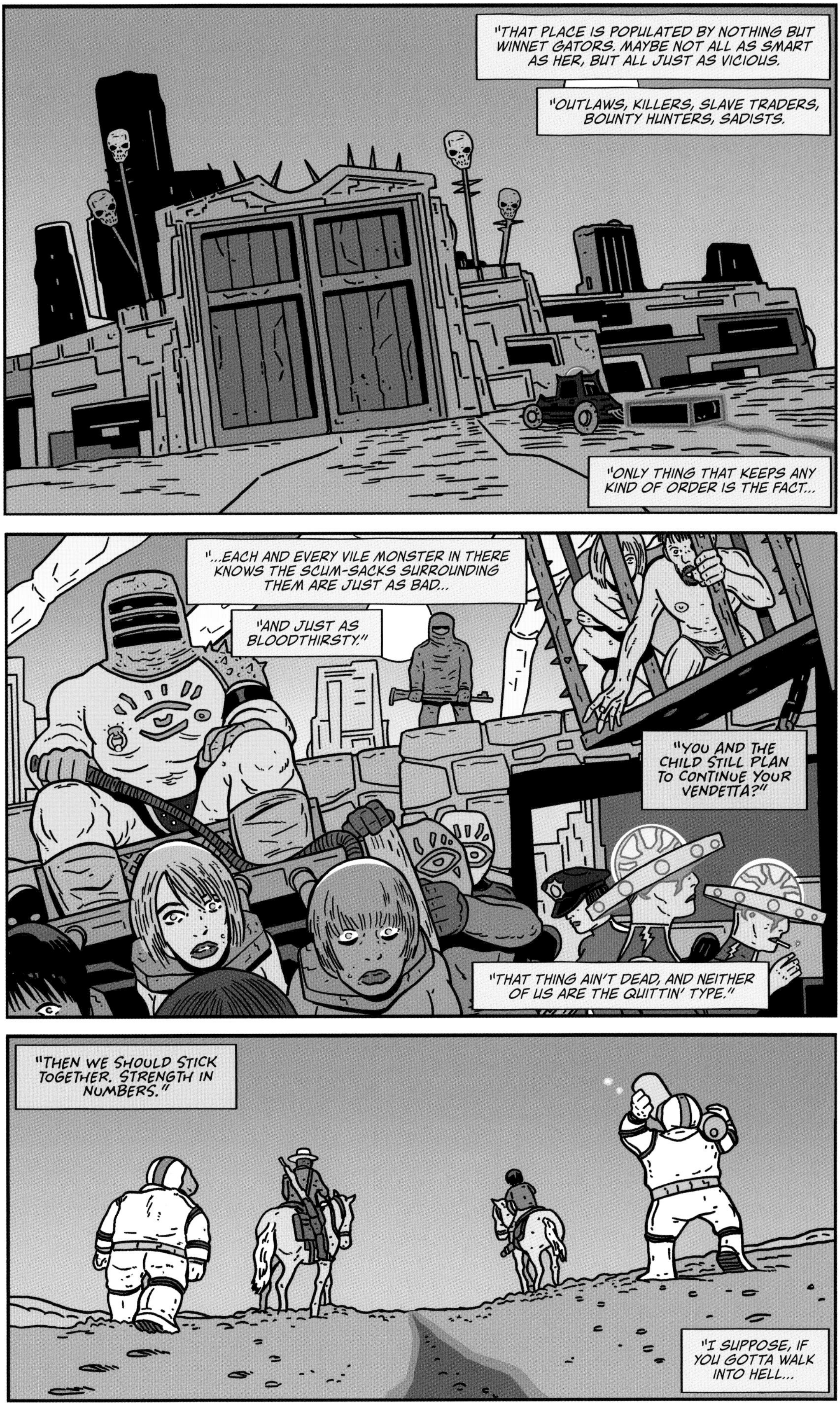
"THAT PLACE IS POPULATED BY NOTHING BUT WINNET GATORS. MAYBE NOT ALL AS SMART AS HER, BUT ALL JUST AS VICIOUS.
"OUTLAWS, KILLERS, SLAVE TRADERS, BOUNTY HUNTERS, SADISTS.
"ONLY THING THAT KEEPS ANY KIND OF ORDER IS THE FACT...
"...EACH AND EVERY VILE MONSTER IN THERE KNOWS THE SCUM-SACKS SURROUNDING THEM ARE JUST AS BAD...
"AND JUST AS BLOODTHIRSTY."
"YOU AND THE CHILD STILL PLAN TO CONTINUE YOUR VENDETTA?"
"THAT THING AIN'T DEAD, AND NEITHER OF US ARE THE QUITTIN' TYPE."
"THEN WE SHOULD STICK TOGETHER. STRENGTH IN NUMBERS."
"I SUPPOSE, IF YOU GOTTA WALK INTO HELL...

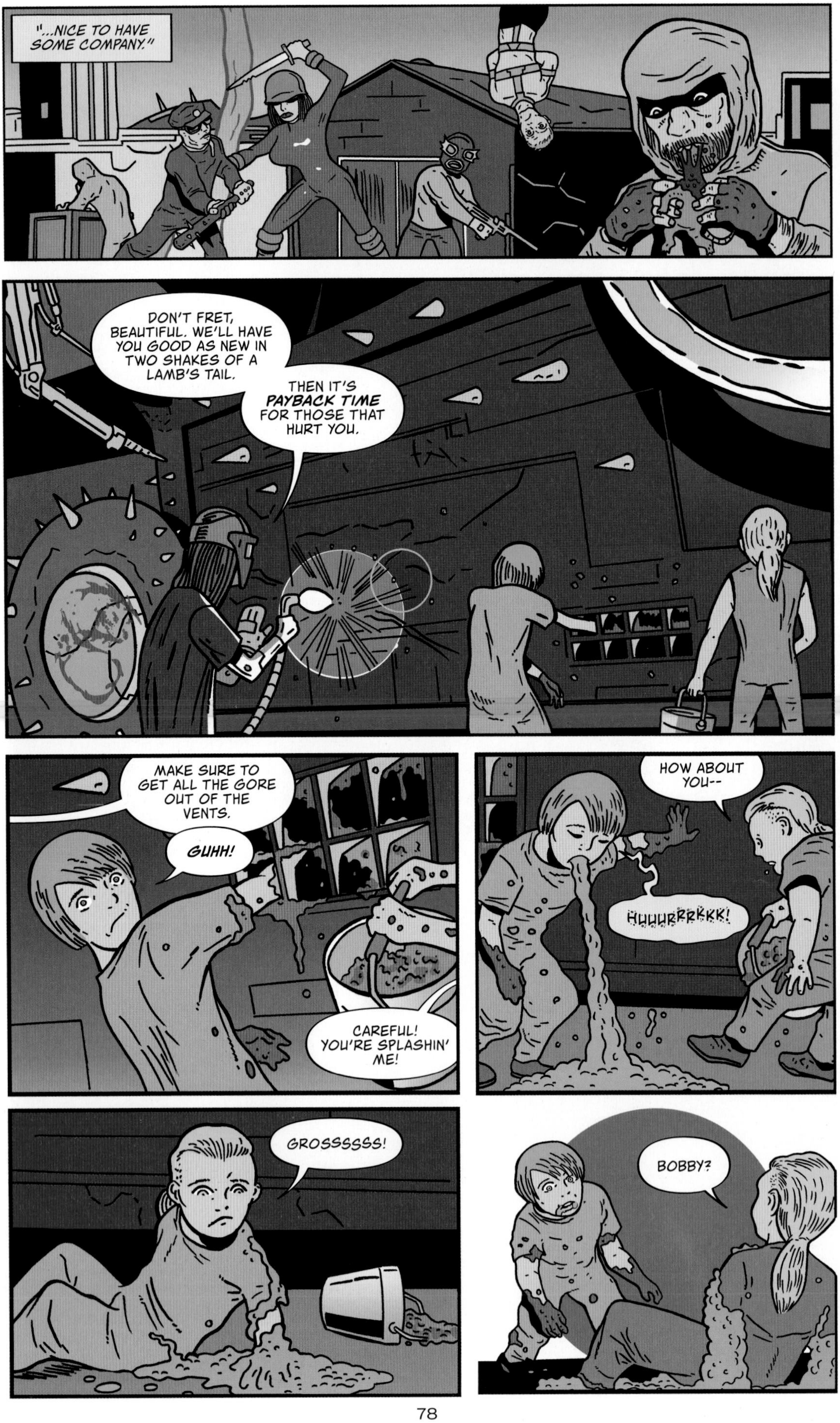
"...NICE TO HAVE SOME COMPANY."
DON'T FRET, BEAUTIFUL. WE'LL HAVE YOU GOOD AS NEW IN TWO SHAKES OF A LAMB'S TAIL.
THEN IT'S PAYBACK TIME FOR THOSE THAT HURT YOU.
MAKE SURE TO GET ALL THE GORE OUT OF THE VENTS.
GUHH!
CAREFUL! YOU'RE SPLASHIN' ME!
HOW ABOUT YOU--
HUUURRRKKK!
GROSSSSSS!
BOBBY?

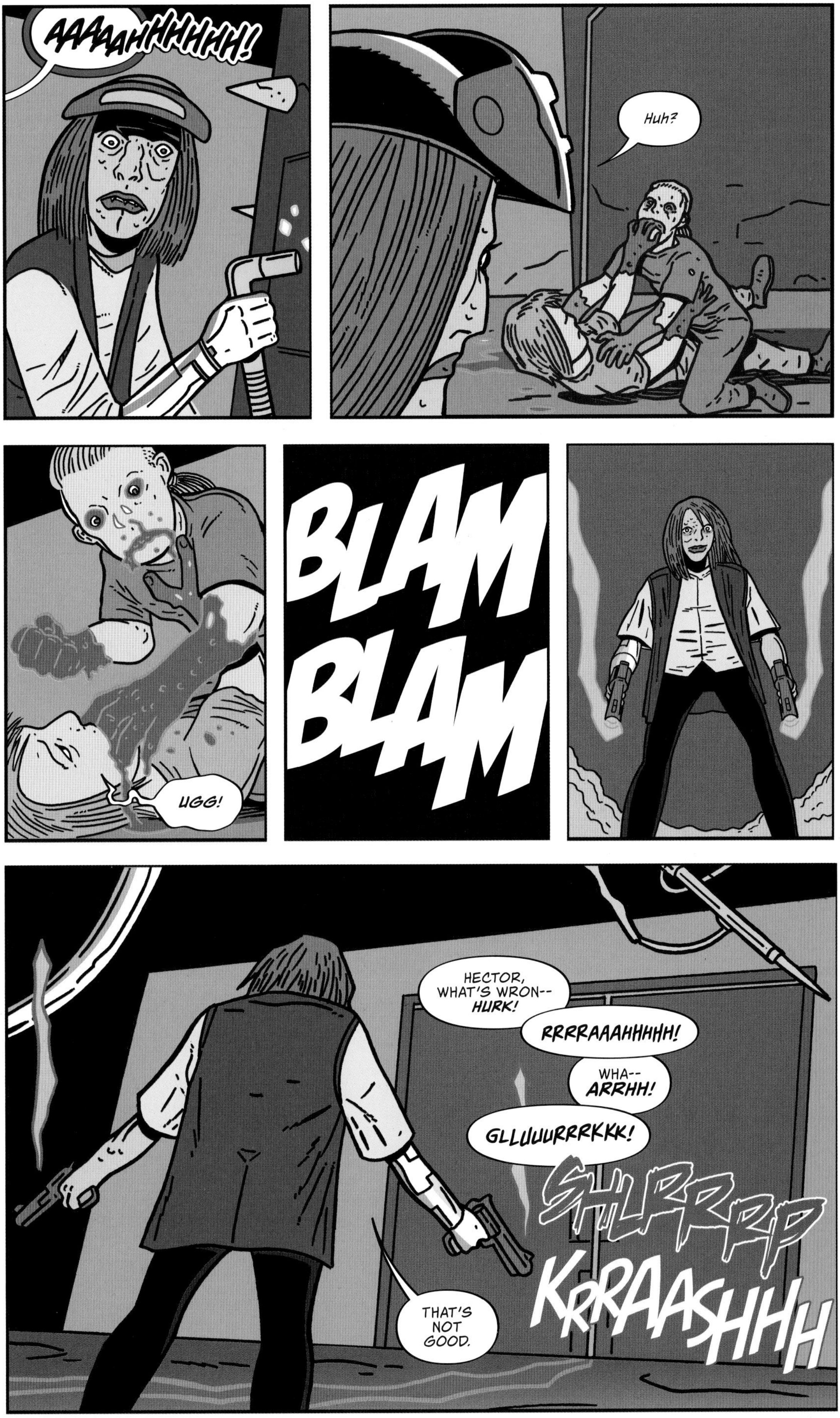
AAAAAHHHHHH!
Huh?
UGG!
BLAM
BLAM
HECTOR, WHAT'S WRON-- HURK!
RRRRAAAHHHHH!
WHA-- ARRHH!
GLLUUURRRKKK!
SHLRRRP
KRRAASHHH
THAT'S NOT GOOD.

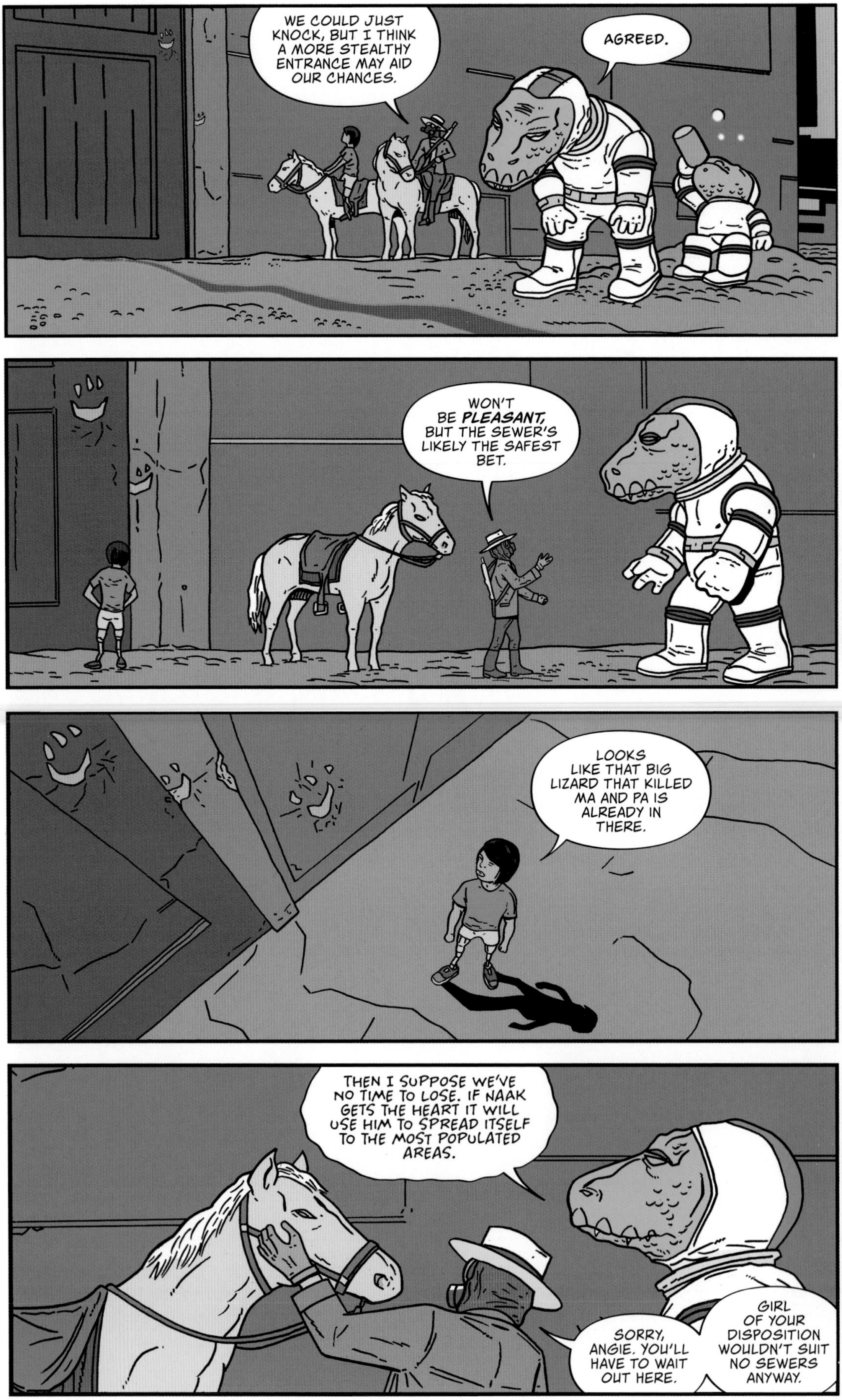
WE COULD JUST KNOCK, BUT I THINK A MORE STEALTHY ENTRANCE MAY AID OUR CHANCES.
AGREED.
WON'T BE **PLEASANT,** BUT THE SEWER'S LIKELY THE SAFEST BET.
LOOKS LIKE THAT BIG LIZARD THAT KILLED MA AND PA IS ALREADY IN THERE.
THEN I SUPPOSE WE'VE NO TIME TO LOSE. IF NAAK GETS THE HEART IT WILL USE HIM TO SPREAD ITSELF TO THE MOST POPULATED AREAS.
SORRY, ANGIE. YOU'LL HAVE TO WAIT OUT HERE.
GIRL OF YOUR DISPOSITION WOULDN'T SUIT NO SEWERS ANYWAY.

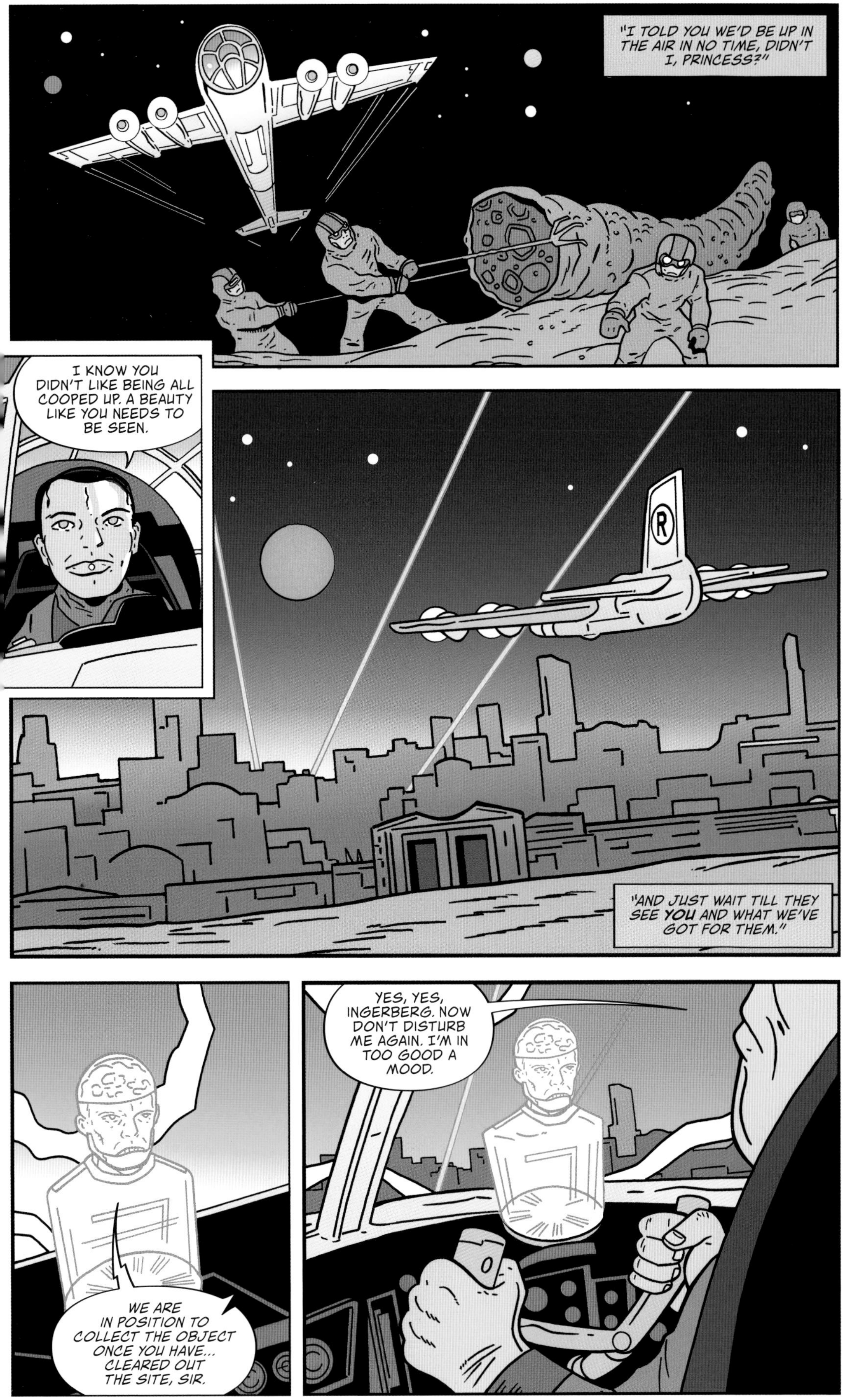
"I TOLD YOU WE'D BE UP IN THE AIR IN NO TIME, DIDN'T I, PRINCESS?"
I KNOW YOU DIDN'T LIKE BEING ALL COOPED UP. A BEAUTY LIKE YOU NEEDS TO BE SEEN.
R
"AND JUST WAIT TILL THEY SEE **YOU** AND WHAT WE'VE GOT FOR THEM."
WE ARE IN POSITION TO COLLECT THE OBJECT ONCE YOU HAVE... CLEARED OUT THE SITE, SIR.
YES, YES, INGERBERG. NOW DON'T DISTURB ME AGAIN. I'M IN TOO GOOD A MOOD.

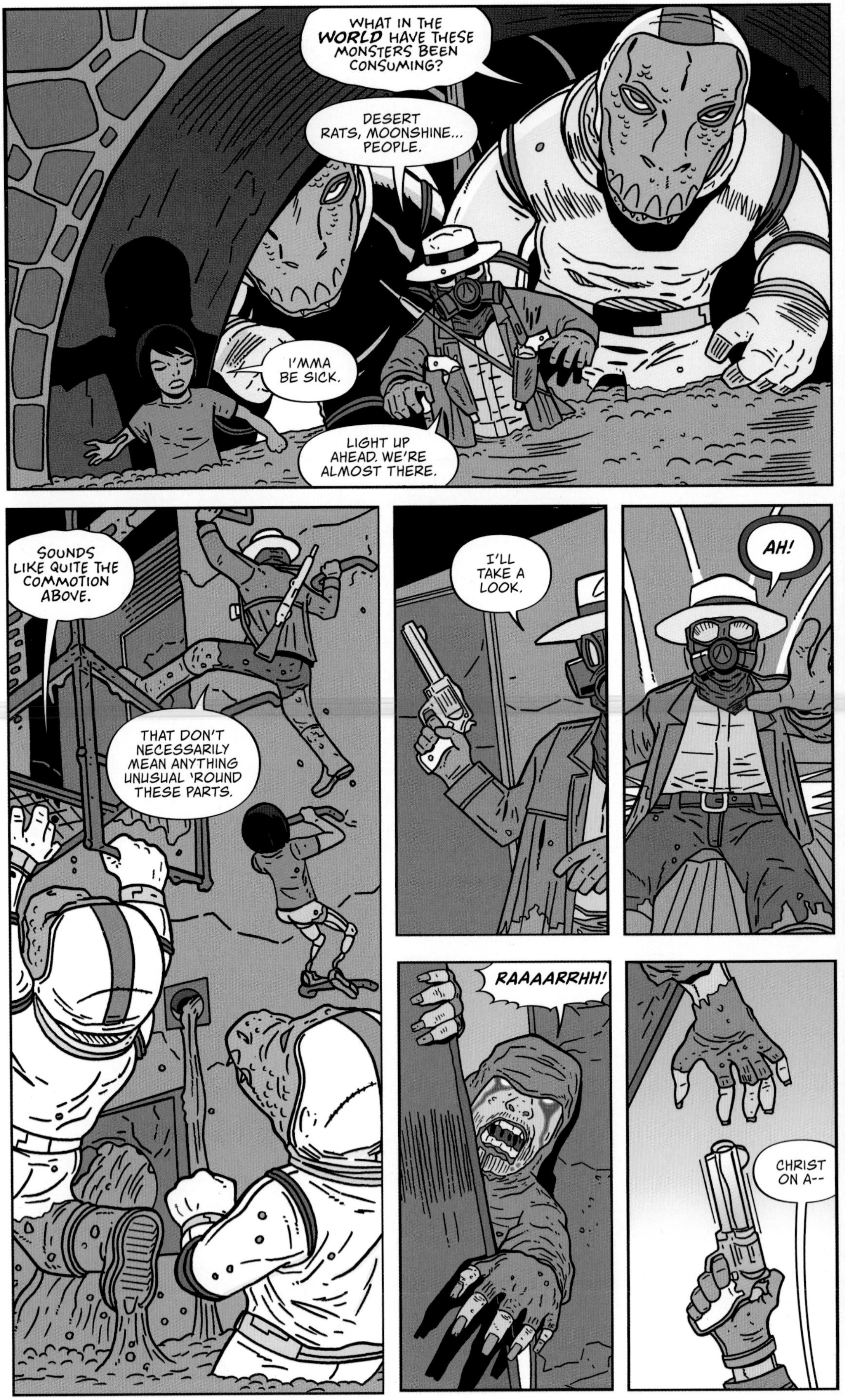
WHAT IN THE WORLD HAVE THESE MONSTERS BEEN CONSUMING?
DESERT RATS, MOONSHINE... PEOPLE.
I'MMA BE SICK.
LIGHT UP AHEAD. WE'RE ALMOST THERE.
SOUNDS LIKE QUITE THE COMMOTION ABOVE.
THAT DON'T NECESSARILY MEAN ANYTHING UNUSUAL 'ROUND THESE PARTS.
I'LL TAKE A LOOK.
AH!
RAAAARRHH!
CHRIST ON A--

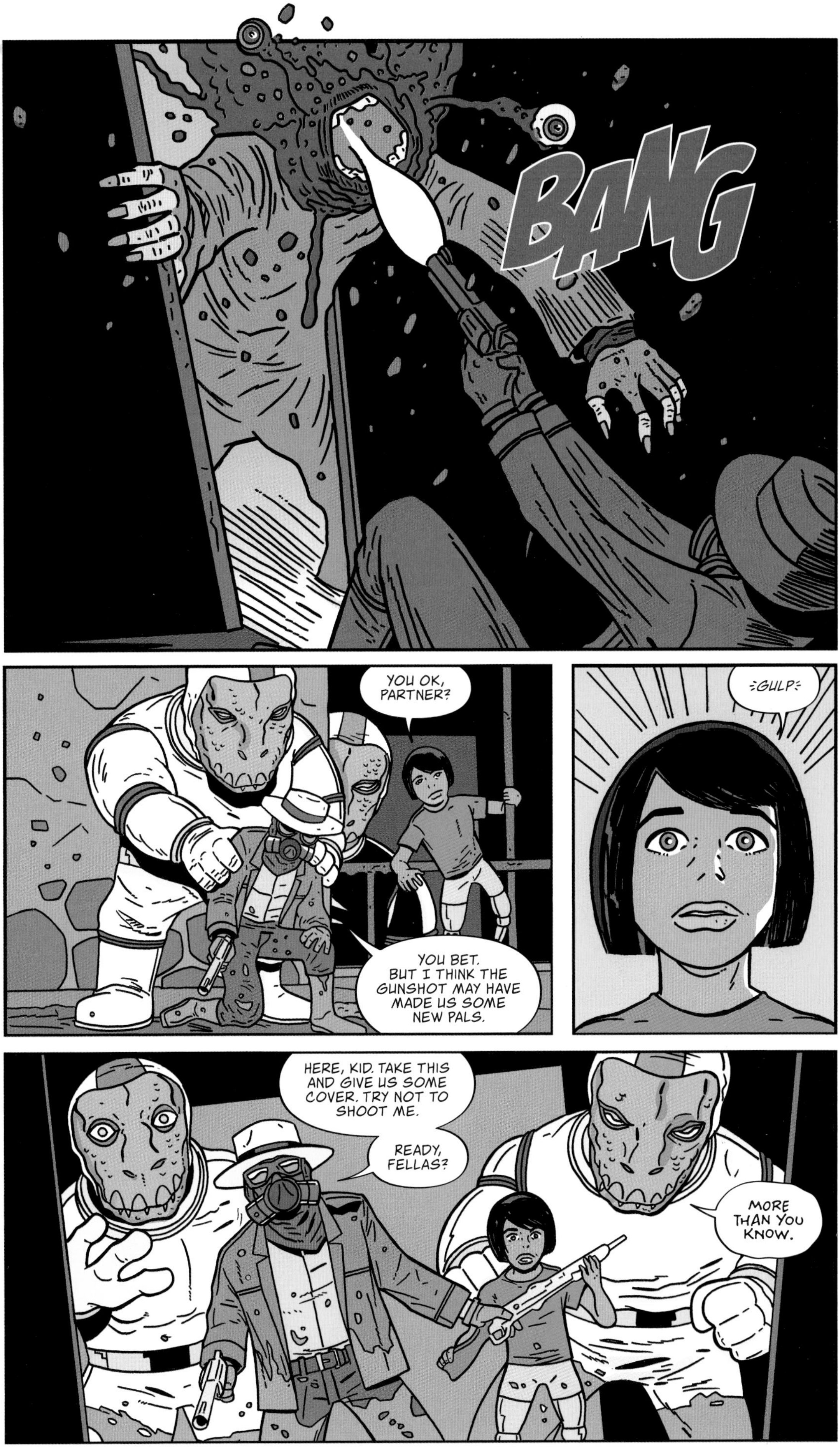
BANG
YOU OK, PARTNER?
YOU BET. BUT I THINK THE GUNSHOT MAY HAVE MADE US SOME NEW PALS.
GULP
HERE, KID. TAKE THIS AND GIVE US SOME COVER. TRY NOT TO SHOOT ME.
READY, FELLAS?
MORE THAN YOU KNOW.

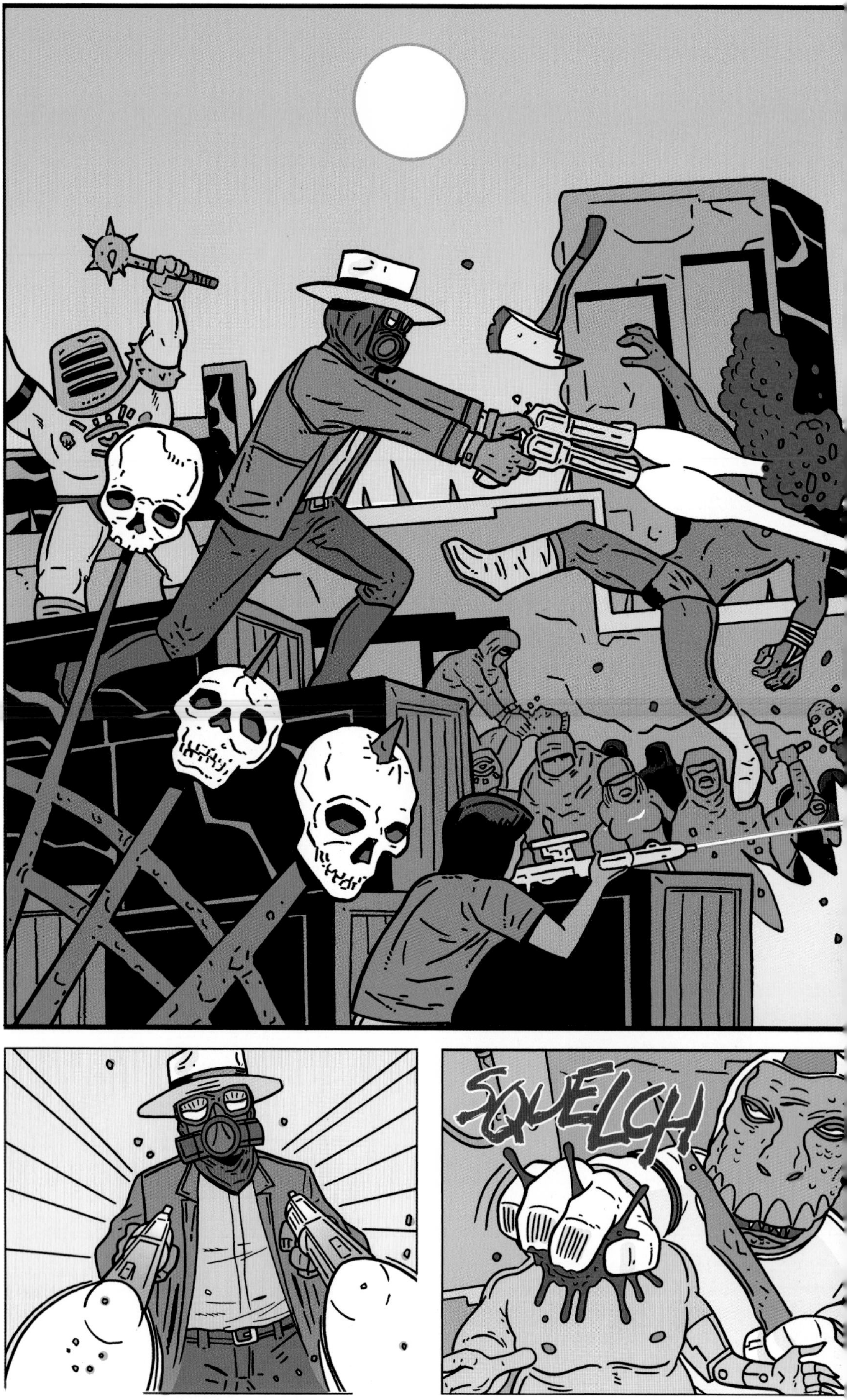
SQUELCH

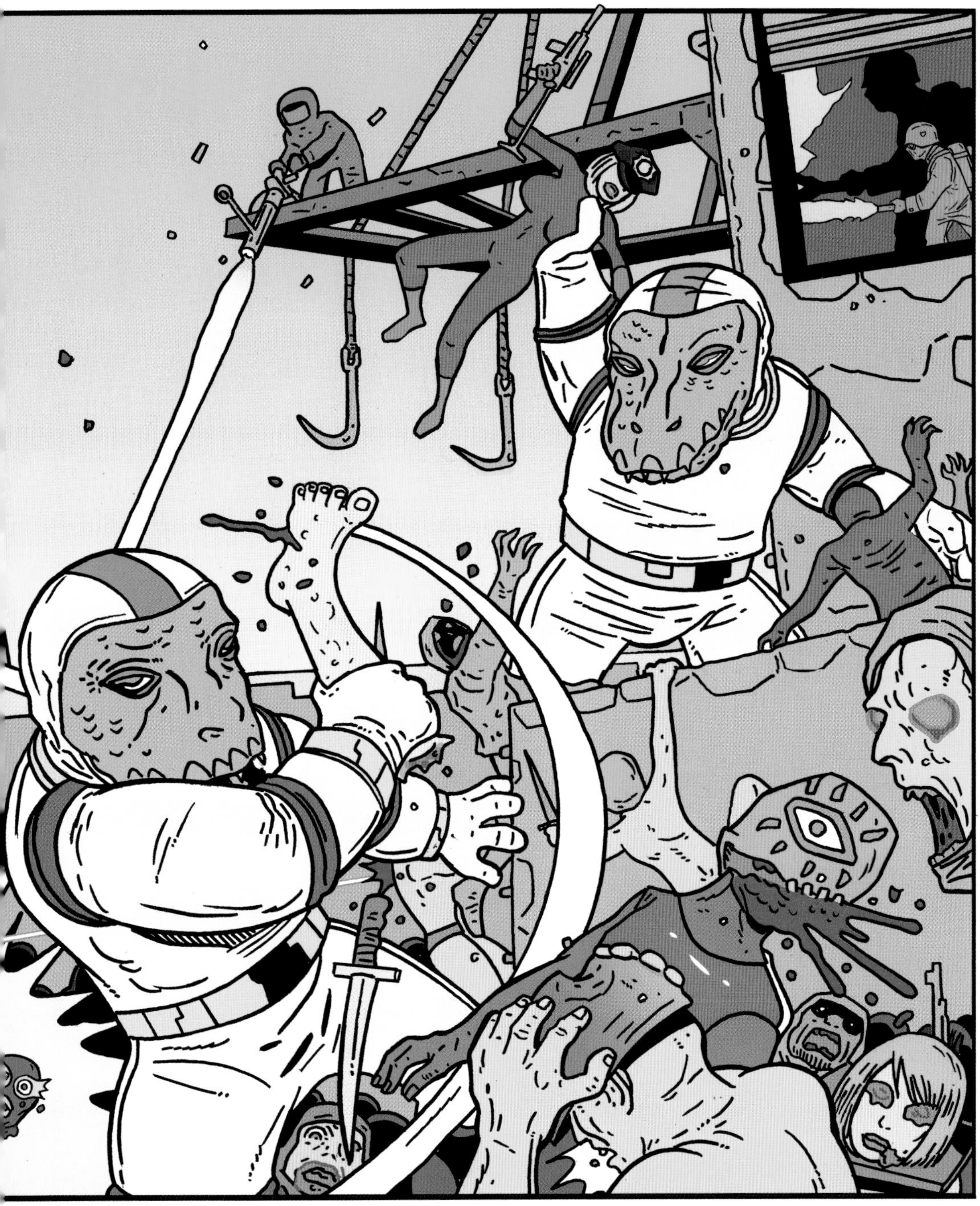

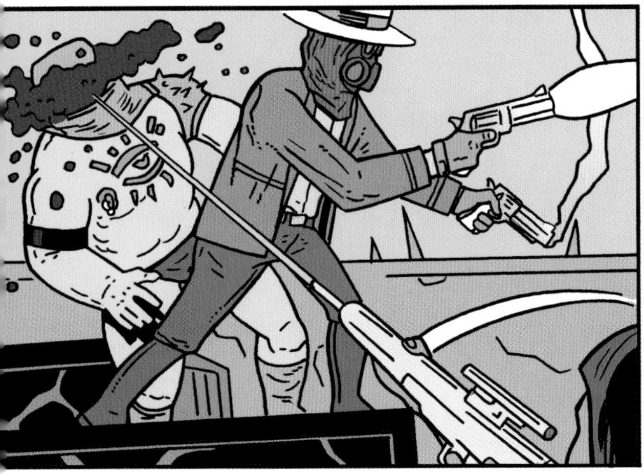

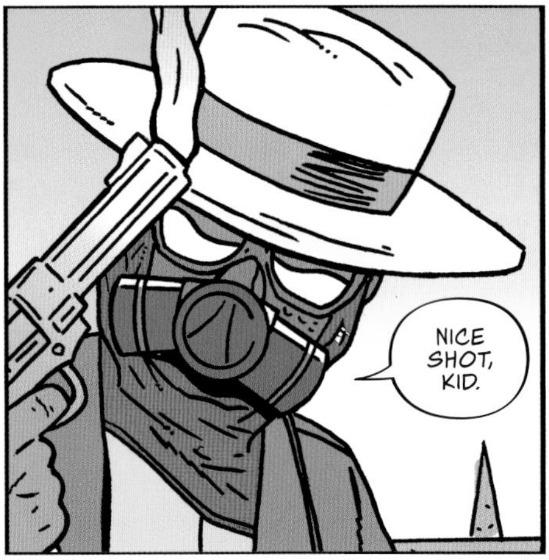
NICE SHOT, KID.

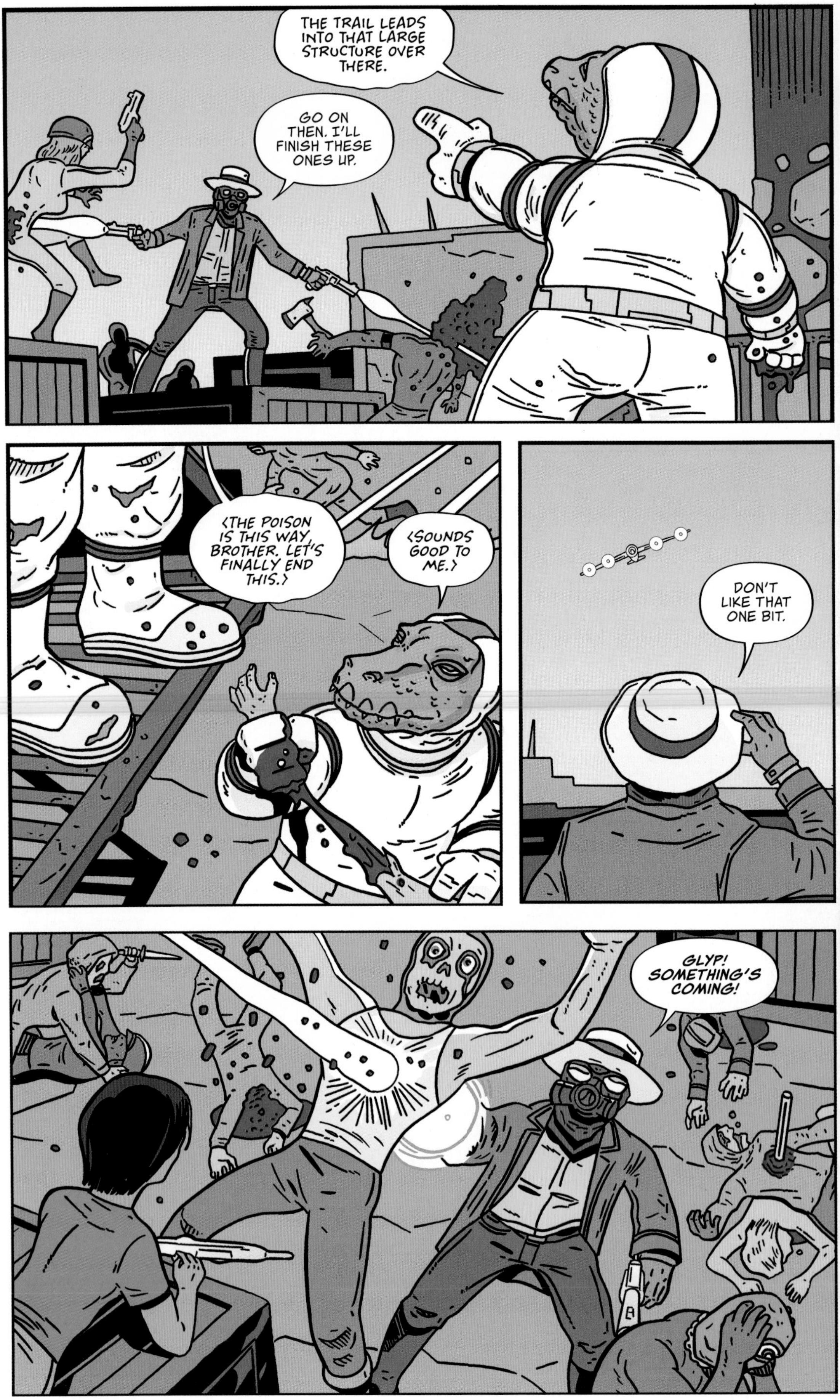
THE TRAIL LEADS INTO THAT LARGE STRUCTURE OVER THERE.
GO ON THEN. I'LL FINISH THESE ONES UP.
<THE POISON IS THIS WAY, BROTHER. LET'S FINALLY END THIS.>
<SOUNDS GOOD TO ME.>
DON'T LIKE THAT ONE BIT.
GLYP! SOMETHING'S COMING!

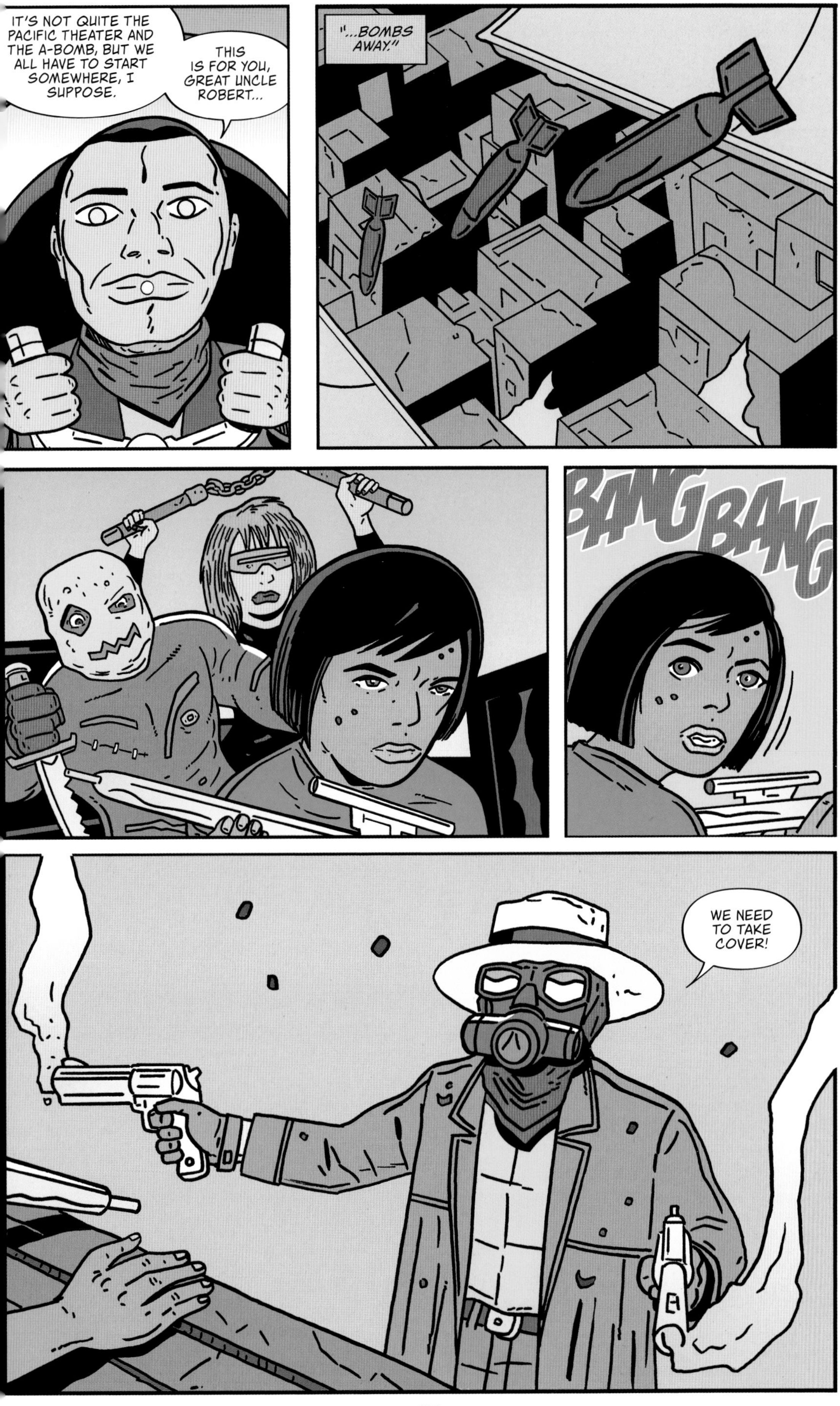
IT'S NOT QUITE THE PACIFIC THEATER AND THE A-BOMB, BUT WE ALL HAVE TO START SOMEWHERE, I SUPPOSE.
THIS IS FOR YOU, GREAT UNCLE ROBERT...
"...BOMBS AWAY."
BANG BANG
WE NEED TO TAKE COVER!

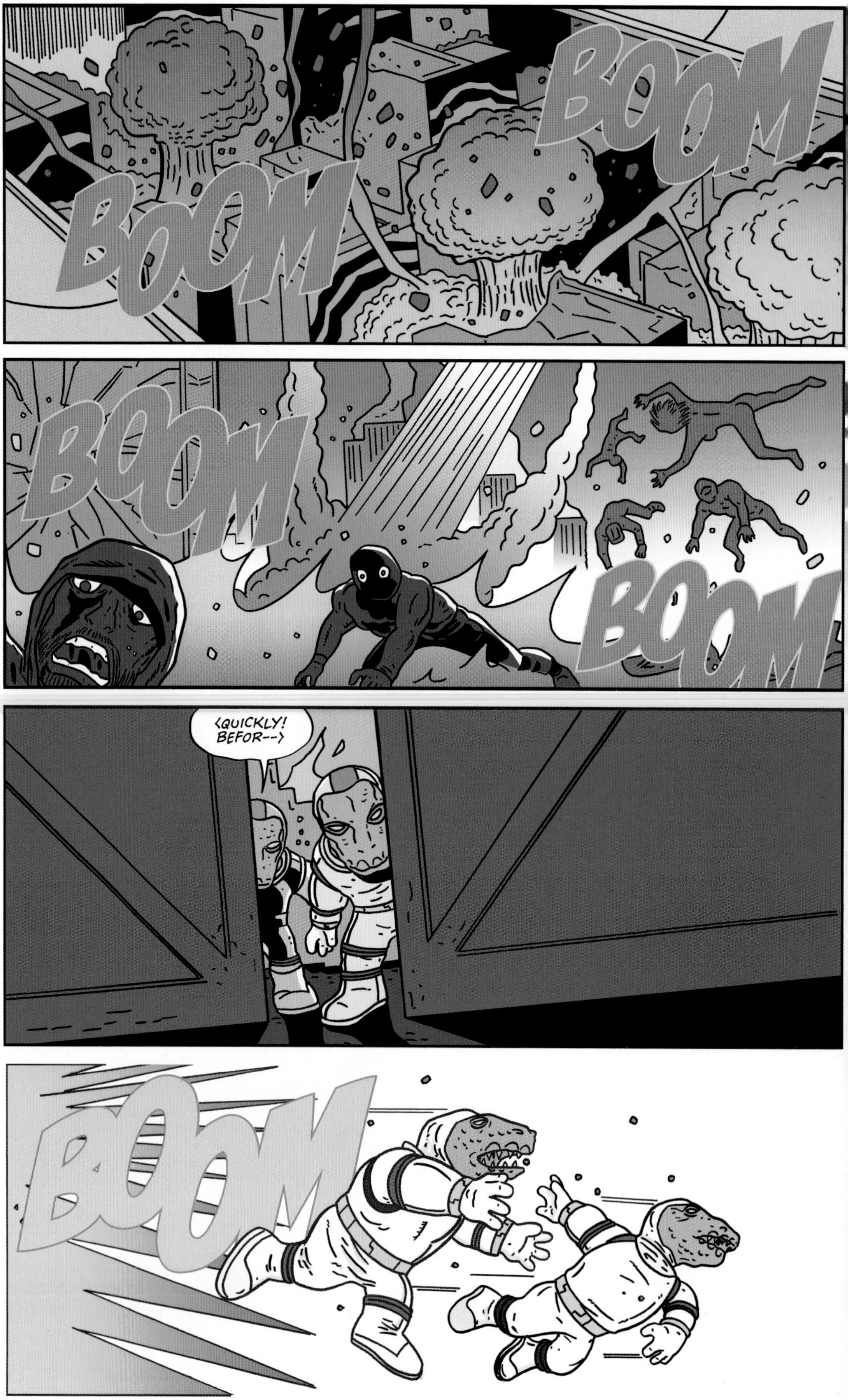
BOOM
BOOM
BOOM
BOOM
‹QUICKLY! BEFOR--›
BOOM

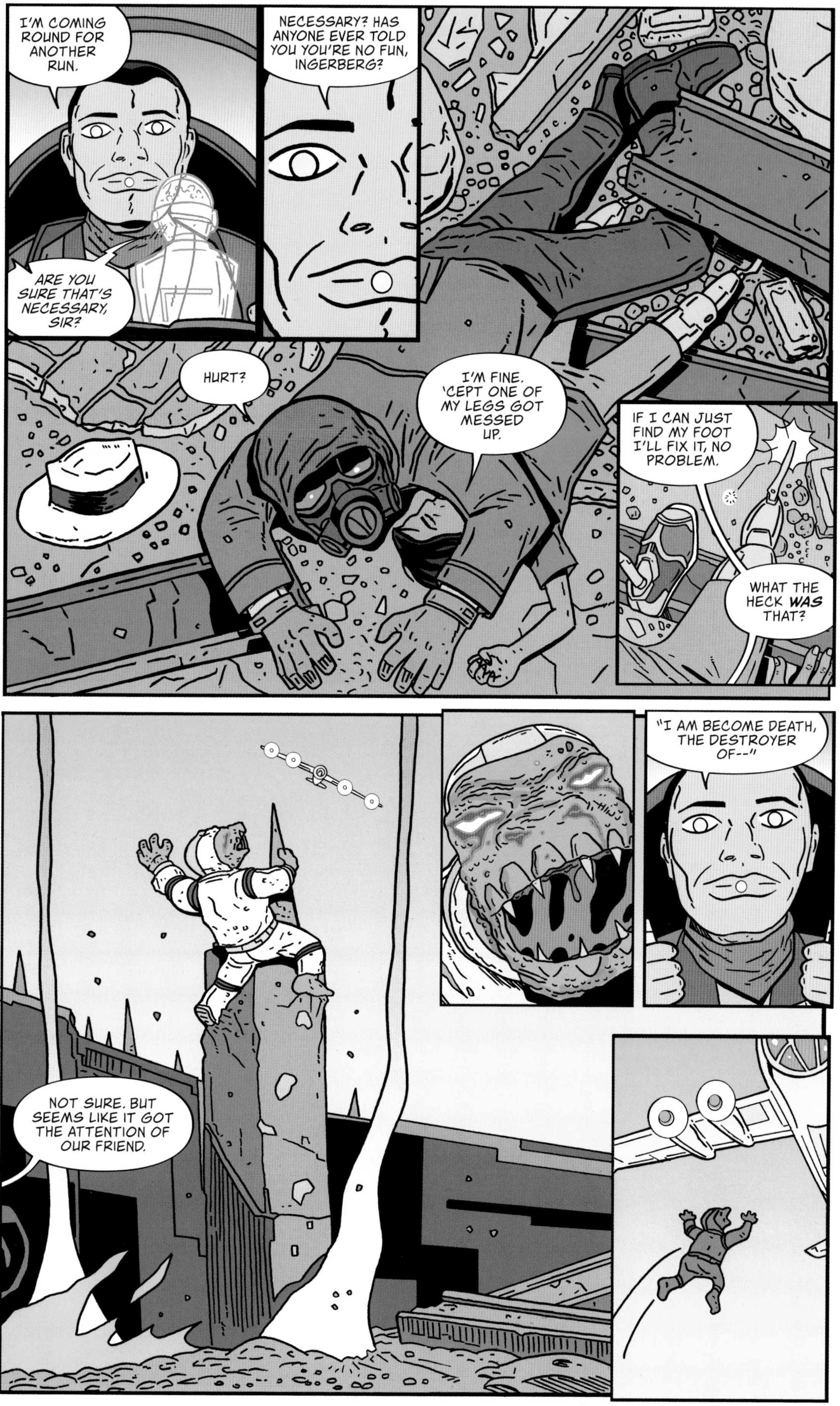
I'M COMING ROUND FOR ANOTHER RUN.
ARE YOU SURE THAT'S NECESSARY, SIR?
NECESSARY? HAS ANYONE EVER TOLD YOU YOU'RE NO FUN, INGERBERG?
HURT?
I'M FINE. 'CEPT ONE OF MY LEGS GOT MESSED UP.
IF I CAN JUST FIND MY FOOT I'LL FIX IT, NO PROBLEM.
WHAT THE HECK WAS THAT?
NOT SURE. BUT SEEMS LIKE IT GOT THE ATTENTION OF OUR FRIEND.
"I AM BECOME DEATH, THE DESTROYER OF--"

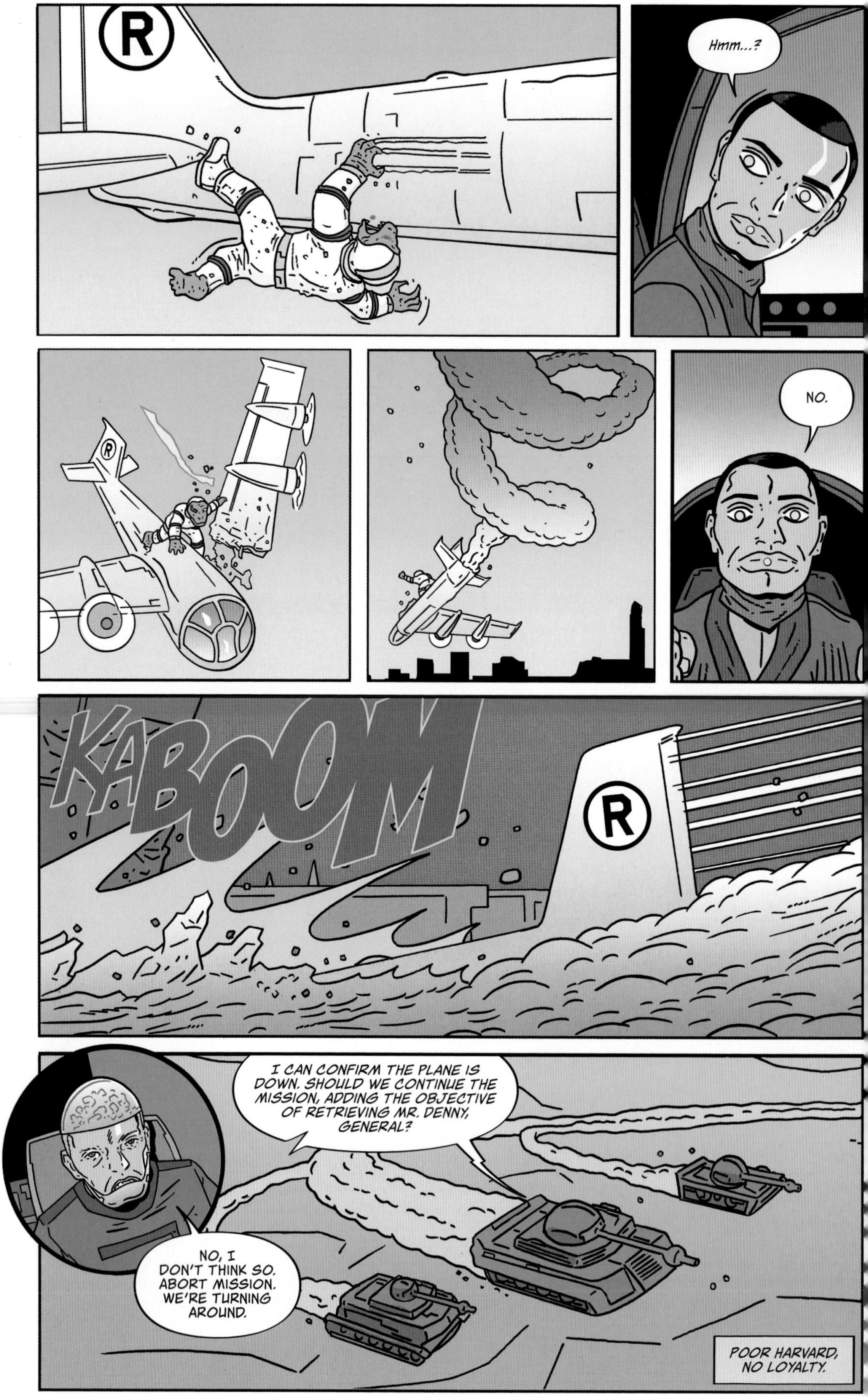

Hmm...?
NO.
KABOOM
R
I CAN CONFIRM THE PLANE IS DOWN. SHOULD WE CONTINUE THE MISSION, ADDING THE OBJECTIVE OF RETRIEVING MR. DENNY, GENERAL?
NO, I DON'T THINK SO. ABORT MISSION. WE'RE TURNING AROUND.
POOR HARVARD, NO LOYALTY.

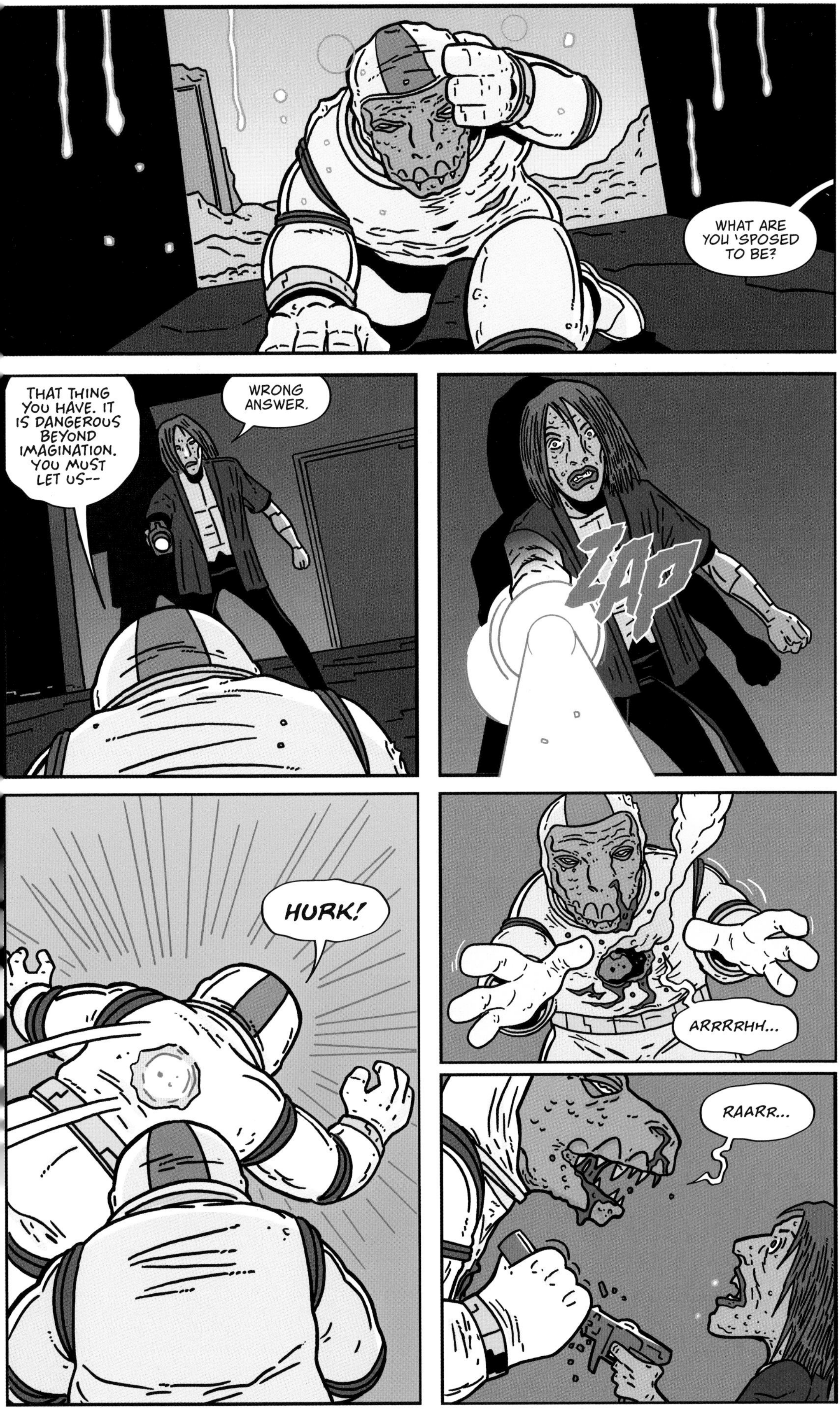
WHAT ARE YOU 'SPOSED TO BE?
THAT THING YOU HAVE. IT IS DANGEROUS BEYOND IMAGINATION. YOU MUST LET US--
WRONG ANSWER.
ZAP
HURK!
ARRRRHH...
RAARR...

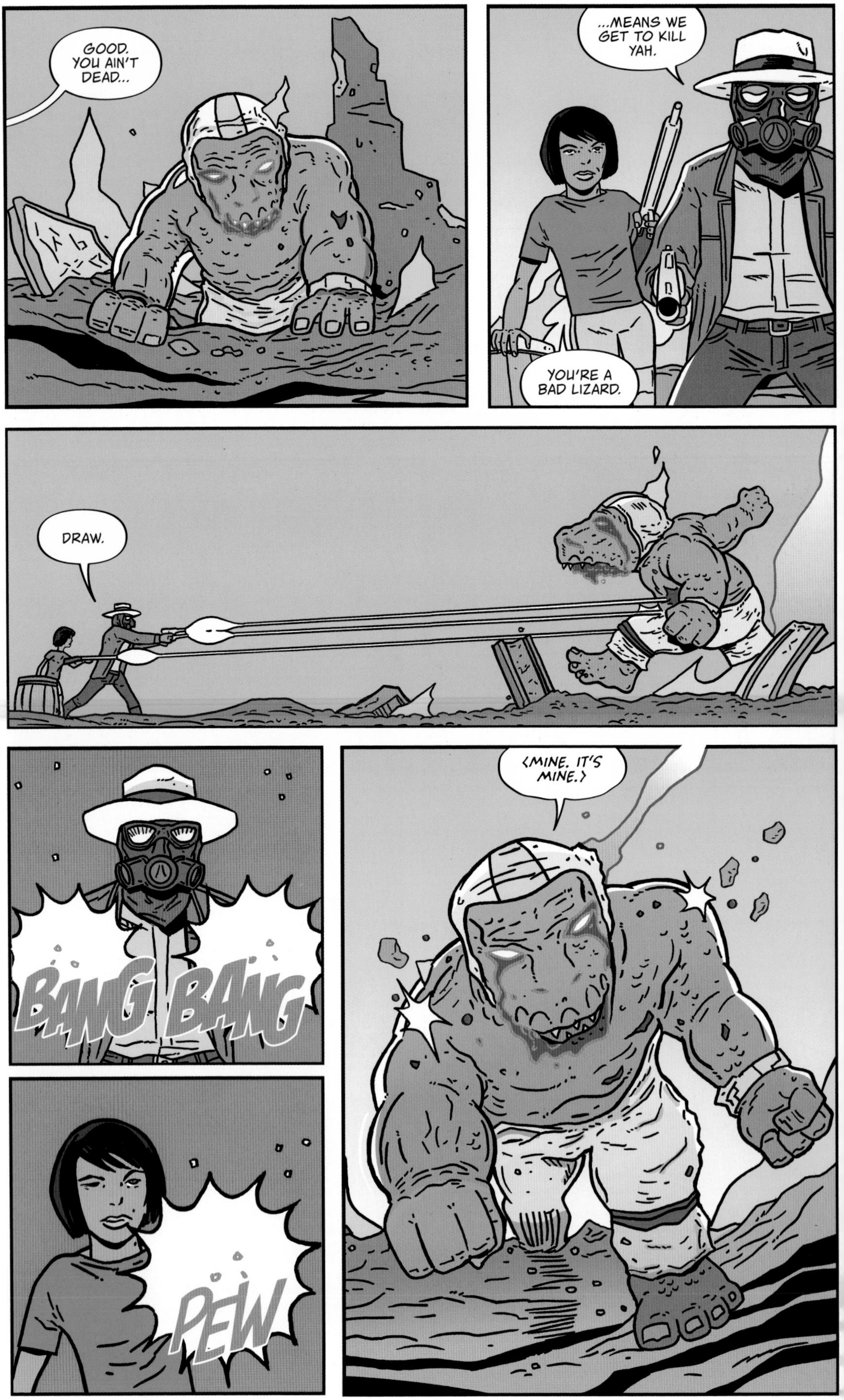
GOOD. YOU AIN'T DEAD...
...MEANS WE GET TO KILL YAH.
YOU'RE A BAD LIZARD.
DRAW.
BANG BANG
PEW
<MINE. IT'S MINE.>

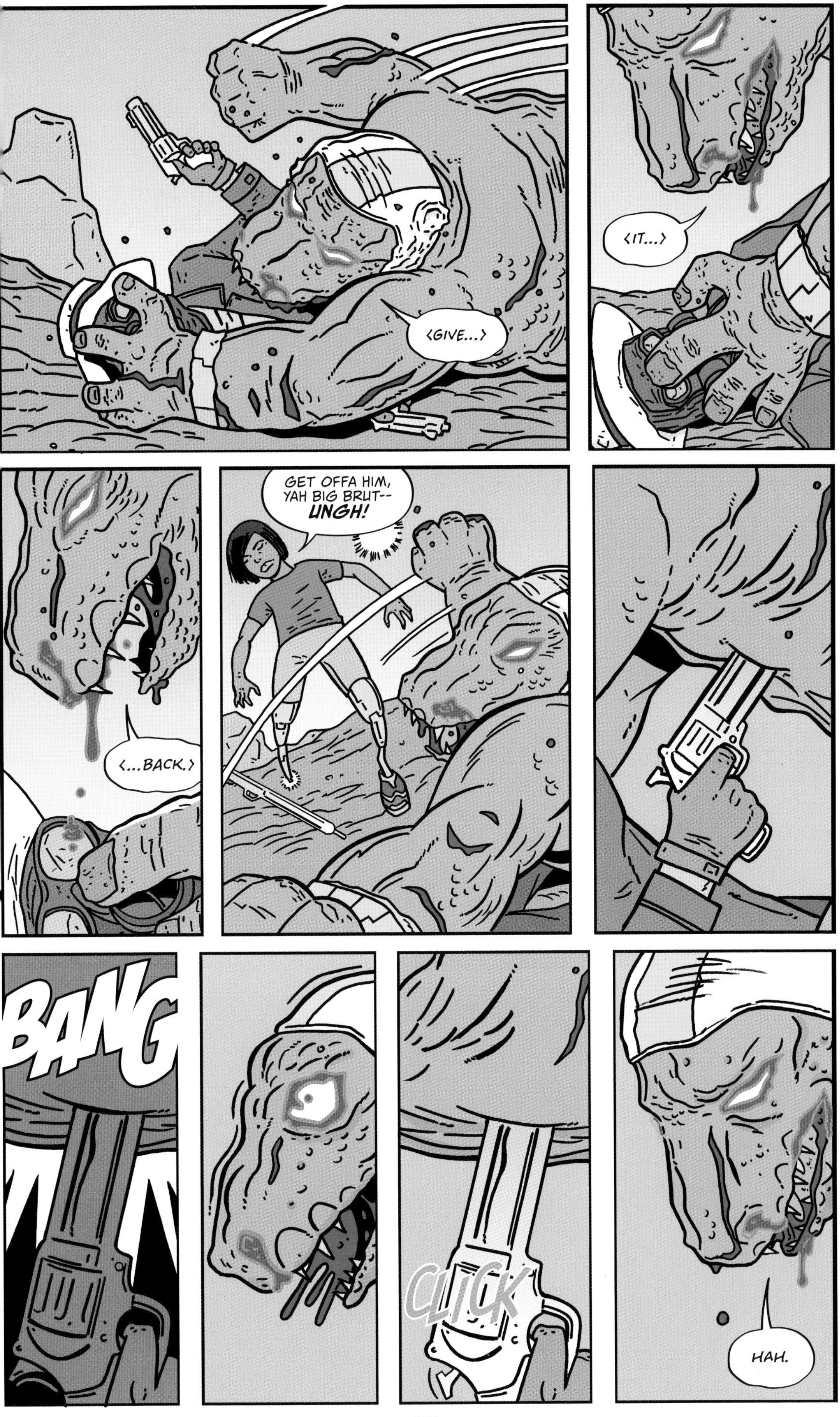
⟨GIVE...⟩
⟨IT...⟩
⟨...BACK.⟩
GET OFFA HIM, YAH BIG BRUT-- UNGH!
BANG
CLICK
HAH.

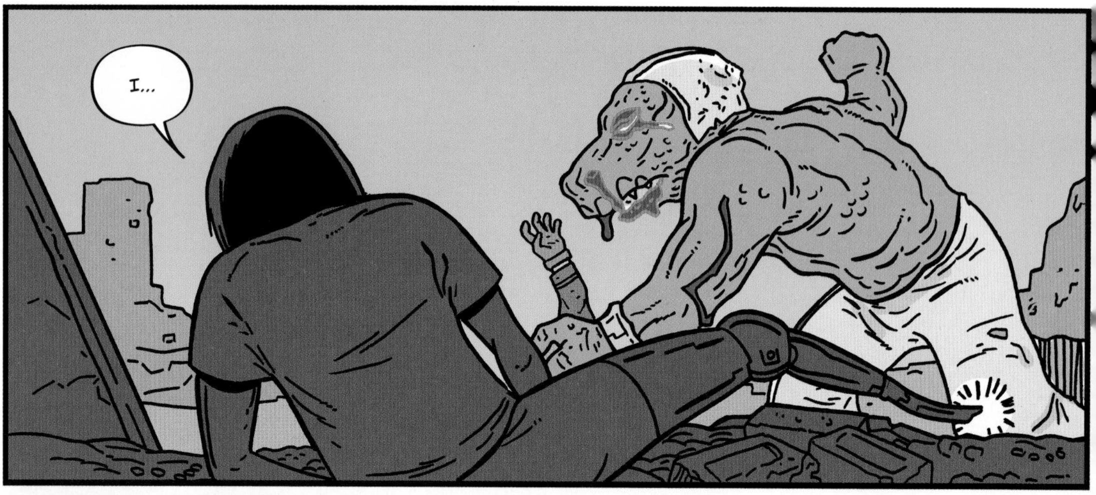
I...

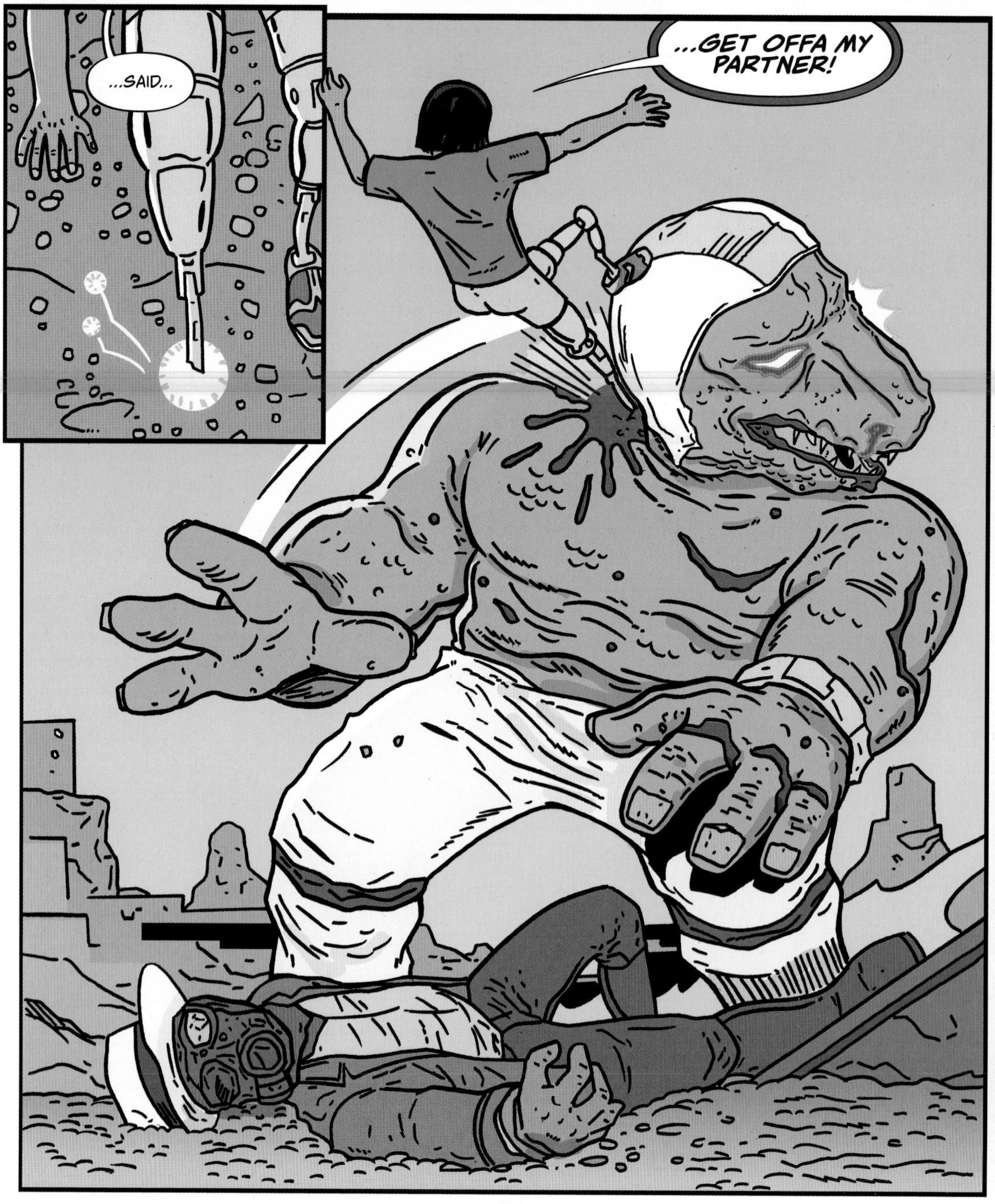
...SAID...
...GET OFFA MY PARTNER!

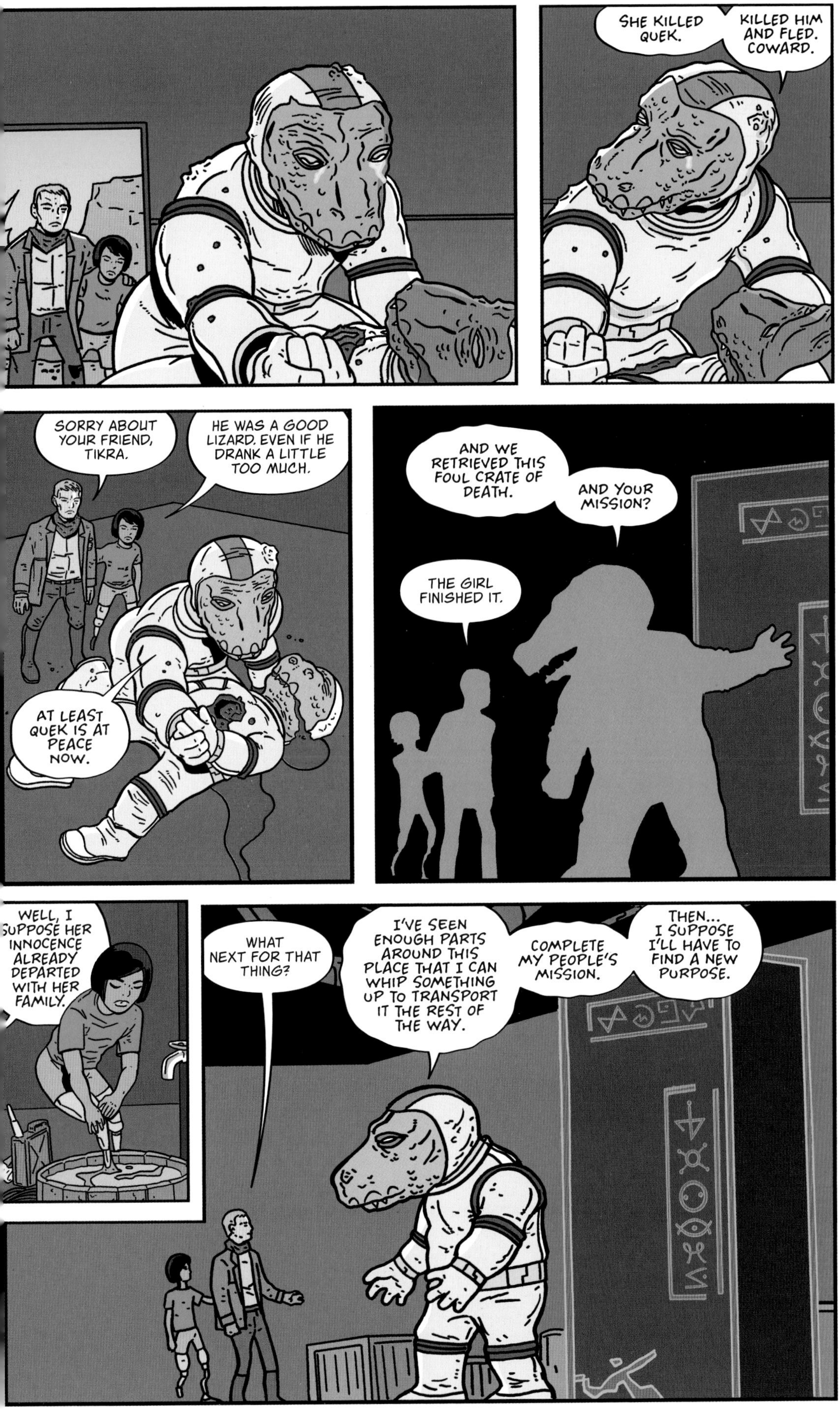
SHE KILLED QUEK.
KILLED HIM AND FLED. COWARD.
SORRY ABOUT YOUR FRIEND, TIKRA.
HE WAS A GOOD LIZARD. EVEN IF HE DRANK A LITTLE TOO MUCH.
AT LEAST QUEK IS AT PEACE NOW.
AND WE RETRIEVED THIS FOUL CRATE OF DEATH.
AND YOUR MISSION?
THE GIRL FINISHED IT.
WELL, I SUPPOSE HER INNOCENCE ALREADY DEPARTED WITH HER FAMILY.
WHAT NEXT FOR THAT THING?
I'VE SEEN ENOUGH PARTS AROUND THIS PLACE THAT I CAN WHIP SOMETHING UP TO TRANSPORT IT THE REST OF THE WAY.
COMPLETE MY PEOPLE'S MISSION.
THEN... I SUPPOSE I'LL HAVE TO FIND A NEW PURPOSE.

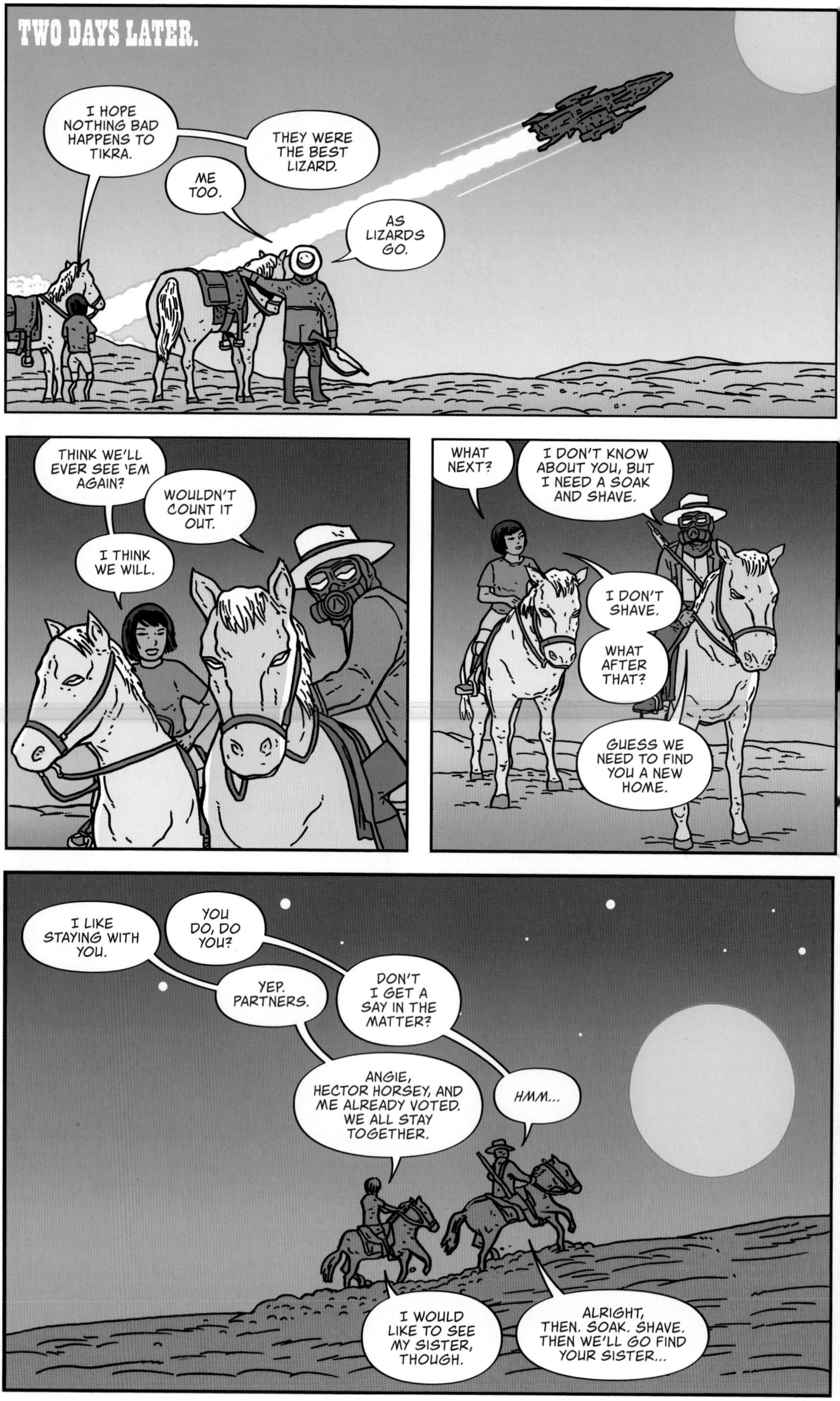
TWO DAYS LATER.
I HOPE NOTHING BAD HAPPENS TO TIKRA.
THEY WERE THE BEST LIZARD.
ME TOO.
AS LIZARDS GO.
THINK WE'LL EVER SEE 'EM AGAIN?
WOULDN'T COUNT IT OUT.
I THINK WE WILL.
WHAT NEXT?
I DON'T KNOW ABOUT YOU, BUT I NEED A SOAK AND SHAVE.
I DON'T SHAVE.
WHAT AFTER THAT?
GUESS WE NEED TO FIND YOU A NEW HOME.
I LIKE STAYING WITH YOU.
YOU DO, DO YOU?
YEP. PARTNERS.
DON'T I GET A SAY IN THE MATTER?
ANGIE, HECTOR HORSEY, AND ME ALREADY VOTED. WE ALL STAY TOGETHER.
HMM...
I WOULD LIKE TO SEE MY SISTER, THOUGH.
ALRIGHT, THEN. SOAK. SHAVE. THEN WE'LL GO FIND YOUR SISTER...

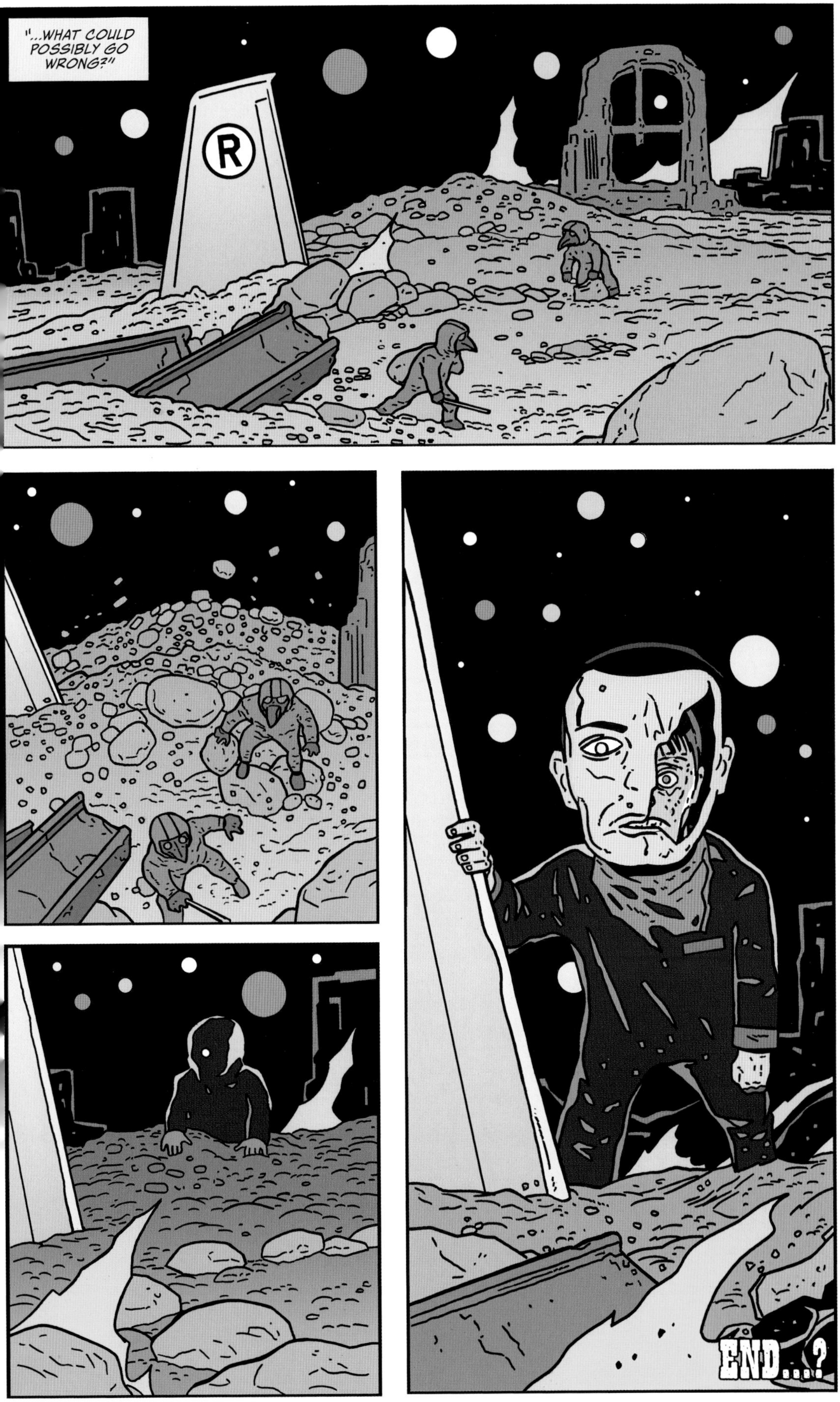
"...WHAT COULD POSSIBLY GO WRONG?"
R
END...?

IN ORDER OF APPEARANCE . . .

ISSUE ONE

COVER A	SHAKY KANE
COVER B	DAVID RUBÍN
COVER C	NICK CAGNETTI
COVER D	SHAKY KANE with Winston Gambro
COVER G	SHAKY KANE

ISSUE TWO

COVER A	SHAKY KANE
COVER B	MARIA LLOVET
COVER C	SHAKY KANE with Winston Gambro

ISSUE THREE

COVER A	SHAKY KANE
COVER B	DAVID LAFUENTE
COVER C	SHAKY KANE with Winston Gambro

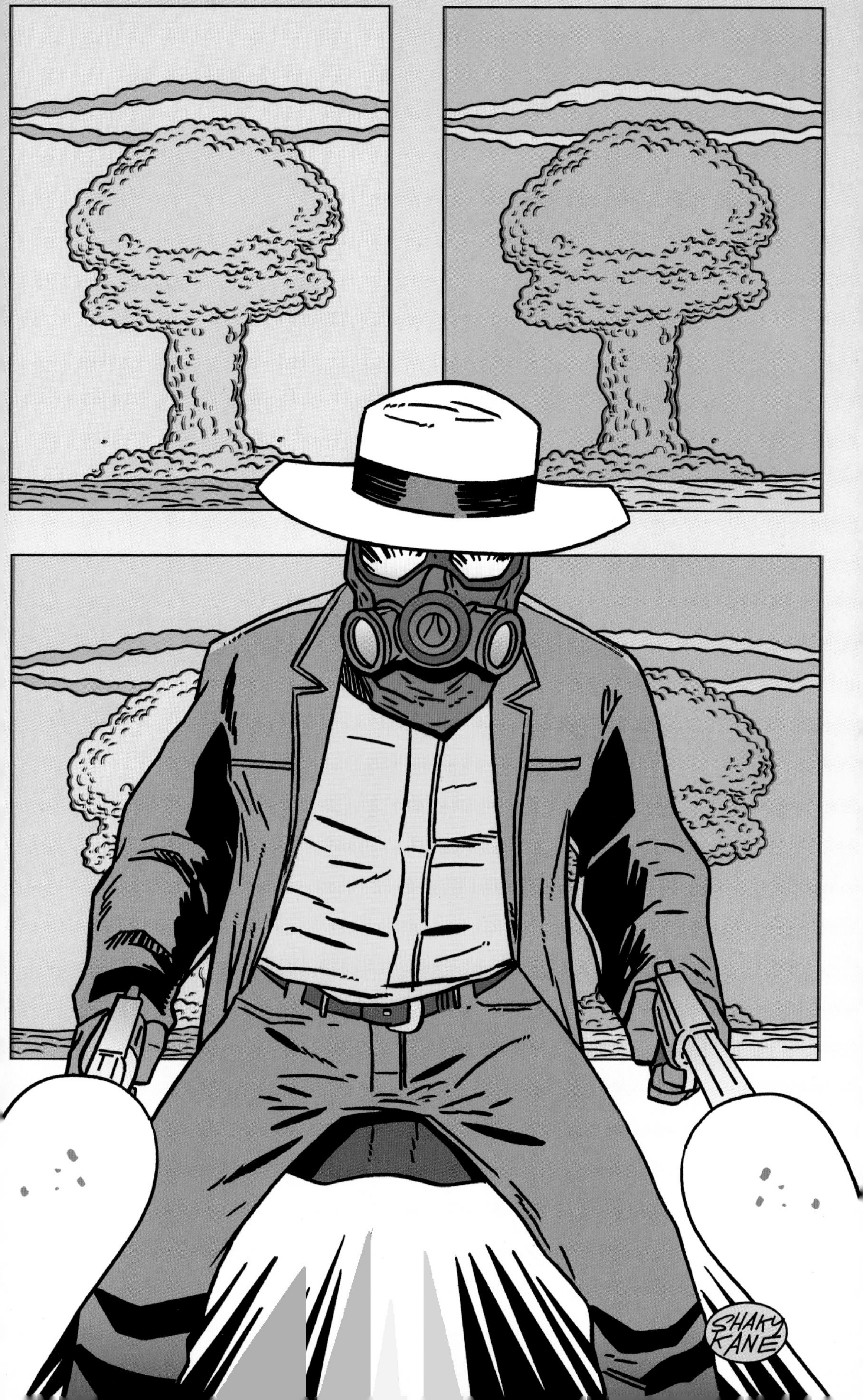
SHAKY KANE

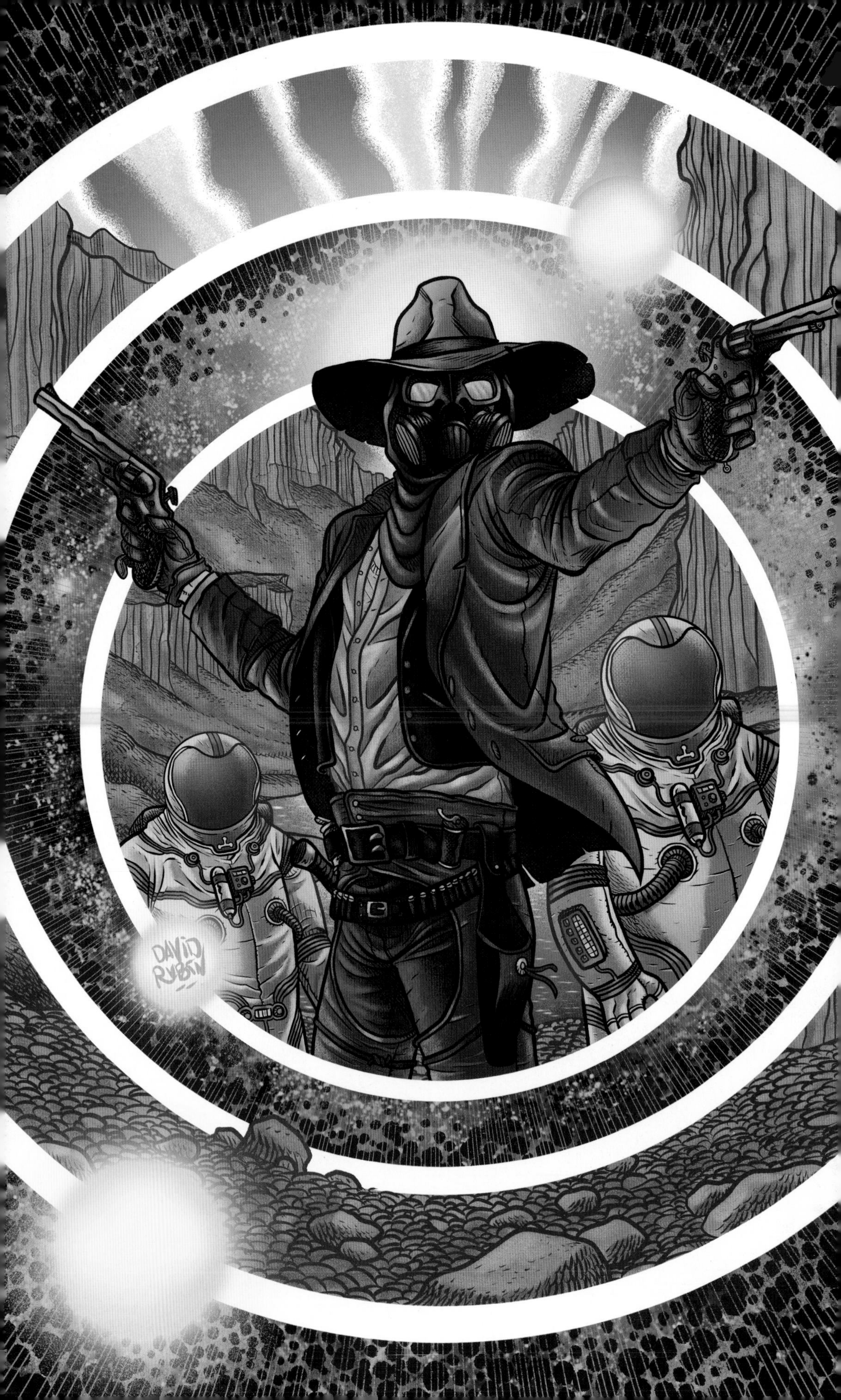
DAVID
RUBIN

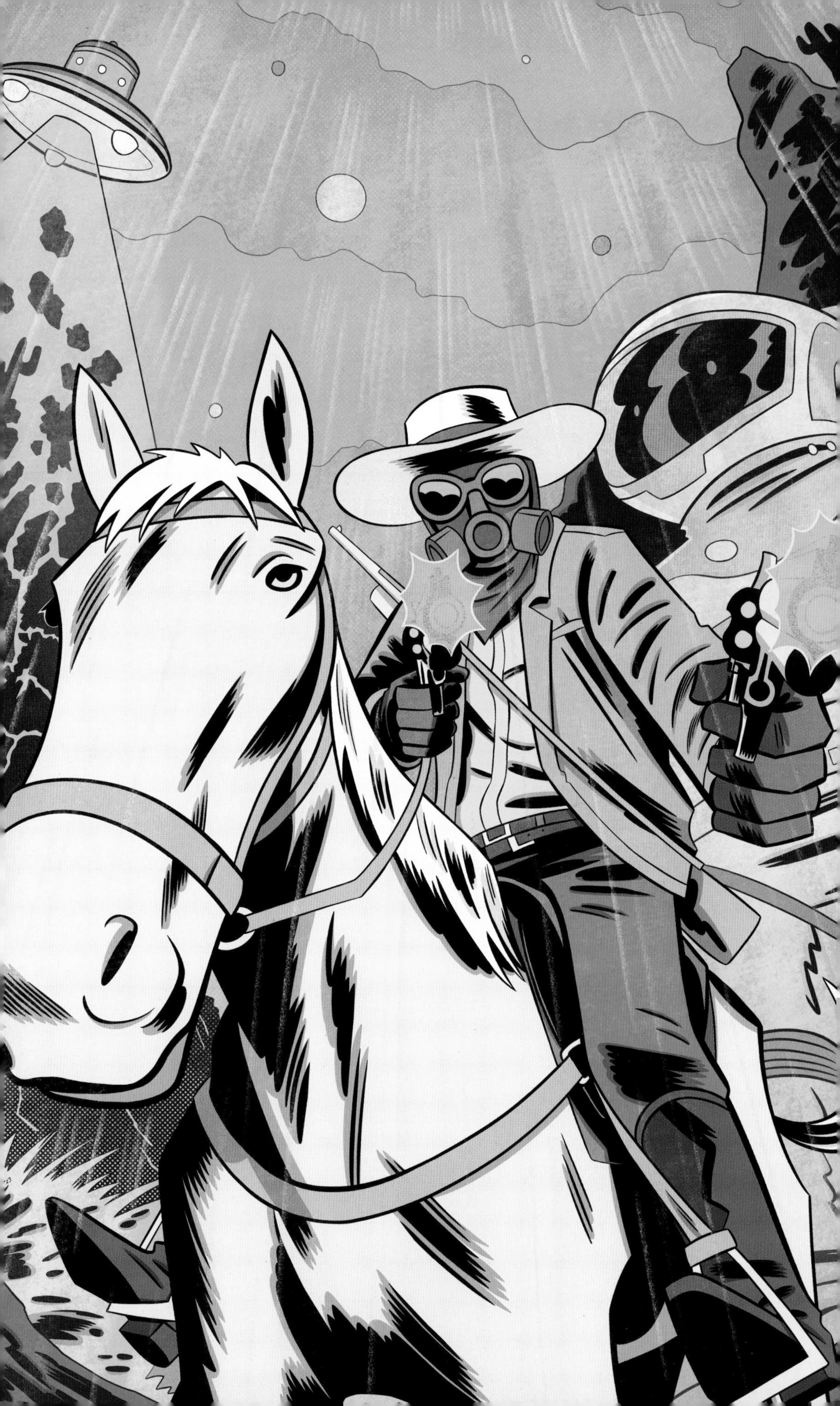

oni PRESS

THOMAS KANE

THE MAN FROM MAYBE

01

Dinonaut Design by SHAKY KANE

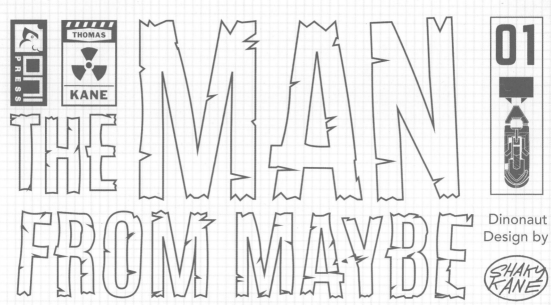

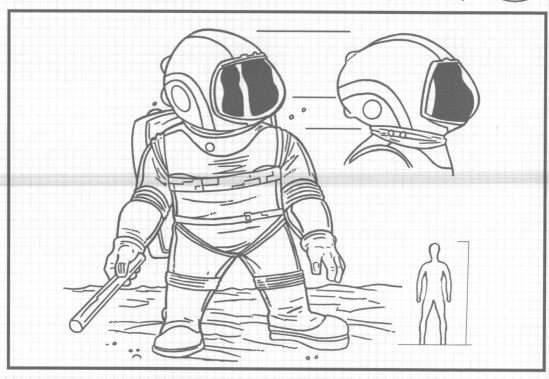

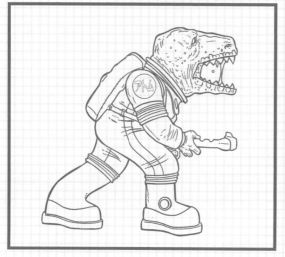

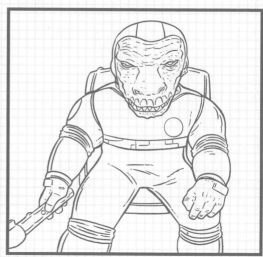

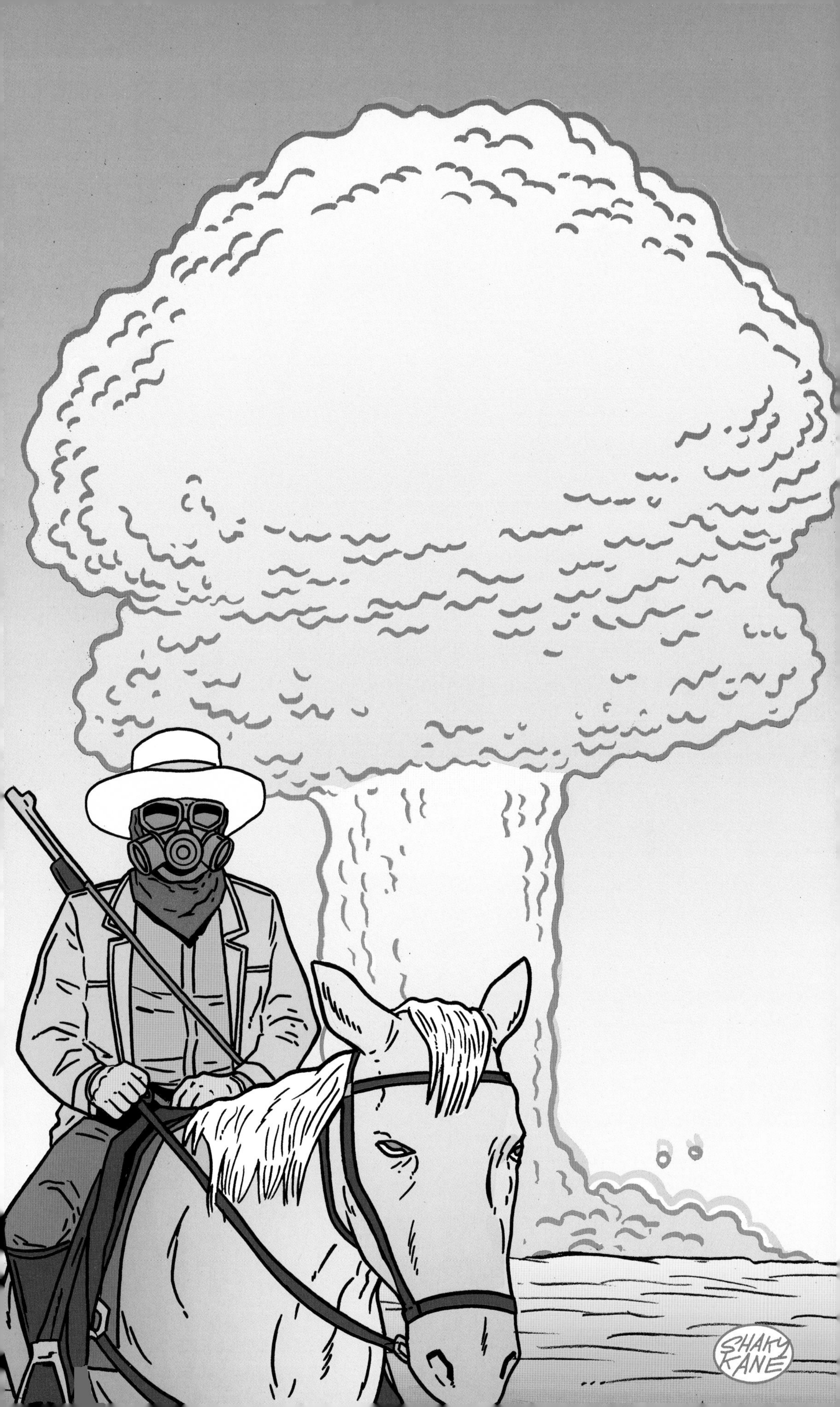
SHAKY KANE

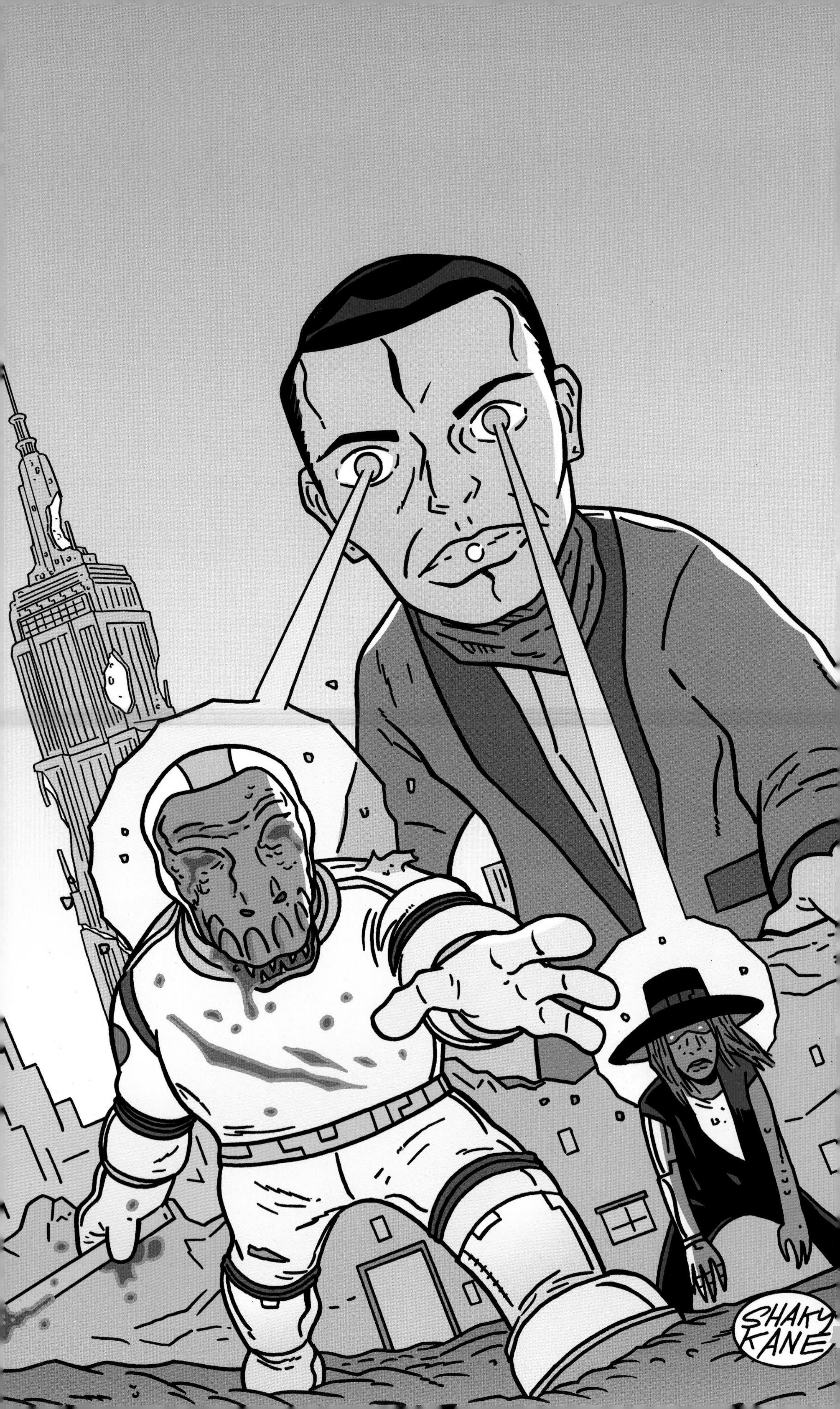
SHAKY
KANE

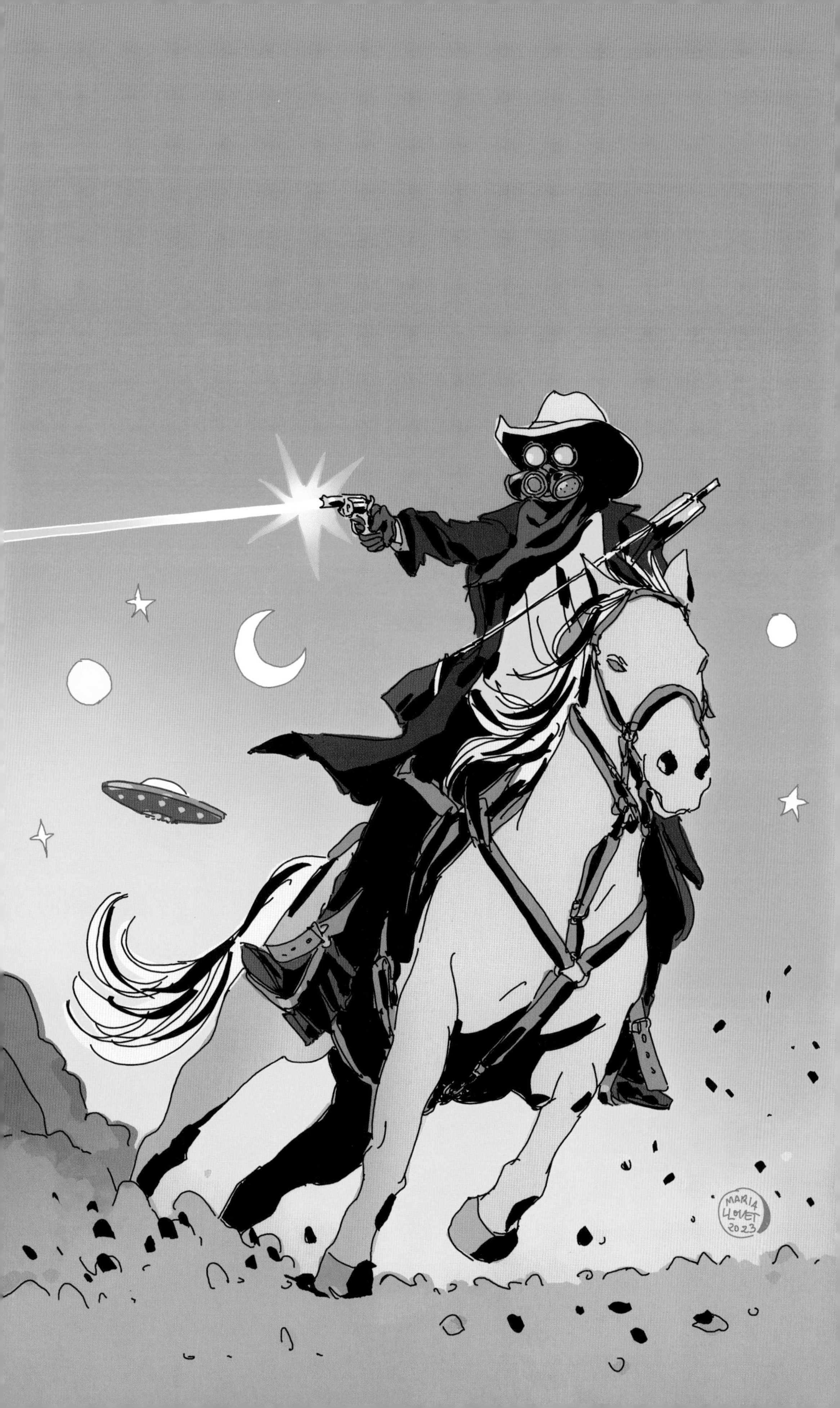
MARIA LLOVET 2023

ONI PRESS

THOMAS KANE

THE MAN FROM MAYBE

02

Man From Maybe & Gopher Designs by SHAKY KANE

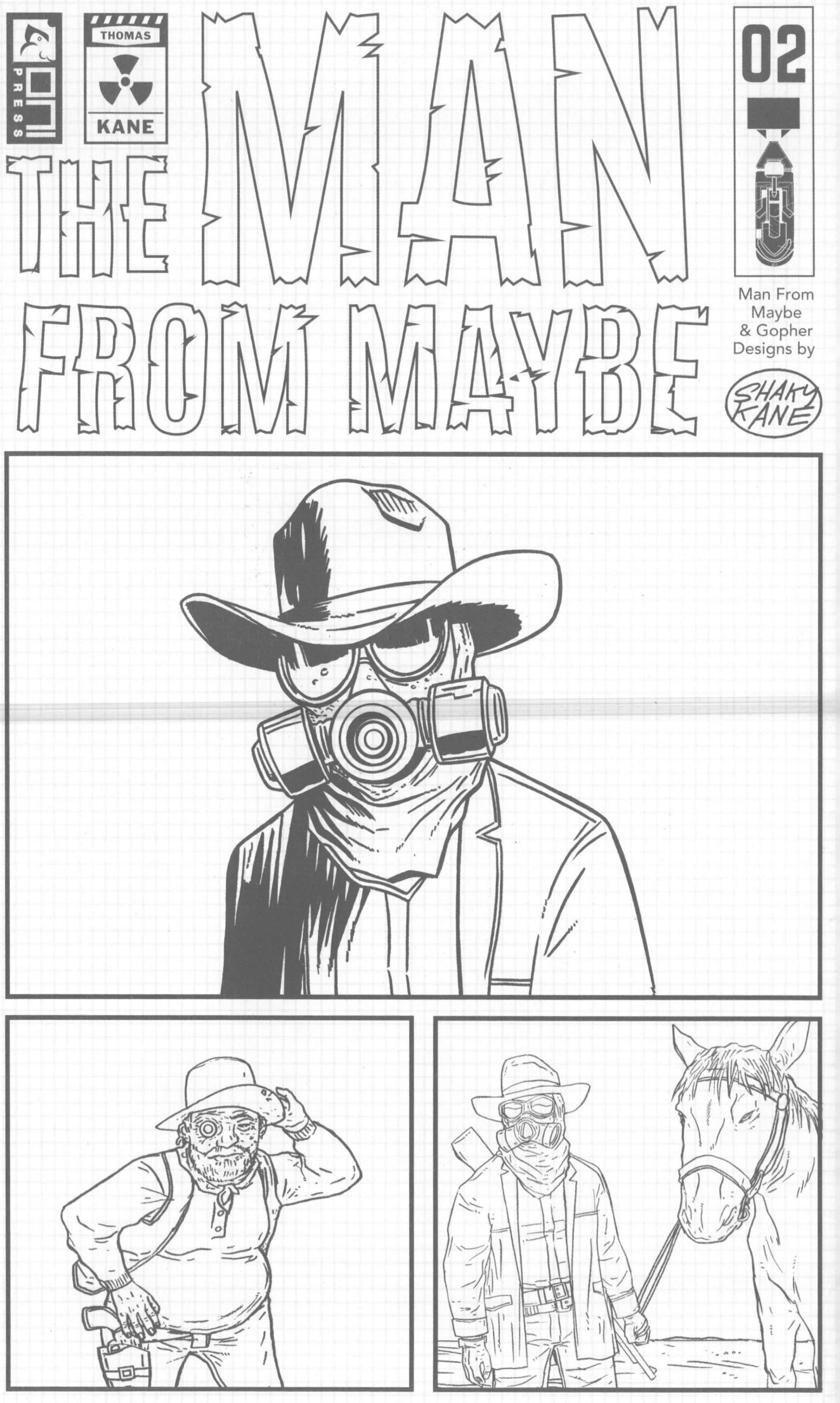

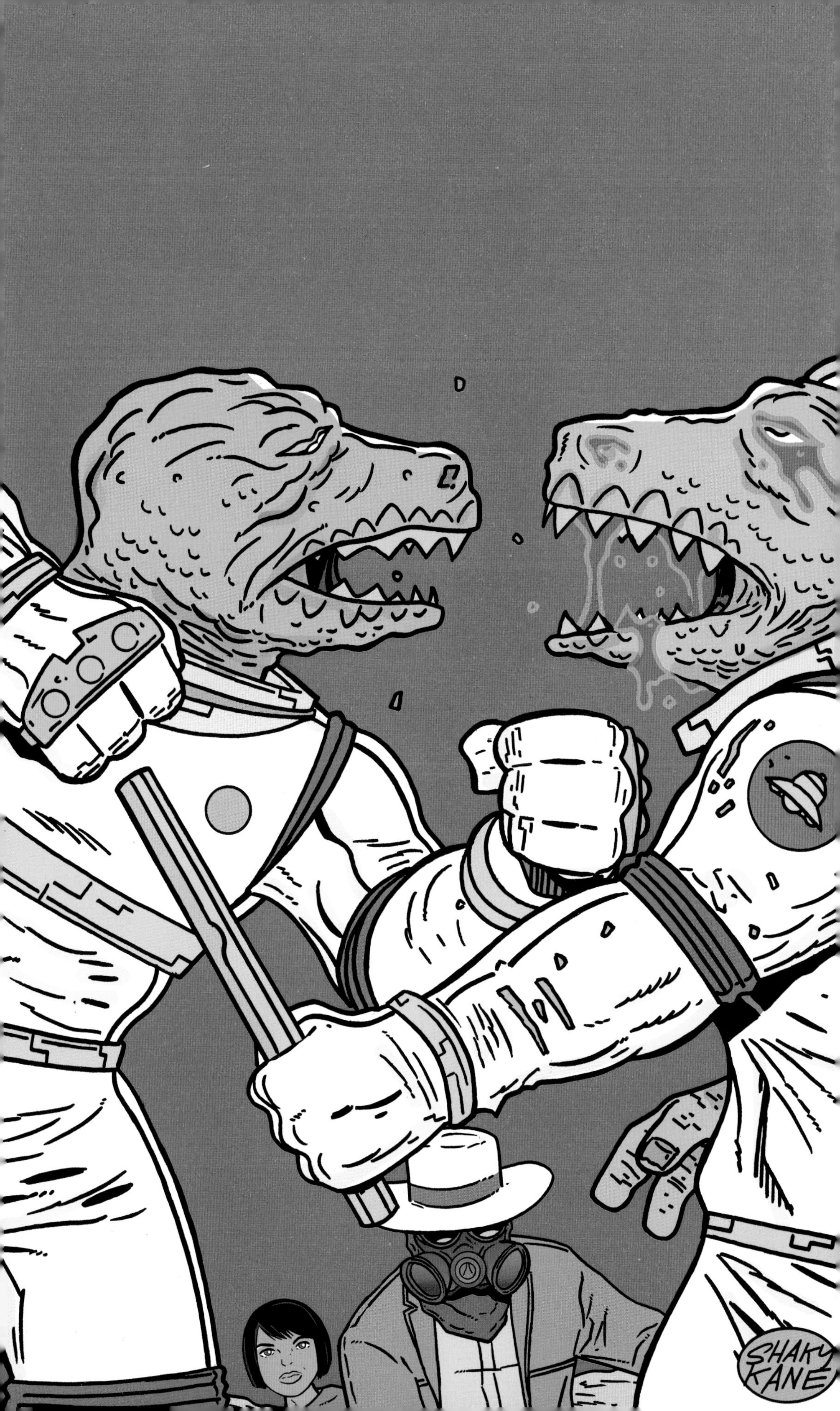
SHAKY
KANE

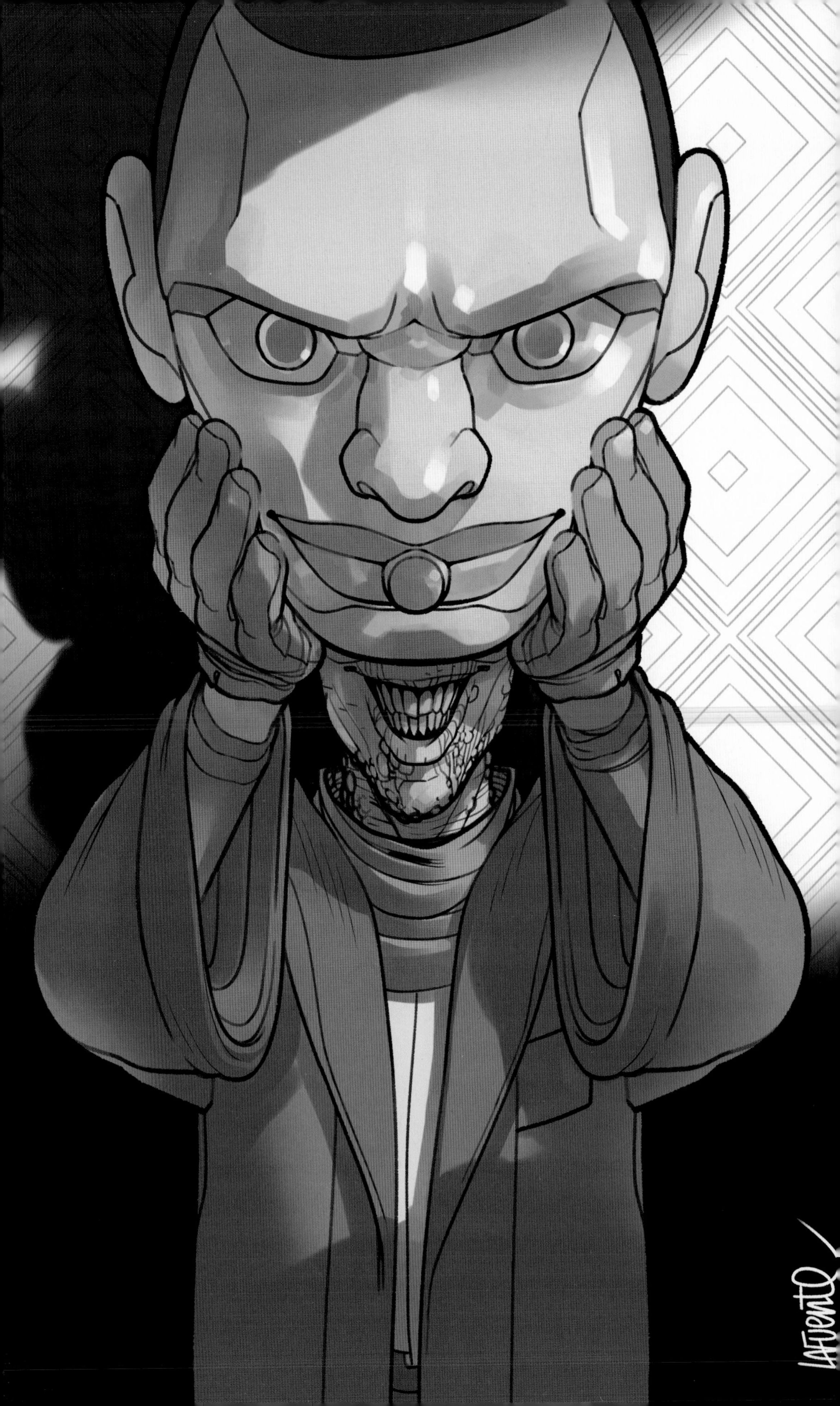

ONI PRESS

THOMAS KANE

THE MAN FROM MAYBE

03

Harvard Denny
Design by SHAKY KANE

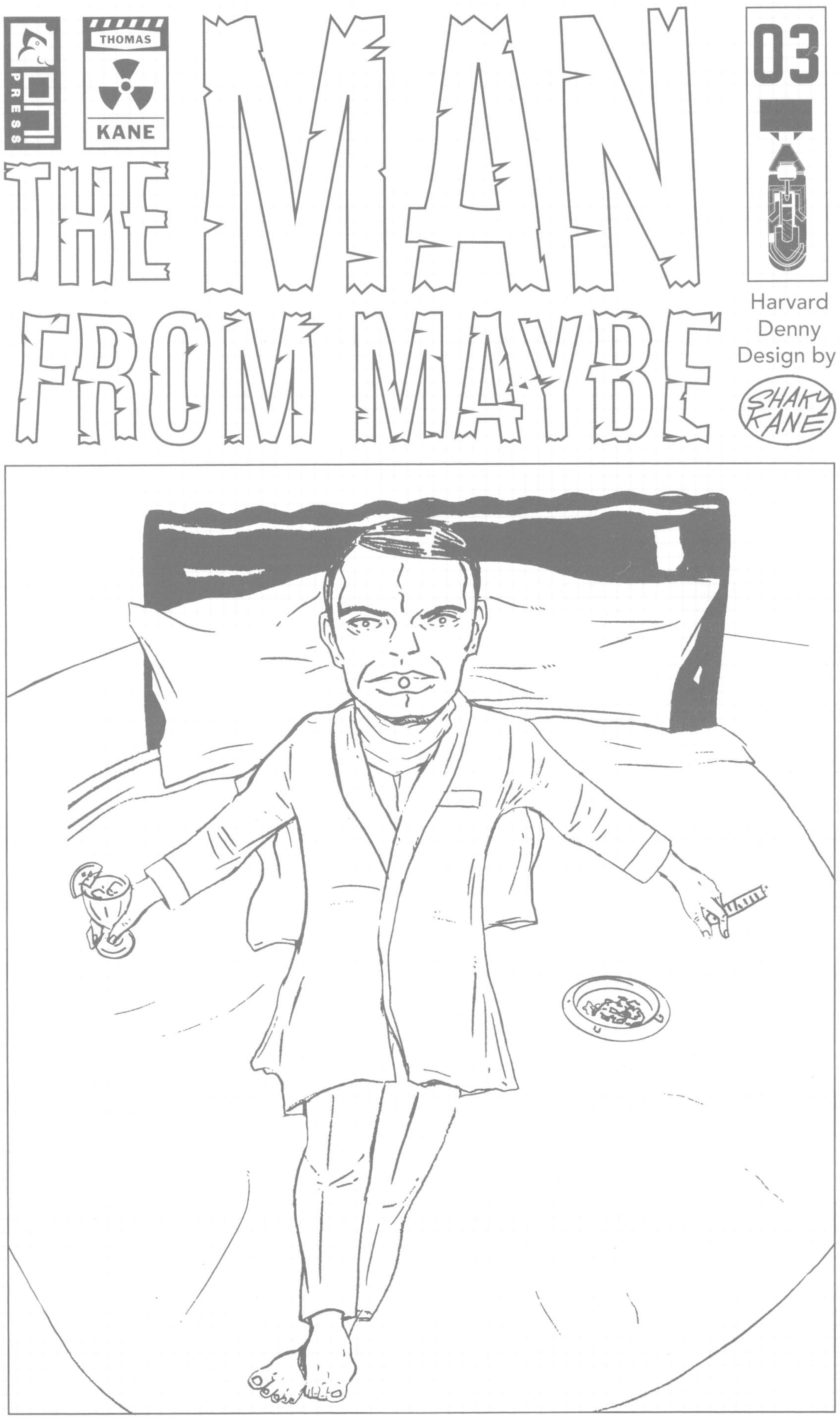

JORDAN
THOMAS

Jordan Thomas hails from the South of England but is currently living in Valencia, Spain. His first published comics work was the 1920s postwar, farm-based horror series *Frank at Home on the Farm*. Since then he has written a sci-fi short for the Oni Press *XINO* anthology and the alien world crime story *Weird Work* at Image Comics, both with Shaky Kane, as well as the UK crime epic *Mugshots* at Mad Cave Studios. He likes dogs, swimming, and swimming with dogs.

SHAKY KANE

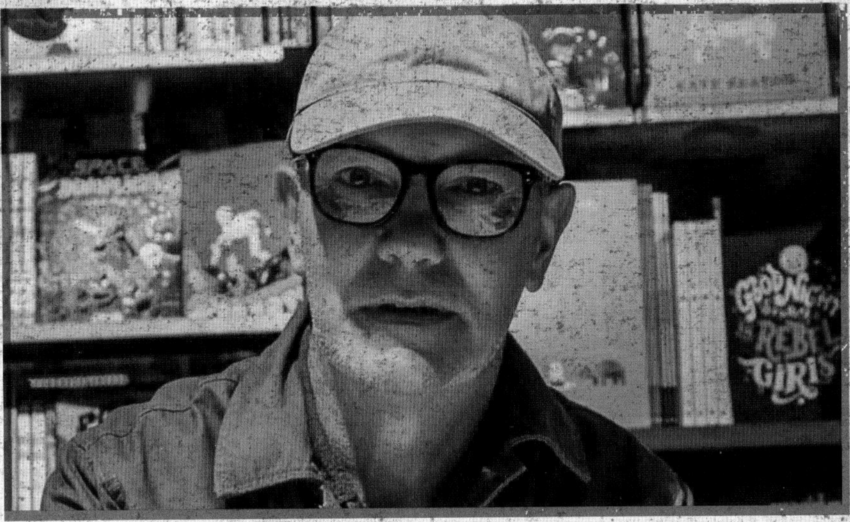
GOOD NIGHT
REBEL
GIRLS

Bathed in the cathode ray thrum of 1960s television, Shaky Kane nurtured a deep love for Americana, in particular the four-color comic books, displayed and wedged into the spinner racks of British newsagents. Inspired by the DIY ethic of the early Punk movement, Shaky contributed to the burgeoning small press scene before finding a spot drawing for British music paper the *NME*. Shaky's work found a home in a whole host of British comic strip publications during the late 1980s to the early 1990s, including *Deadline*, *Revolver*, *Judge Dredd the Megazine*, and *2000 AD*. Returning to comics in 2010, Shaky collaborated with writer David Hine on the highly acclaimed *Bulletproof Coffin* series for Image Comics. Finding a new readership and a reappraisal of his art, brought about by the growth of online communication, Shaky has produced artwork for a number of comic book publications, including *The Bulletproof Coffin Disinterred*, *Cowboys and Insects* (David Hine), *Elephant Men*, *The Beef* (Richard Starkings), *Last Driver* (Chris Baker), *That's Because You're a Robot* (David Quantick), *Cap'n Dinosaur* (Kek-W), *Weird Work* (Jordan Thomas), and has teamed up with *Vice* magazine regular Krent Able on the oversize anthology *Kane and Able*. True to his early artistic inspirations, Shaky continues drawing for independent publications to this day, and is regularly published on both sides of the Atlantic.

More Titles from ONI PRESS

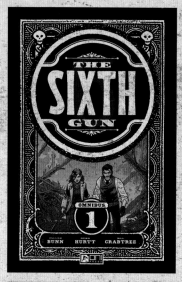

The Sixth Gun

by Cullen Bunn and Brian Hurtt

During the darkest days of the Civil War, there existed six pistols of otherworldly power. When the most dangerous of them, the Sixth Gun, comes into the possession of an innocent girl, it's up to a lone gunfighter with a checkered past to keep her out of harm's way.

Pink Lemonade

by Nick Cagnetti

Threatening doppelgangers! Extra-terrestrial fanboys! nefarious corporate machinations! These are but some of the ingredients to be found in the story of Pink Lemonade, the newest hero on the scene!

Wonton Soup

by James Stokoe

Join Johnny Boyo and Deacon as they cruise the intergalactic super-highway in search of legendary ingredients and amazing high adventure!

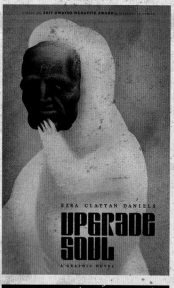

Upgrade Soul

by Ezra Claytan Daniels

When Hank and Molly undergo an experimental rejuvenation process, their hopes are dashed when faced with the results: severely disfigured, yet intellectually and physically superior duplicates, prompting the question: Can they live with themselves?

Dega

by Dan McDaid

A crashed ship—a lone survivor—and a monstrous secret that lies hiding in the darkness beneath the world!

Xino

by Various

Don't miss this all-new, big-swing, big-idea sci-fi anthology series presenting that unique brand of speculative fiction that made us fall in love with the genre in the first place!